101 Best Tech
Resumes

OTHER BOOKS BY JAY A. BLOCK AND MICHAEL BETRUS:

101 Best Resumes

101 More Best Resumes

101 Best Cover Letters

101 Best Resumes for Grads

2500 Key Words to Get You Hired

101 Best Tech Resumes

JAY A. BLOCK, CPRW
MICHAEL BETRUS, CPRW

McGraw-Hill
New York   Chicago   San Francisco
Lisbon   London   Madrid   Mexico City   Milan
New Delhi   San Juan   Seoul   Singapore
Sydney   Toronto

The McGraw·Hill Companies

2 3 4 5 6 7 8 9 0   QPD/QPD   0 9 8 7 6 5 4 3

ISBN 0-07-140886-X

McGraw-Hill books are available at special quantity discounts to use as premiums and sales promotions, or for use in corporate training sessions. For more information, please write to the Director of Special Sales, Professional Publishing, McGraw-Hill, Two Penn Plaza, New York, NY 10121-2298. Or contact your local bookstore.

 This book is printed on recycled, acid-free paper containing a minimum of 50% recycled, de-inked fiber.

Library of Congress Cataloging-in-Publication Data
Block, Jay A.
    101 Best Tech Resumes / by Jay Block and Michael Betrus
        p.   cm.
    ISBN 0-07-140886-X (alk. paper)
1. Resumes (Employment)   2. Cover letters.   3. Job hunting.   4.
Technologists.   5. Industrial technicians.   I. Title: One hundred one
best tech resumes.   II. Title: One hundred and one best tech resumes.
III. Betrus, Michael.   IV. Title.
    HF5383 .B5346   2003
        650.14'2—dc21   2002013558

Contents

Contributors

Pages That Resumes Appear on
Karen Baird-Eaton, CPRW   84, 123, 155, 214, 216, 240
Effortless Resumes
631 Fifth Street, Suite 2060   4040 Civic Center Drive, Suite 200
Santa Rosa, CA_95404   San Rafael, CA 94903
(415) 479-6531 / (707) 528-0589
kb@effortlessresumes.com
www.effortlessresumes.com

Alesia Benedict, CPRW, JCTC   102, 105
VIP Contributor
CAREER OBJECTIVES
151 W. Passaic Street,
Rochelle Park, NJ 07662
(800) 206-5353 / (800) 206-5454—fax
gethired@getinterviews.com
www.getinterviews.com

Liz Benuscak, CPRW, IJCTC   80, 89, 134, 141, 149, 179, 184, 189
Bi-Coastal Resumes, Inc.
32 Old Schoolhouse Road, New City, NY 10956
(800) 813-1643—voice / (800) 813-1898—fax
bi-coastal@prodigy.net
www.bi-coastalresumes.com

Tracy A. Bumpus, CPRW, JCTC   91, 93, 99, 128, 137, 143, 153, 161,
RezAMAZE.com   165, 177, 212, 217, 236, 246
1807 Slaughter Lane #200, PMB366, Austin, TX 78748
(888) 277-4270 / (512) 291-1404
tbumpus@rezamaze.com
www.rezamaze.com

Diane Burns, CPRW, IJCTC, CCM   112, 114, 119, 194, 203, 219,
Career Marketing Techniques   231, 248
5219 Thunder Hill Road, Columbia, MD 21045
(410) 884-0213
dianecprw@aol.com
www.polishedresumes.com

Nita Busby, BA, MS, CPRW, CAC   139, 205, 224, 226, 242
Owner/General Manager, Resumes, Etc.
438 E. Katella, Suite J, Orange, CA 92867
(714) 633-2783
Resumes100@aol.com
www.resumesetc.net

Acknowledgments

We would like to thank all the members of the Professional Association of Resume Writers (PARW) who collectively have raised the bar of excellence in the area of resume writing and job coaching. Their contributions have made it possible for more people around the globe to find passion and purpose in their work.

We would like to thank Philip Ruppel and Michelle Howry for sponsoring and editing the *101 Best ...* series, and enabling our message to reach career designers everywhere.

Alphabetical Listing of Resumes/Cover Letters

1

How to Use This Guide

Welcome to the newest installment in the *101 Best Resumes* series. This book is a departure for us, as well as all other resume sampling books available, because it addresses the new flourish of opportunities that has sprung from the Internet-based economy. Our past resume books have been focused on traditional occupations, such as general management, sales, finance, etc. However, with the multitude of new positions created out of the technology of the last decade or two, we had many requests for a resource that would meet the needs of these new occupations.

This guide offers a variety of tools for you. As we did in our earlier books, we review the different sections and components of a resume, the different resume formats, and which to use for various occasions. The largest portion of the book is dedicated to showcasing the best resumes that members of the Professional Association of Resume Writers have created for their clients. Every resume has been produced by a Certified Professional Resume Writer and was actually used by a client.

We have done enough research on this subject to know that most people buy a book like this for the sampling it provides, and the instruction that accompanies it may or may not be read. So, if you choose not to read the guidelines we have set forth, please consider the following tips in using the book:

- Even if a particular sample resume is not in your area of expertise, look it over anyway. It may include an appealing format or approach that you may like. For example, many different headlines and title styles are sampled.

- Take a good look at the box of hints for a given resume. We've tried to make it easy for you to see the strategy the Certified Professional Resume Writer used in designing that resume.

- Notice the relaxed writing style in the cover letters. Try not to write in too stiff or formal a manner.

- Really look over "Tips to Get You Hired" starting in Chapter 11. They will provide you with savvy tips that you won't find anywhere else.

- Look at the many sample resumes provided by the Certified Professional Resume Writers. Whatever you do for a living, you should still look at the formats of all the resumes for ideas on layouts, different ways of writing, and the impact of including graphics and clip art in your resume. The resumes also exemplify a variety of different ways that people have utilized the "five Ps" of resume writing you learn about in Chapter 6.

2

Finding Job Openings

For students and recent graduates, there are several primary sources of job leads:

- Networking
- Online services
- Career fairs
- Contacting companies directly
- Classified advertisements
- Executive recruiters and employment agencies

There are several unique elements to job searching fresh from school compared to those with several years of experience. There are differences in the tactical approaches to the job search, and we will provide some suggestions and guidelines for you to help get that resume in front of the right people.

NETWORKING

The buzzword of job searching is *networking*—connecting with people. And it's your best strategy today. Networking *is* people-connecting, and when you connect with people you begin to assemble your network. Once your network is in place, you will continue to make new contacts and communicate with established members. People in your network will provide advice, information, and support in helping you to achieve your career goals and aspirations.

Networking accounts for up to 70 percent of the new opportunities uncovered. So what is networking? Many people assume that they should call all the people they know, personally and professionally, and ask if they know of any companies that are hiring. A successful networker's approach is different.

College grads and seniors should use their college's alumni for networking sources. Generally speaking, most people are pretty willing to help you network if they can be managed by you to have them do something specific, or for general advice. The trick is getting in the door to those connected professionals. Here are some tips on networking with alumni.

- If you hear of alumni presenting at your college in your area of interest, go there, and make sure you contact the presenters and ask for their cards for future reference.

- Ask professors in your discipline if they know of any graduates who work in the area in which you are interested, or for companies that you are targeting. Here is another trick—suppose you are interested in obtaining an accounting job with Ford Motor Company. Go to other professors, such as in the engineering department or marketing department, etc., who may be connected with alumni or managers within Ford. Large companies employ countless disciplines, and you need to leverage any "in" that you can uncover.

- Focus on recent graduates/alumni. They were more recently in your shoes, and may be better sources of tips and leads than more established alumni.

- Go to alumni gatherings, such as football games at sports bars, etc. In Dallas, the Michigan State University alumni association has over 100 members, to put it in some perspective. Alumni, especially from major universities, are *everywhere*. Visit them in the market in which you wish to live and work. Become friendly with the chapter president.

Make sure you treat alumni as respected networking sources and utilize the principle outlined later in this section. Don't send them your resume, and don't ask them for a job. Be well organized and think through what you want to ask them so they can give you very targeted advice. If you are not focused, they will not be able to help, and may find the whole exercise frustrating.

A successful networker starts by listing as many names as possible on a sheet of paper. These can include family, relatives, friends, coworkers and managers (past and present), other industry contacts, and anyone else you know. The next step is to formulate a networking presentation. Keep in mind that it need not address potential openings. In networking, the aim is to call your contacts asking for career or industry advice. The point is, you're now positioning yourself not as a desperate job hunter, but as a *researcher*.

It is unrealistic that you will go far asking people for advice like this:

John, thanks for taking some time to talk with me. My company is likely to lay people off next month, and I was wondering if your company had any openings or if you know of any.

This person hasn't told John what he does, has experience in, or wants to do. John is likely to respond with a *"No, but I'll keep you in mind should I hear of anything."* What do you think the odds are that John will contact this person again?

A better approach is to ask for personal or industry advice and work on developing the networking web:

John, Amanda Mancini at BMI suggested I give you a call. She and I have worked together for some time, and she mentioned that you work in finance and are the controller of Allied Sensors. I work in cost accounting and feel you'd likely be able to offer some good career advice. I'd really appreciate some time. Could we get together for lunch some time in the next week or so?

You have now asked for advice, not a job. People will be much more willing to help someone who has made them feel good about themselves or who appears genuinely to appreciate their help. This strategy can be approached in many ways. You can ask for: job search advice (including resume or cover letter advice); overall career advice (as shown above); industry advice; key contacts they may know; information about various companies/people/industries; or other people they may know. It is important that the person you network through likes you. When someone gives you a reference, it is a reflection of that person. They will not put themselves at personal or professional risk if they aren't confident that you will be a good reflection on them. Finally, send each person you speak with a thank-you letter. That courtesy will be remembered for future contacts.

In addition to traditional networking for opportunities, there is another very effective way to leverage networking in today's economy. Suppose you go to Monster.Com and uncover a great opportunity with Cisco Systems, Bristol-Myers Squibb, or some new e-commerce company. Before blindly sending in your resume and a brief cover letter to that company (or recruiter), immediately ask around and try to find a reference you can leverage to get to them.Following the rules of "six degrees of separation," there is a good chance you can ask around and get a personal introduction to that hiring manager.

When you do, you have engineered a reference and network from the back door.Another terrific strategy to help you in this quest is to proactively have your best references send in letters of recommendation to that hiring manager during the interview process.The determination you demonstrate by developing these references from your network will be perceived as the kind of determination you will demonstrate on the job. Companies desperately need good employees. Sell yourself as one of these, and most companies will find a place for you.

A client of ours, Mark, was looking to find a position with Voice-Stream, a fairly new wireless telecommunications company. Their Web site had a posting for a position they wanted that was located in Atlanta. But, how do you avoid being batched in the plethora of resumes that these companies receive for each posting, especially in today's economy (2002)? Here is what we did. We worked with the candidate to see if he knew *anyone* at VoiceStream. After a few days of asking around, it turned out that Mark's girlfriend's friend (in Chicago) used to work there. So, we called her and got the name of her VP.

Mark called him in Seattle and he actually picked up the phone, in part because Mark called before hours, when things were slow, and he waited until he answered the phone, not leaving a voice mail. Mark gave him a quick "elevator pitch" of his background and what his goals were, and the VP referred him to that region's VP. Mark then reached that VP, and by now had a few names to drop, positioning himself as a referred candidate.

The new VP had Mark get in touch with an HR recruiter in Kansas City, and weeks later secured an interview and a position. That whole networking exercise took just two days, but enabled Mark to scoop thousands of other candidates. You too should think of creative ways to network "internally."

ONLINE SERVICES

When searching for a job opportunity in the "dot.com" industry, online sites will be a huge resource for you. In fact, it may be a primary for this industry, compared to more traditional means for more traditional jobs.

Many resources exist today that specialize in guiding you through the maze of job searching online. Though a comprehensive direction is beyond the scope of this publication, you should recognize that after networking, online searches will probably be your best resource for uncovering a high number of quality "dot.com" job opportunities.

The top sites that house these opportunities include:

- Monster.com (*www.monster.com*)
- Headhunter.net (*www.headhunter.net*)
- Jobs.com (*www.jobs.com*)
- America's Job Bank (*www.jobsearch.org*)
- JobOptions (*www.joboptions.com*)
- Career mosaic (*www.careermosaic.com*)
- CareerBuilder (*www.careerbuilder.com*)

Though there are many great resources to help you in your online search, here are a few tips to keep in mind:

1. Have a good idea of what types of job you are seeking. That will make the search on these online sites more narrowed in scope and productive. Have geography and keywords prepared in advance. These two

objectives should be complete anyway as part of developing your resume.

2. Have two resumes ready at hand: a "finished" Microsoft Word document to send as an attachment, and a nonformatted text-only resume to copy and paste in an email. The content should be the same, but the latter should be stripped of formatting that will not be preserved through the email exchange.

3. Plan to post your resume at these sites as well as send them directly to recruiters and employers.

4. Take the time to read and understand how the sites work before jumping in head first.

5. Print out copies of everything you see of interest on a site. It will help you for future reference. Also, catalog whom you send emails and resumes to, so you won't send redundant "applications."

6. Provide a personal email address, not the one of your current employment. Check your email daily, as that is a common first reply you will receive.

7. We will cover this later in more detail in Chapter 7, but make sure that your resume is very tight in your experience and what you want to do. The folks reading these resumes are doing so online and will not lend a lot of time to each, so make it easy for them to get to your qualifications and objectives quickly and effortlessly.

CAREER FAIRS

Career fairs are very overlooked opportunities to uncover good career options. In 1997, Grace Matherly, 26, was looking for a new marketing job in Dallas. She networked with some former colleagues, checked the classified ads, and contacted some executive recruiters. Still, she had not yet uncovered the position that was the best fit. Then she heard of a career fair for engineers and technical managers. Though she was not looking for that type of position, she went anyway to network.

There she met some recruiters from Sprint, and they informed her that Sprint had a big marketing presence in Dallas, and that they were hiring. They put her in touch with them, and within 60 days she secured exactly the position for which she was looking. She uncovered an opportunity that had not been advertised and had no executive recruiter supporting.

Even if the career fair is for a different specialty than your own, it still provides excellent networking opportunity to uncover new leads. Generally, career fairs are advertised in local papers and held at hotels or convention centers, and from 5–15 companies may be participating, even more in large ones in major markets.

Career fairs can sometimes be crowded, with long lines of candidates waiting to interview. You can maximize your productive time with good preparation. Try to register electronically at the organizer's Web site if possible. This eliminates standing in line at the entrance. Get there early before the long lines if you can. No matter what time you show up, go first to the companies that your research has indicated will be the best match—then hit the rest. Do take the time to visit as many companies as you can. Below are some tips to ensure that you get noticed.

TIPS

- Develop your "elevator pitch." This is a two-minute overview of your background and the type of position for which you are looking. It should include professional/academic information, not personal information. However, when delivering, you can interject some personal information to build rapport, demonstrate a high energy personality, and distinguish yourself. Just don't overdo it.
- Bring at least one good copy of your resume for each company participating in the fair, as well as a few extras in case you network in other areas.
- Research the employers attending. Learn more about each company, its product/services, etc., and current challenges. You can find terrific information on their Web sites and in media reviews. Some of these can be garnered from going to the company's trading symbol on financial Web sites and looking in the "news" sections. Also, just type in the name of the company in a good search engine, and click on what comes up.
- Bring a folder to carry resumes and a notepad for notes.
- Dress professionally. Dress professionally. Dress professionally.
- Prepare for the interviews. Review the tips for interviewing section in this book.
- Prepare questions that you want employers to answer.
- Go alone; if you go with friends or family, walk the fair by yourself.
- Be aware of time demands on employers. Do not monopolize an employer's time. Ask specific questions and offer to follow up after the fair, as appropriate.
- Be direct. Introduce yourself. If you are job seeking, state the type of position in which you are interested. If you are gathering information, let employers know that you are only interested in materials and information.
- When greeting a recruiter, introduce yourself and look confident by initiating a handshake with a smile.
- Ask the company what the next step is and how to follow up.
- Get appropriate contact info and ask for a business card.
- After the career fair, send a thank-you card and reconfirm interest in the position and company. In the note, include exactly when *you* will follow up, and then do so. Put the burden of follow-up on yourself, because they may intend to but be too busy and put it off or forget.

CONTACTING COMPANIES DIRECTLY

Aren't there one or two companies that you've always been interested in working for? Ideally, you may know someone who will introduce you to key contacts there or inform you of future openings. The best way to get introduced to a targeted company is to have a current employee personally introduce you or make an introductory phone call for you. You could make the introduction and reference the employee you know. We'll get into this later, but if you don't know anyone at a targeted company, a recruiter may be a good source of contact for you, even if it involves no job order for them.

You could send an unsolicited resume, but the likelihood of this materializing is low. Most large-profile companies receive thousands of resumes a year, and few are acted on. Corporate recruiters Jackie Larson and Cheri Comstock, authors of *The New Rules of the Job Search Game*, don't regard mass-mailed resumes very seriously. Part of the problem is that too many resumes are written as past job descriptions and are not *customized* toward a targeted position.

Conrad Lee, a retained Boca Raton recruiter, believes "information is the most important thing in contacting companies directly. Don't call just one person in the company and feel that is sufficient. That person may have their own job insecurities or be on a performance improvement plan. You should contact 5 to 10 people and only then can you say you contacted that company directly." New job search strategies all suggest targeting a select few smaller companies (under 750 employees, as larger companies are still downsizing) intensely rather than blanketing a thousand generically. Contacting the head of your functional specialty in that company is a good start. Is it hard? Of course. You're facing rejection, probably feeling like you're bothering busy people, begging, or maybe even feeling inferior. Would you feel inferior if you were calling hotels and ticket agencies for Super Bowl information? Of course not. What if some can't help you? You just get back on the phone until you achieve your goal. These contacts should be approached the same way. You have a great product to sell—yourself. Position yourself as someone of value and as a product that can contribute to the target company.

The key is to position yourself for individual situations. This requires specialized letters, resumes, and strategies tailored for each situation.

When you do contact the company, you can do it directly through yourself, or through a reference/networking source. A third-party endorsement lends credibility to you, and will differentiate you from the other applicants. The networking section in this chapter is a good guideline on how to contact companies directly.

CLASSIFIED ADVERTISEMENTS

When you depend on classified advertisements to locate job openings, you limit yourself to only 7-10 percent, or less, of all available jobs, plus you are competing with thousands of job hunters who are reading the same ads. Keep in mind that the majority of these ads are for lower-wage positions. Do not disregard the classifieds, but at the same time, don't limit your options by relying too heavily on them. Answering ads is more effective at lower levels than higher. An entry-level position or administrative support position is more likely to be found using this method than a director's position. But it is easy to review advertisements. Check the local paper listings on Sunday, the paper of the largest metropolitan area near where you live, and even a few national papers like the *Wall Street Journal* (or their advertisement summary, *The National Business Employment Weekly*) or the *New York Times*.

You may gain company insight by looking at the ads that don't necessarily match your background. You may see an ad that says "Due to our expansion in the Northeast we are looking for _____." You have just learned of an expanding company that may need you. Review papers that have good display ads like the *Los Angeles Times, The Chicago Tribune*, or any other major Sunday edition.

EXECUTIVE RECRUITERS AND EMPLOYMENT AGENCIES

Employment agencies and executive recruiters work for the hiring companies, not for you. There are thousands of employment agencies and executive recruiters nationwide. Employment agencies generally place candidates in positions with a salary range under $40,000, which may bode well for many recent graduates. Executive recruiters place candidates from temporary service at the administrative or executive level to permanent senior-level management. Recruiters can be a great source of hidden jobs, even if they do not have a position suitable for you at a given time.

Recruiters and agencies will have a greater chance of successfully locating a position for you if your professional discipline is of a technical or specific nature, such as accounting, engineering, or sales.

All of the above methods are excellent and necessary in your career design.

3

Taking an Inventory of Your Skills

Have you ever known any highly successful sales professionals who didn't have a firm grasp and knowledge of their product? Ask experienced salespersons what the "secret to success" is, and they will say that it's knowing the product, knowing the customer, and matching the benefits of the product to the needs of the customer. This is a powerful success formula.

The job search is a sales and marketing endeavor. There is simply no way around this: *You* are the product, *you* are the salesperson, and you must define your customers and promote yourself to them. So, like the highly successful salesperson, the key to your success is to know your product (you) inside and out, and match the benefits of the product to the needs of your potential customers (prospective employers). In sales, we call this "selling features and benefits." You must know the features of the product, known as *marketable skills*, and determine what specific benefits result from those features that would interest a prospective employer. In other words, the only reason for someone to hire you is for the benefit you offer that person or company. When interviewers ask you what your strengths are, what skills you bring to the table, or what contributions you feel that you could make to the company, they are actually asking you to identify your features and the benefits that the company would realize by hiring you.

In order to communicate effectively the features and benefits of the product, namely you, you must first take an inventory of your skills. In the simplest of terms, there are three categories of skills:

- Job-related skills
- Transferable skills
- Self-management skills

JOB-RELATED SKILLS

There are four categories of job-related skills: (1) working with people, (2) working with data and information, (3) working with things, and (4) working with ideas. Though most of us work with all four categories at one time or another, we tend to be attracted to one or two areas in particular. Successful teachers, customer service representatives, and salespeople must be particularly skilled at working with people. Financial controllers, weathermen, and statistical forecasters possess outstanding skills in working with data and information. Engineers, mechanics, and computer technicians enjoy using their skills to work with things. Inventors, writers, and advertising professionals must have solid creativity and idea skills.

Which category do you tend toward? *You need to determine which job-related skills you are strongest in and which you enjoy the most. Then write a brief paragraph stating why you feel you are skilled and qualified to work with the category you selected.*

TRANSFERABLE SKILLS

Transferable skills are just that—transferable from one environment to another. If you enjoy working with people, your specific transferable skills might include leadership, training, entertainment, mentoring, mediation, persuasion, public speaking, conflict resolution, or problem solving. If you enjoy working with data and information, your specific transferable skills might include research, analysis, proofreading, editing, arranging, budgeting, assessing, measuring, evaluating, surveying, or pricing. If you enjoy working with things, your specific transferable skills might include knowledge of equipment, repair, maintenance, installation, setup, troubleshooting, or building. And finally, if you enjoy working with ideas, your specific transferable skills might include creating, developing, reengineering, restructuring, painting, writing, problem solving, planning, or brainstorming.

So take 15 minutes, sit down with a pen and paper, and write down all the skills and abilities you possess *that have value to another company*. Transferable skills are marketable and tangible qualifications that will have value to many organizations. An accountant, human resources manager, or logistics manager at General Motors has tangible transferable skills that are of value to many companies both in and out of the automotive industry.

SELF-MANAGEMENT SKILLS

Self-management skills are skills that are personality and value oriented. Self-management skills are those that describe your attitude

Taking an Inventory of Your Skills

and work ethic. They include creativity, energy, enthusiasm, logic, resourcefulness, productive competence, persistence, adaptability, and self-confidence. One cautionary note, however: *Try not to be too general in describing your self-management skills*. When you identify a specific skill, always be prepared to explain how that skill will benefit a prospective employer. For example, if you're analytical, how does that make you better prepared for a position you have designed for yourself?

When you identify and recognize your skills, you begin to know your product. If you know your product inside and out, you will never be caught off guard in an interview. In fact, you will be able to reinforce your value by emphasizing specific accomplishments you've achieved in the past, using those specific skills.

In summary, writing a powerful resume requires that you identify your marketable skills because they represent the heart of the resume. Your ability to sell yourself confidently in an interview despite stiff competition depends on knowing your skills and communicating the benefits of those skills to the interviewer. Strategic resume preparation begins with identifying what you have to offer based on where you plan to market yourself. It is the foundation for developing a powerful resume, and it will be the foundation of successful interviewing as well.

4

What Is a Resume?

The resume is the driving force behind career design. Ironically, it's not the resume itself that is critical; it's the energy, planning, strategy, and commitment behind the resume. For a professional athlete or actor, it's the preparation that makes or breaks the performance. In career design, the effort that goes into the preparation of your resume will play a major role in the outcome of your campaign. If you invest quality time and energy in developing a comprehensive and focused resume, you'll get quality results! On the other hand, if you put your resume together without much thought or reason, simply writing down your life's story and distributing it to potential employers, chances are you'll experience less than impressive results. In fact, you'll probably end up in the un-enviable position of joining the 80-percent club—those who are dissatisfied with their jobs.

The resume is the driving force of career design if it is constructed in a strategic and methodical manner. With this in mind, let's define resume. Dictionaries define it variously as "a summary" or as "a statement of a job applicant's previous employment experience, education, etc." This definition is hardly adequate, so let us offer you a clear and concise definition:

> *A resume is a formal written communication, used for employment purposes, notifying a potential employer that you have the skills, aptitude, qualifications, and credentials to meet specific job requirements. A successful resume is a marketing tool that demonstrates to prospective employers that you can solve their problems or meet their specific needs, and thus, warrant an employment interview in anticipation of being hired.*

In order to demonstrate that you can meet the needs of employers, you must have specific goals and objectives. Too many job seekers have vague, ambiguous, or uncertain career goals. They say, "I want a well-paying job with a progressive organization," or "I'm open to most anything." Forget that approach! You wouldn't say to a travel agent, "I'd like to go on a vacation somewhere interesting," or "I'm open to most anything." The age-old question applies: If we don't know where we're going, how will we ever get there, or know when we've arrived? There is no doubt that the quality of your career—the quality of your life—is a matter of choice and not a matter of chance only if a choice is made.

How does all this tie into writing resumes? There are only two types of resumes that have proved to be effective in career design, and most people use neither type. If you took every resume in circulation today and put them end to end, they would circle the Earth over 26 times. That amounts to about 650,000 miles of resumes. And here is a statistic that is truly astonishing: Approximately 98 percent of all resumes being circulated today don't do justice to the candidates they describe. In other words, most of the resumes are autobiographical in nature, describing just the background and experience of a candidate. The problem with autobiographical resumes is that they simply don't work.

Hiring managers and personnel professionals don't read resumes for education or entertainment. The bottom line is this: If you can identify an employer's needs or problems and explicitly demonstrate that you can fill those needs or effectively solve those problems, you'll be interviewed and eventually hired. It's logical and makes good common sense. In Chapter 5, we'll explain which resumes work, and why.

5

Successful Styles and Formats for Resumes

Here are the two types of resumes that are powerful and that work:

- The Targeted Resume
- The Inventory Resume

If you know the job classification and/or the industry or environment in which you want to work, you are a candidate for a targeted resume. In essence, you can identify (target) what you want to do either by job title or by industry or by both.

If you are a generalist, open to a number of options, or unable to identify clearly what you want to do, but are able to identify your marketable skills, you are a candidate for an inventory resume. An inventory resume promotes one's marketable skills to a diversified audience.

THE TARGETED RESUME

If you know your target audience, you must create a resume that emphasizes your skills, abilities, and qualifications that match the needs of your target. Position the text on your resume to match the job requirements as closely as possible. For example, if you're seeking a sales position but are not fussy about what industry you sell in, you would identify the key assets and value that you bring to the table. Five such assets might be:

1. Possessing exceptional closing skills.
2. Having an active network in place that would be especially enticing to a future employer who is looking for a candidate to ignite a sudden surge of new business.
3. Having been trained by a reputable company so a new learning curve is literally nonexistent.
4. A proven and verifiable track record of specific sales accomplishments.
5. The ability to turn around a flat and phlegmatic territory into a flourishing one.

The problem with most resumes, according to hiring authorities, is that people simply list responsibilities. You will seldom be hired based on past responsibilities, but you have an excellent chance of being hired based on former accomplishments.

THE INVENTORY RESUME

If you cannot clearly identify your target, then your resume should highlight your accomplishments and skills in a more generic manner. What benefits will a prospective employer receive in return for employing you? What skills do you bring to the table that will enhance and contribute to the organization?

Let's take the example of a branch manager of a bank who is making a career change. He might have five specific skills that he can market to any number of industries, so he would develop an inventory resume with a portfolio of inventory assets that might include the following:

1. Solid sales and marketing skills
2. Excellent financial and budgeting skills
3. Training and development abilities
4. Seasoned operations management skills
5. Strong computer aptitude

After advertising these specific skills on the resume, the balance of the document would focus on specific achievements in these five areas.

Regardless of which resume type you choose, you must incorporate pertinent information that addresses the needs, concerns, and expectations of the prospective employer or industry. Samples of both resume types are included in this book.

COMMUNICATING CRITICAL MESSAGES

A resume must communicate critical messages. What are critical messages? A resume is a 30-second advertisement. Understanding that, critical messages are likened to "hot buttons," using marketing terminology. Critical messages are messages that the reader of your resume needs to read. They ignite enthusiasm and eventual action—which is an interview.

Career design is an exercise in self-marketing, and it's okay to be creative and to get excited about your future. When it comes to marketing yourself, there is just one ironclad rule for resume writing, and here it is:

There can be no spelling or typographical errors, and the resume must be well organized and professionally presented, consistent with the industry you are pursuing.

That's it! Yes, brief is better, one or two pages unless you have a very unique situation. Today, many successful career designers are incorporating graphics in their resumes, packaging them in a vibrant, exciting, and professional manner. For the first time, career designers are getting enthusiastic and excited about their resumes. After all, if you can't get excited about your resume, how do you expect anyone else to get excited about it?

So to this end, there are two main objectives to a resume. The obvious one is that the resume is a hook and line, luring a prospective employer to take the bait and invite you to an interview. The second objective of the resume is to get you pumped up, and prepare you for the interview and the process of securing a job.

RESUME FORMATS

Your resume can be written in any one of five formats: chronological, functional, combination, curriculum vitae, and resumap.

Chronological Format

The chronological format is considered by many employment professionals and hiring authorities to be the resume format of choice because it demonstrates continuous and upward career growth. It does this by emphasizing employment history. A chronological format lists the positions held in a progressive sequence, beginning with the most recent and working back. The one feature that distinguishes the chronological format from the others is that under each job listing, you communicate your (1) responsibilities, (2) skills needed to do the job, and, most important, (3) specific achievements. The focus is on time, job continuity, growth and advancement, and accomplishments.

Functional Format

A functional format emphasizes skills, abilities, credentials, qualifications, or accomplishments at the beginning of the document, but does not correlate these characteristics to any specific employer. Titles, dates of employment, and employment track record are deemphasized in order to highlight qualifications. The focus is squarely on what you did, not when or where you did it.

The challenge of the functional format is that some hiring managers don't like it. The consensus seems to be that this format is used by problem career designers: job hoppers, older workers, career changers, people with employment gaps or academic skill-level deficiencies, or those with limited experience. Some employment professionals feel that if you can't list your employment history in a chronological fashion, there must be a reason, and that reason deserves close scrutiny.

Combination Format

This format offers the best of all worlds—a quick synopsis of your market value (the functional style), followed by your employment chronology (the chronological format). This powerful presentation first addresses the criteria for a hire—promoting your assets, key credentials, and qualifications, supported by specific highlights of your career that match a potential industry or employer's needs. The employment section follows with precise information pertaining to each job. The employment section directly supports the functional section.

The combination format is very well received by hiring authorities. The combination format actually enhances the chronological format while reducing the potential stigma attached to functional formats. This happens when the information contained in the functional section is substantive, rich with relevant material that the reader wants to see, and is later supported by a strong employment section.

Curriculum Vitae

A curriculum vitae (CV) is a resume used mostly by those professions and vocations in which a mere listing of credentials describes the value of the candidate. A doctor, for instance, would be a perfect candidate for a CV. The CV is void of anything but a listing of credentials such as medical schools, residencies performed, internships, fellowships, hospitals worked in, public speaking engagements, and publications. In other words, credentials do the talking.

The Resumap

The resumap is a new format that clearly breaks with tradition. The writing of the resume is a left-brain exercise where thoughts occur in a rational, analytical, logical, and traditional manner. By engaging the right brain in this endeavor (the creative, imaginative, and stimulating side of the brain), the resume becomes a more dynamic document.

HOW TO SELECT THE CORRECT FORMAT

Consider using a chronological format if you have an impeccable work history and your future ties to your past. Contemplate using a combination format if you have few deficiencies in experience, education, or achievements. Consider a functional format if you are a student, returning to the workforce after an extended absence, changing careers, have worked many jobs in a short period of time, have had employment breaks, or have any other history that would make using a chronological or combination format challenging. Feel free to use a CV if your credentials speak for themselves and no further information is required of you until the interview. Use a resumap when you want to be different and make a statement.

In the end, exercise common sense and design a resume that best promotes you. There are no rules, only results. Select the format that will afford you the best chance of success.

6

The Five Ps of Resume Writing

Now it's time to review the five Ps of an explosive resume:

- Packaging
- Positioning of Information
- Punch or Power Information
- Personality
- Professionalism

PACKAGING

Packaging is a vital component to sales success. Most people wouldn't think of purchasing something from a store if the packaging was slightly broken. Paper stock, graphics, desktop publishing, font variations, and imaginative presentations and ideas are part of the packaging process. Most resumes are prepared on white, ivory, or gray paper. Conforming may be a recipe for disaster, so package your resume to stand out from the crowd. You'll want to remain professional and, in some cases, on the conservative side. There are various paper styles and presentation folders that are professional but unique and that still provide a competitive edge. Office supply stores or your local printer will be good sources of different paperstocks.

POSITIONING OF INFORMATION

Positioning means organization. Organize the data on your resume so that it's easily accessible to the reader, and the reader is able to grasp significant information quickly. You need to create a section of the resume (the Introduction, which we discuss in Chapter 7) where the key information will be displayed. In other words, by creating a highly visible section within the resume, you manipulate the reader's eyes to hone in on information that you deem essential to getting an interview. By doing this, you make the best use of the hiring authority's 10 to 20 seconds of review time.

You can have the best credentials in the world, backed by a powerful personality, complemented by the strongest references, but these career-making credentials are useless if your resume is sloppy, poorly organized, and difficult to read. No matter how superior you are to your competition, the prospective employer will almost never read a poorly presented document.

PUNCH OR POWER INFORMATION

This "P" is by far the most important. When you deliver the punch, you deliver the power information that the hiring manager wants to see. It means that you are supplying the reader with *information that matches a career designer's skills, abilities, and qualifications to a prospective employer's needs*. Quite simply, power information delivers the knockout punch, indicating to a prospective employer that you meet the criteria for hire.

The employer's task is to locate candidates whose overall credentials and background meet the organization's needs. Your task is to demonstrate, in your resume and later during an interview, that you have what the employer is looking for. So the starting point of all career design resumes is projecting and anticipating hiring criteria. You need to be aware of the type of person who will be reviewing your resume. Furthermore, you must determine what kind of information that person seeks that will provide you with a clear competitive advantage and spark enough interest to warrant an interview.

The challenge for those people writing resumes is to address directly the concerns of hiring authorities. The challenge is to get into the employers' heads. What are they thinking? What do they want? What can you show them that will make them react? In many instances, it's specific, quantifiable achievements.

This is a good time to emphasize the importance of noting specific accomplishments on your resume. The fact that you were responsible for doing something in a past job in no way assures anyone that you were successful! If your resume is full of generalities, responsibilities, and job descriptions, and lacks specific successes and achievements, how do you expect a prospective employer to differentiate your resume from the other 650,000 miles of documents? The majority of attention should be placed on your accomplishments and achievements. Responsibilities don't sell. Benefits, results, and success sell. What you were responsible for in the past has little impact on your future. *What you specifically accomplished highlights your past and determines your hireability.*

PERSONALITY

Hiring managers want to hire people with pleasing personalities. Your resume can have its own personality. Packaging can convey a unique personality, and so can words. We are suggesting that by the use of sumptuous vocabulary, you can turn a rather dull sentence into a more lavish and opulent one. Substitute the word "ignited" for "increased." Change the term "top producer" to "peak performer." Instead of "being responsible for something," show that you were "a catalyst for major improvements in _____."

Remember, words are power. Make use of the more than 750,000 available to you in the English language. A resume does not have to be a lackluster instrument. Lighten up and let your resume dance a bit, sing a little, and entertain the reader. By displaying a personality, you display emotion. And more than any other single element, emotion sells!

PROFESSIONALISM

Countless hiring managers believe that how people present themselves professionally will determine how professionally they will represent the company. We purchase expensive clothing, practice good hygiene, and make sure we look our very best when going to an interview because we want to make a good, lasting, and professional first impression. The resume must do the same. Once again, you are the product, and you are the salesperson. Your resume is your brochure. Would you hire yourself, based on the professionalism of your resume?

What is professionalism? Well, would you:

- Send your resume out without a cover letter, or would you enclose a personal cover letter addressed specifically to a targeted individual on matching stationery?
- Fold your resume into thirds and stuff it in a business envelope, or would you send the resume out in an attractive flat envelope without folding it at all?
- Send the resume by regular mail, or use overnight or two-day air mail to make a more powerful entry into the organization of destination?
- Expect the prospective employer to call you after receiving your resume (reactive responsibility), or would you make it clear that you will telephone that person within a week to arrange an interview?

Think about these questions for just a moment. What would seem more professional to you? There is a tremendous shortage of professionalism out there. Embrace professionalism, and you'll discover that you'll be invited to more and more interviews. That means more opportunities.

7
Anatomy of a Career Design Resume

Regardless of the resume type you choose or the format you decide upon, there are five primary sections that make up a successful career design resume, along with numerous subsections that can also be incorporated. The five primary sections are:

1. Heading
2. Introduction
3. Employment
4. Education
5. Miscellaneous

THE HEADING

The heading, also referred to as your *personal directory*, consists of your name, address (with full zip code), phone number (with area code), and personal email. If you carry a portable phone or pager or have a fax machine, you can include these phone numbers in your heading. We do not recommend that you include a work number. Many hiring managers do not look favorably upon those who furnish a work number. They may conclude that if you use your present company's phone and resources to launch a job search campaign on company time, you might do the same while working for them.

There are two basic methods for setting up your heading: the traditional, and the creative. The traditional method is the centered heading. This is effective for any resume, including those that will be scanned by a computer. The creative style consists of any heading that is not centered. Look at some of the many different examples of headings in the sample resumes. For style and layout ideas, look at resumes even if they do not represent your profession.

THE INTRODUCTION

An effective, power-packed introduction consists of two or three sections. The introduction sets the tone of the resume and swiftly connects your areas of expertise with the prospective employer's needs. It must answer the initial query, "What do you want to do?" or "What value can you provide my company?"

It identifies who you are and what you have to offer, and can take any of the following three forms:

- Title
- Objective
- Summary

For target resumes, consider using a title or an objective. An objective should not be used if it limits your scope. For example, if you work in operations, an objective might exclude opportunities that you don't even know exist. However, if you work as a nurse or accountant, your objective may be clearly defined. When developing an inventory resume, you should incorporate a summary to kick off your introduction. The purpose of the summary is to convey the scope of your experience and background and to indicate to the reader your key strengths and areas of expertise. *The first section of the introduction must ignite initial interest and make the reader want to continue.*

THE EMPLOYMENT SECTION

The employment section is, in the majority of cases, the most important section of your resume. (Resumes of recent college graduates are among the exceptions, when academic achievements and extracurricular activities are given more weight than employment experience.)

The employment section will have the most influence on a prospective employer in determining if you get an interview, and ultimately, a job offer. This section highlights your professional career and emphasizes experience, qualifications, and achievements. The employment module normally begins with your most recent position and works backward (allocate the most space to the most recent positions and less space as you go back in time). If you have a sensible and strategic reason to deviate from this guideline, and it enhances your document, go for it. Otherwise, reference the following information for each employer:

1. Name of company or organization
2. City/town and state where you worked
3. Dates of employment
4. Titles or positions held

How far back do you have to go? That's entirely up to you. You do not have to go back more than 10 to 12 years unless you have a good reason to do so. For instance, if you want to get back into a particular career, something you did 18 years ago but stopped doing to raise your children, you'll want to go back 18 years. But the rule of thumb is 10 to 12 years. For the most part, what we did 15 years ago is of little consequence to an employer today.

Experience is not limited to paying jobs. Include volunteer work if it is applicable and it enhances your candidacy. Do not include salary, reasons for leaving, or supervisor's name unless you have a very specific reason for doing so. Salary history and requirements, if requested, should be addressed in the cover letter.

Content

When using a chronological or combination format, provide specific information for each employer you worked for and for each job you performed. Include three pieces of information for each employer or job:

1. Basic responsibilities and industry- or company-specific information
2. Special skills required to perform those responsibilities
3. Specific accomplishments

The listing of your job responsibilities should read like a condensed job description. Bring out only the highlights, not the obvious. Finally, use positive and energy-oriented words. The words you choose should reflect your energy level, motivation, charisma, education level, and professionalism. Emotion and action sell; use action and power words.

Briefly describe any special skills you used in carrying out past responsibilities. These skills might include computers that you operated, special equipment used, and bilingual capabilities. Other examples of skills that you might have employed include problem solving, communications, and organizational or technical mastery. Review your daily tasks, and you'll be surprised at the skills you use every day but take entirely for granted.

The major focus of the employment or experience section should be on your specific accomplishments, achievements, and contributions. What you did in terms of day-to-day functions has little impact. *What you accomplished through those functions determines hireability.* Achievements vary from profession to profession. You need to consider:

- Revenue increases
- Profit improvements
- Expense savings
- Reengineering successes
- Productivity improvements
- System enhancements
- Awards and recognitions
- New policies and procedures
- Quality improvements
- New technology introduction
- Start-ups and turnarounds
- Reducing employee turnover
- Mergers and acquisitions
- Inventory reductions
- Adding value to the company
- Problems identified
- Contributions made and resolved

When using a functional format, simply list the information—company name, city and state, dates of employment, and titles—and leave it at that.

Other Employment

Your employment history may quite possibly go back 20 years or more. Focus the majority of your resume on the most recent 10 to 12 years, and provide a brief synopsis of the rest. You are not obligated to account for every minute of your life, so use this section to summarize activities performed many years ago if it will round out your employment background.

THE EDUCATION SECTION

The education section, as any other section, should position your credentials in the very best light without being misleading. List your highest degree first and work back. If you have attended six different colleges but have no degree, you might think that these efforts indicate that you are a lifelong learner. But it could also be interpreted as *project incompletion*, and work against you. Think carefully, strategize, and do what's right for you.

Generally, the education section appears at the beginning of your resume if you have limited work experience. A recent high school, technical school, or college graduate will, in most cases, fall into this category. As your portfolio of experience and achievements gains momentum, the education section will drop toward the end of the resume as newly formed experiences, skills, and accomplishments begin to outweigh educational experience in the eyes of a prospective employer. Finally, if your educational credentials are seen as critical, or are superior to those of competing candidates, you'll want to introduce this section early in the resume.

If you have a postsecondary degree, you need not list high school credentials on the resume. A job seeker with no postsecondary degree should include high school graduation on the resume. Particular details you might want to address under the heading of education include:

- Grade point average (GPA), if 3.0 or higher
- Class ranking
- Honors and awards
- Scholarships
- Intramural or varsity sports
- Clubs and special classes
- Relevant course work if directly related to your target profession (mostly for recent graduates)
- Special theses or dissertations
- Internships
- Research projects
- Extracurricular activities (tutoring, volunteer work, student activities, working on school newspaper)
- Career-related jobs and activities while attending school

This is a good place to talk about hiding information. There are some very imaginative methods of trying to hide weaknesses, and without exception, they all fail. But that doesn't mean you should accentuate any flaws in brilliant colors for all to see. The best way to overcome a weakness is to identify a corresponding strength that will more than make up for the weakness. If you have an associate's degree in business when a bachelor's degree is required, what can you do? Pinpoint areas of experience where you've proved yourself, especially where practical experience and a proven track record stands out. Demonstrate high energy and enthusiasm and stress your commitment to give 200 percent. Also, enroll in a community school and begin earning your bachelor's degree, and state this in your resume and/or cover letter.

You need to address your weakness honestly by demonstrating powerful strengths and assets. Even if you are successful in initially fooling a hiring authority, you can be sure that the interview will be quite uncomfortable. If questions are asked that you can't answer satisfactorily, you're in for an embarrassing, defensive, and unproductive meeting. You will come across as conniving and unethical.

MISCELLANEOUS SECTIONS

Military

If you served your country and received an honorable discharge, it is fine to mention this briefly in your resume. Unless your experience in the military is directly related to the profession you are pursuing (e.g., U.S. Navy aircraft mechanic applying for a job as a mechanic with an airline), then keep it very short, one to two lines at most. The more your military background supports your future career goals, the more emphasis you should give it. Underscore key skills and achievements.

Finally, and this is very important, translate military jargon into English. Many civilian employers were not in the military and can't relate to or understand military vernacular. If you are not sure of the proper equivalent civilian terminology when translating military verbiage to business terminology, seek out assistance. After going through the painstaking effort of getting a hiring or personnel manager to read your resume, you want to be absolutely certain that this person can easily understand the messages you are sending.

Interests

Interests are inserted to add a human element to the resume; after all, companies hire people, not robots. This is a section that should be kept brief, tasteful, and provocative insofar as the interviewer can use this information as an "ice breaker" and to set the tone of the interview. It helps to build rapport.

Obviously, you will want to use an interest section when your interests match job requirements, skills, or related activities that enhance your chances of getting an interview, and a job offer. A country club manager may want to include tennis, golf, and swimming as hobbies. A computer teacher may want to list reading, attending motivational workshops, and surfing the Internet as hobbies. A salesperson may want to include competitive sports because many sales managers view strong competitive skills as a valuable asset in the highly competitive sales arena.

Provide one line (no more, unless you have a compelling reason to do so) of information to show the reader your diversification of interests. You might try two or three athletic interests, two to three hobbies, and/or two to three cultural interests. This gives the prospective employer a good profile of who you are outside of work.

Community Service, Special Projects, and Volunteer Work

Many organizations place a high degree of importance on community service. They value fund-raising efforts, volunteering time to charities, and contributing to community improvement. In many cases, it is good public relations and enhances a company's image. Organizations that value these activities believe in the adage that "what we get back is in direct proportion to what we give." If you feel that supporting community activities, the arts, and other such causes will enhance your overall credentials, then by all means, include them on your resume.

Professional and Board Affiliations

Memberships and active participation in professional and trade associations demonstrate to a prospective employer that you (1) are a contributing member of your profession, (2) desire to advance your own knowledge and improve your skills, and (3) are committed to the future of your vocation. Pertinent affiliations should appear in your resume.

If you sit on boards of directors, this also indicates that you are well respected in your community and that you give of your time to other organizations, be they profit or nonprofit entities. These distinguishing credits should be included in your resume.

Awards, Honors, and Recognitions

No doubt these are critical to your resume because they represent your achievements in a powerful and convincing manner. It's one thing to boast about your accomplishments—and that's good. But flaunt your accomplishments *supported by specific awards and recognitions*, and that will often be the one thing that separates you from your competition.

You can illustrate your honors and recognitions:

1. In the introduction section of your resume
2. Under professional experience
3. As a separate section

Technical Expertise/Computer Skills

Incorporating a section describing your specific technical and computer skills may be an effective way to introduce your skills quickly to the reader. In a high-tech, ever-changing business environment, employers are looking for people with specific skills and, even more importantly, for people who have the ability to learn, adapt, and embrace new technologies.

In this section, consider using short bulleted lists so the information is easily accessible. Information and data tend to get lost and confused when lumped together in long sentences and paragraphs.

Teaching Assignments

If you have conducted, facilitated, or taught any courses, seminars, workshops, or classes, include this on your resume, whether you were paid for it or not. Teaching, training, and educating are in-demand skills. They exhibit confidence, leadership, and the ability to communicate. If you have experience in this area, consider stating it on your resume.

Licenses, Accreditation, and Certifications

You may choose to include a section exclusively for listing licenses, accreditation, and certifications. Consider using bulleted lists as an effective way to communicate your significant qualifications quickly and effectively.

Languages

We live and work in a global economy where fluency in multiple languages is an asset in great demand. Be sure to list your language skills at the beginning of the resume if you determine that these skills are critical to being considered for the position. Otherwise, clearly note them toward the end.

Personal

Personal data consists of information such as date of birth, marital status, social security number, height, weight, and sex (if your name is not gender-specific), health, number of dependents, citizenship, travel and relocation preferences, and employment availability.

Employers, by law, cannot discriminate by reason of age, race, religion, creed, sex, or color of your skin. For this reason, many job seekers leave personal information off the resume. Unless you have a specific reason to include it, it's probably a good idea to limit or eliminate most personal information. For example, if you are applying for a civil service position, a social security number might be appropriate to include on the resume. Or, if you are applying for a position as a preschool teacher and have raised six children of your own, you may want to include this information on the resume.

Here's a good test for determining whether or not to include personal information on a resume: Ask yourself, "Will this information dramatically improve my chances for getting an interview?" If the answer is yes, include it. If the answer is no, or I don't know, omit it.

8

An E-Guide to the Electronic Resume

We have been discussing how to develop a resume primarily in the traditional way. Nearly everyone is used to writing up their resumes as word processing documents, finding nice stationery, printing up the resume, and sending it out in the mail with a stamp.

Today, along with the advent of all the new dot-com job opportunities, comes a new way of distributing your resume. Mail with a stamp is still useful, to be sure, but so is email and Web site postings. In fact, for those of you in the Internet-related industries, email and Web site communications are so prevalent that you should consider those communications vehicles your first priority.

There are two kinds of electronic resumes. One is the resume that is sent as an email attachment. The other is a text copy inserted into a Web site input field or directly pasted into an email.

E-RESUMES AS ATTACHMENTS

When you send your resume as an email attachment, you take the file of your resume that you created in a word processing software program, like Microsoft Word, and "attach" it to the email. We assume that you know how to perform the task of attaching a document in an email.

We would always recommend that you attach your resume in email or posting communications, where possible. Hiring managers and recruiters will invariably print the email with your resume. If you have a good version attached, it will be easier to read than a text-only file, which might be graphically displeasing or difficult to sort through.

If you attach your email, all the guidelines previously discussed still hold true.

E-RESUMES AS TEXT FILES

Another way you can offer your resume is as a text file. This means that you are providing the bare content of your resume in text, but without the graphical enhancements. This can mean that you no longer get to use tabs, bullets, certain spacing, boxes, shading, bold print, etc. This can make the creation of the resume both easier and more difficult.

It can be easier to create a resume in text-only format because you are in fact eliminating the graphical enhancements and formatting. You're simply writing in straight text. However, making an effective presentation without that ability to format actually makes it a more difficult task. This is very important! You need to make your resume appealing given the limitations just described.

MODIFICATIONS FOR WRITING E-RESUMES AS TEXT FILES

For the next few sections, please refer back to Chapter 7, "Anatomy of a Career Design Resume." We will take each section that defined how to write up the resume and offer up tips on modifying that for the text-only version.

The Heading

Keep the heading free of any bullets, change in fonts, and underlines. Use commas instead. Your new text-only heading might look something like this:

> Joe Pascual, 3628 Eastmore Street, San Francisco, CA 94123, 415-555-1257, jpascual@winklink.com

The Introduction

Since this is going to be reviewed online, you need to get to the point as concisely as possible. A good introduction is very important here. Try to boil your accomplishments down to three or four, preferably quantifiable ones, and make them as concise as possible. A reader's attention span is shorter when reading plain text on a monitor than it is when reading on paper.

> 5 years' experience in telecommunications
>
> Accomplished background in telecommunications engineering and product development
>
> Sales and product management background in wide area network (WAN) design, ATM, Frame Relay, and Internet services

The Employment Section

Keep this section free of any bullets, changes in fonts, and underlines. Use commas instead. An entry in your new text-only employment section might look something like this:

SPRINT CORPORATION, San Francisco, CA, 1996 to Present

Advanced Sales Support Manager/Field Product Manager

*Provided technical and product-related support for Sales Support divisions on leading-edge technologies for approximately 200 engineering and sales management employees.

*Led sales support for data services for highest-performing region in Sprint, which in 2000 was 213% of plan.

*Developed analyses of competitors' product offerings and evaluated customer demand for new product feature offerings through market surveys. Provided recommendations to Marketing and Business Development on needed enhancements to product portfolio.

The Education Section

Keep this section free of any bullets, changes in fonts, and underlines. Use commas instead. Your new text-only education section might look something like this:

EDUCATION

COLLEGE OF WILLIAM AND MARY, Williamsburg, VA,
Bachelor of Science, May 1996

The Finished Product

The following is an example of how the completed resume would appear:

Joe Pascual, 3628 Eastmore Street, San Francisco, CA 94123, 415-555-1257, jpascual@winklink.com

PROFESSIONAL PROFILE

– *5 years' experience in telecommunications*

– *Accomplished background in telecommunications engineering and product development*

– *Sales and product management background in wide area network (WAN) design, ATM, Frame Relay, and Internet services*

SPRINT CORPORATION, *San Francisco, CA, 1996 to Present*

Advanced Sales Support Manager / Field Product Manager

– *Provided technical and product related support for Sales Support divisions on leading-edge technologies for approximately 200 engineering and sales management employees.*

– *Led sales support for data services for highest-performing region in Sprint, which in 2000 was 213% of plan.*

– *Developed analyses of competitors' product offerings and evaluated customer demand for new product feature offerings through market surveys. Provided recommendations to Marketing and Business Development on needed enhancements to product portfolio.*

EDUCATION

COLLEGE OF WILLIAM AND MARY, Williamsburg, VA,
Bachelor of Science, May 1996

9
Cover Letters

You must include a cover letter when sending your resume to anyone. Resumes are impersonal documents that contain information about your skills, abilities, and qualifications, backed by supporting documentation. In most cases, you'll send the same resume to a host of potential employers. A resume is a rather rigid instrument, and unless you customize each document for a specific audience, the resume is, for the most part, inflexible.

Phoebe Taylor, in her 1974 publication, *How to Succeed in the Business of Finding a Job*, provides advice on cover letters that, after so many years, still holds true:

> *If you stop to think about it for a moment, all resumes have basic similarities. Librarians' resumes are look-alikes; accountants' resumes have much in common; and so on. To get the employer to single out the "paper you," you'll have to demonstrate some ingenuity to separate yourself from the crowd.*

> *The cover letter provides additional pertinent information and reemphasizes your qualifications consistent with the employer's needs. As your "personal messenger," it shows your uniqueness and your ability to express yourself on paper and gives a glimpse of your personality. Addressed to a real person, "Dear Mr. Johnson" or "Dear Ms. Winters," it becomes a personal communiqué. It proves to the reader that you made the effort and used your resourcefulness to find out his or her name and title.*

A cover letter allows you to get more personal with the reader. It is the closest you can get to building rapport without meeting in person. It is a critical component in getting an interview and, eventually, the job.

Cover letters should be brief, energetic, and interesting. A polished cover letter answers the following questions concisely and instantaneously:

1. Why are you writing to me, and why should I consider your candidacy?
2. What qualifications or value do you have that I could benefit from?
3. What are you prepared to do to sell yourself further?

Cover letters work best when they are addressed to individuals by name and title. They should be written using industry-specific language and terminology. And finally, you must initiate some future action. Specifically, you want to let readers know that you will be contacting them for the purpose of arranging an interview, or whatever the next step will be. Be proactive! Don't expect people to call you; when possible, you should launch the next step, and do so with confidence and an optimistic expectation.

ANATOMY OF A COVER LETTER

What follows is the skeletal structure for a successful cover letter:

1. Your heading and the date
2. Person's name and title
3. Company
4. Address
5. Salutation
6. First paragraph: Power opening—talk about the organization, not you
7. Second paragraph: Purpose of this correspondence and brief background
8. Third paragraph: Punch the "hot buttons"—what precisely can you do for them?
9. Fourth paragraph: Closing and call to action (initiate your next move)
10. Sign-off

Consider the following quotation:

> I would be lying if I told you that I read every resume that crossed my desk. But I have almost never not looked at a resume that was accompanied by a solid, well-written cover letter. The lesson here is that you must learn how to write a strong letter. A cover letter should do more than serve as wrapping paper for your resume. It should set you apart from other candidates.

This quote comes from Max Messmer, CEO of Robert Half International, Inc., one of the world's largest staffing firms. Messmer suggests that most cover letters emphasize what candidates are looking for and not enough about the contributions a candidate can make to an organization. Therefore, when you are composing your letters, avoid overusing the pronoun "I," and focus instead on the contributions that you will make to the company. Don't rehash what you deliver in the resume. Whenever possible, mention information that reflects your knowledge of the organization you are writing to or the industry as a whole. Bring current news or events into the letter that will show the reader you are up-to-date and current with industry trends.

COVER LETTERS AND THE INTERNET

If you are sending an electronic or emailed resume, your email will open with a note. This is your new cover letter. The dynamics of an on-line cover letter probably vary more from the traditional than the changes in your resume. Emailed cover letters should be considered short introductions. They should be not nearly as long as what you might put in the mail.

Your emailed cover letter might also be used as a source of key words for computer searches, so make them rich with at least a few key words (nouns) that will give the reader an overview.

The same general principles of a cover letter hold true for an emailed one. However, it is critical to keep it short and maintain the same formatting guidelines as for the electronic resume. This means that you need to choose a monotype font (one equally spaced for each letter) so the spacing won't get lost in the data transport. When you email a note, the networks transport in an ASCII format, which means it is converted into a generic format and loses formatting such as underlining, bold type face, italics, and creative font choices. ASCII recognizes only spacing and tabs.

Finally, the key steps in Chapter 7, "Anatomy of a Career Design Resume," won't apply here, because when you email a letter, the headings and address formats are embedded in the email itself.

Keep your email cover letter short and simple, but make sure it still contains enough punch.

THE BROADCAST LETTER

There are times when a career designer is gainfully employed, content with the job, but restless enough to want to explore alternatives. Maybe you're bored, not earning what you feel you deserve, foresee trouble ahead, or just want a career change to try something different. The challenge in this situation is that you don't want to take the chance of your current employer's finding out that you're looking for other work. That could cause really big trouble. The day you send out your first resume, you risk exposure. You can never be 100 percent sure where your resume will end up. Consequently, the moment you broadcast to anyone that you are exploring employment opportunities, you run the risk of exposing this to your present employer. The broadcast letter is a means to protect you to a certain degree, though even the broadcast letter is not foolproof.

The broadcast letter can also be used by those who have had 16 jobs in the past three years, who take time off from work on occasion, or who are returning to the workplace following an extended absence. The broadcast letter becomes half cover letter, half resume. Though you'll need a resume some time down the road, a broadcast letter is a technique used to attract initial attention without providing extensive detail or exposing information you'd rather not divulge at this time. Some career designers use this letter format because they feel that people are more apt to read it than a resume. Secretaries, for instance, who screen incoming mail may not screen out broadcast letters as quickly as they do resumes.

Broadcast letters provide an effective means for discreetly communicating your employment intentions to executive recruiters or employment agencies or for informing key people in your network of your goals and objectives. The broadcast letter, by definition, broadcasts your strengths and abilities in more depth than a cover letter but in less detail than a resume. Many advantages to sending out a broadcast letter include the following:

- Broadcast letters avoid chronology of employment.
- They provide a partial listing of former employers.
- These letters communicate that you are presently employed and are, therefore, uncomfortable in advertising your present employer until there is interest in you as a viable candidate.
- They emphasize your strong employment record and accompanying assets without mentioning educational credentials that may be viewed by others as weak.
- Broadcast letters allow you to overcome a challenging past, including alcohol or substance abuse difficulties, time spent in jail, physical or emotional encounters, or other similar obstacles.

A broadcast letter can be an effective way to introduce yourself and spark interest in your candidacy. You must be prepared, however, to address any challenges in subsequent communications with employers who show an interest in you after having reviewed the broadcast letter.

Chapter 10 offers 16 sample cover letters for your review. Notice how many are written less formally than you might expect, and how they allow the writer more creativity than a resume might. Try not to write the cover letter in too formal a style. Many entry-level candidates tend to write very stiff "professional" letters that prevent the reader from getting to know them.

OTHER COLLATERAL MATERIALS

Personal Calling Cards

It may not be practical to carry your resume everywhere you go or to every meeting or event you attend. But everywhere you go and at every meeting or event you do attend, you should be networking. If you connect with an individual who might be of some assistance to your career design efforts, you must be prepared to leave a calling card. We highly recommend that you have 500 to 1000 personal calling cards printed (they are not expensive), and make it a point to hand out 100 to 150 a week for starters! Include just the basic information: name, address, phone number, and your career objective or short summary of qualifications.

Thank-You Notes

You should send thank-you notes to every person who makes even the most infinitesimal impact on your career design. Stock up on some stylish, classy notecards because even a small item like a thank-you note can make a huge difference in the outcome of your labors.

10

16 Action-Oriented Cover Letters

RADIO FREQUENCY ENGINEER COVER LETTER

To: jobsearch.net;employment.com;engineeringnetworking.com

Date: October 2, 1999

Subject: Seeking radio frequency (RF) engineering position

I am interested in networking through this group to find an RF engineering position in either Denver or Phoenix with a cellular or PCS wireless organization.

I have worked with AT&T Wireless services in their TDMA deployment in two new PCS markets (Chicago and Milwaukee). I am very skilled with the latest forecasting tools and optimization methods for both TDMA and CDMA platforms. Attached is my resume for those interested. My references and work history are both very solid. Any tips or suggestions you may have are welcomed.

Thanks!

Steve Windsor

steve.windsor@worldnet.net   Attachment: [*resume.doc*]

ADVERTISING ACCOUNT EXECUTIVE COVER LETTER

To: advertisingjobs.net;jobsearch.net

Date: May 14, 1998

Subject: Seeking advertising account executive position

I am interested in finding a position with a Big 6 advertising firm in the capacity of advertising account executive. I have worked in advertising for three years, and past accounts include Procter and Gamble, Dave and Busters, Cisco, and Ethan Allen.

I am the lead account manager for Dave and Busters and Cisco. Duties include contract negotiation, liaison between clients, and creative development.

Please see attached resume if you are interested. If you know of any relevant contacts, please forward leads to me, or feel free to forward this email and the attached resume. I really appreciate it!

Sincerely,

Mary Beth Rouse

mbrouse@sprintmail. com   Attachment: [*resume. doc*]

MARKETING DEVELOPMENT COVER LETTER

Dear Ms. Pappas:

My experience in business management and marketing is an excellent fit for your new telecommunications start-up in Houston. I have watched with much envy as you launched your PCS network in other markets and want to take this opportunity to introduce myself.

Though I did not see a market development opening on your Web site, I am confident that I am a good fit and would like to be available for consideration should an opening come along.

I am currently employed, but I am very interested in Sprint, and would like the opportunity to discuss your future market developments.

Sincerely,

RG Matherly
rgmatherly@91215225251521.com

CHEMICAL PRODUCT DEVELOPMENT COVER LETTER

3255 Phillips Street
Irving, TX 77299
(214) 555-5687

Dear Ms. Lane:

Please allow me to introduce myself. I am new to the Michigan area. I have worked in the chemical products industry for the last six years, and I am interested in continuing in that industry here. I spent the last seven years in Chicago, but a recent engagement has brought me to central Michigan.

I worked for ABC Chemical in Chicago, moved on to XYZ Chemical for two years, and received promotions en route with each company. Considering that Dow is such a prominent player in the industry, I feel lucky to have been moved here.

My background lies in product development within the industry. I was on the market launch team that rolled out synthetic covering for wet weather shields. We gained a 17 percent share within 18 months of our launch, which is very strong by XYZ standards.

I will stop by your office next Tuesday between 2 p.m. and 3 p.m. to fill out your formal application. If you can take a few moments to see me at that time, I would be very grateful. I will call you on Monday to see if this can be arranged.

Thank you for your attention. I am excited about the possibility of joining Dow Chemical Company.

Sincerely,

Mary Beth Rouse
mbr@aol.com
4799 E. Deckerville Road
Saginaw, MI 48569
(517) 555-5682

Kathy Lucy Morris

504 Orange Circle, Crystal, MN 55428 (612) 555-8978

March 4, 1996

Mr. Tom Jensen, Executive Director
Palm Beach Visitors and Convention Bureau
122 Convention Plaza
West Palm Beach, FL 33408

Dear Mr. Jensen:

Palm Beach County, according to reliable publications, is one of the fastest-growing counties in the United States. I applaud the tremendous work you are doing at the Palm Beach Visitors and Convention Bureau to attract major events, further improving the economic climate of our thriving area. Your achievements, showcased as the cover story in the latest *Convention Center, International*, are impressive, and I for one would like to be a contributing sales member of your professional team.

I understand from the article that you are looking to become the number-one convention center in Florida, and I feel that my sales skills and abilities can help tip the scales from Orlando to Palm Beach! I offer you:

* **Nine years of proven experience in convention/event sales**
* **A verifiable track record for closing major national events**
* **Strong market analysis and strategic planning skills**
* **A personable, team-spirited professional with a strong network (national) in place**

I will be in West Palm Beach next month. If possible, I would like to visit and personally meet with you to introduce myself and my qualifications. I will take the liberty of calling you next week to arrange such a meeting.

Thank you for your time and consideration. I look forward to speaking and meeting with you soon.

Sincerely,

Kathy Morris

Kathy North

215 Hartman Drive

Portsmouth, NH 03801

(603) 555-4606

January 26,1996

Mr. Mike Desa, General Sales Manager
Speller Automobiles, Ltd.
325 Rolling Woods Highway
Dover, NH 03723

Dear Mr. Desa:

I am a recent college graduate with a **B.A. Degree in Automotive Marketing and Management**. I have also been part of a family-owned automobile distributorship for nearly all my life, so cars are my life!

I noticed your advertisement for *Automotive Sales and Marketing Assistant* in the *Dover Star* on June 14, and I am submitting my resume for your consideration.

You mentioned in the advertisement that the successful candidate must have:

1. A Bachelor of Arts degree   **I do**
2. Excellent communications skills   **I do**
3. Ability to work well with people at all levels   **I do**
4. Eagerness to learn and "pay my dues"   **I am and I will**

This is a job that I believe was made for me. I am familiar with your operation, as I am originally from this area. I am available immediately, and offer you competence, dedication, and a good work ethic. If you don't mind, I will call you next week to see if a personal interview can be scheduled.

Thank you for your consideration, and I look forward to speaking with you next week.

Sincerely,

Kathy North

Enclosure

Christine Pantoya

9981 Southern Boulevard • West Palm Beach, Florida 33409 • (561) 555-5719

March 29, 1999

Ms. Theresa Mascagni
Vice President Technical Operations
4800 Oakland Park Boulevard
Fort Lauderdale, FL 33341

Dear Ms. Mascagni:

After completing much research on the wireless communications industry over the last few months, it has become apparent that NextWave holds a unique position in the market. NextWave has secured multiple C-Block licenses across the country, and when built out will have a national presence comparable to AT&T and Sprint.

In order to meet your aggressive growth goals of launching this market by next fall, you will certainly need a strong RF team that has experience in the CDMA platform. Specifically, you will need a team that has experience optimizing the Lucent and Nortel base stations.

As a consultant, I led RF teams from network design to launch with both PrimeCo and Sprint PCS in the Chicago and Dallas MTAs, both of which were on a Lucent platform. I can provide excellent references from both. I think NextWave is a cutting-edge operation, one in which ingenuity, creativity and drive can make a material impression. I want to be a part of your team.

My experience is in perfect line with your needs right now and what you will need after launch. I will give you a call next week to set up some time for us to talk further.

Sincerely,

Christine Pantoya

David Hines

2357 Golf Drive Lane
Coppell, TX 75220
(817) 555-5974

June 9, 1999

Mr. Grant D. Powers, CEO
Golden Bear International
Golden Bear Plaza
11712 U.S. Highway 1
North Palm Beach, FL 33412

Dear Mr. Powers:

Your Controller, Mr. Gerald Haverhill, told me over golf a few weeks ago that you are
looking for an MIS director. He told me some very interesting things about GB and I
was impressed, not only with the growth and profitability, but in the similarities between
GB and Diversified Centers, my current employer. GB has added 23 new training centers in the United States and is overseeing the design of all Jack Nicklaus courses. With
that much widespread activity, MIS needs must surely be exploding.

With that much national activity, you must need each site to be networked with your
home office for both voice and data transport as well as to establish a WAN to improve
real-time connectivity. The design aspect of the business must eat up a lot of bandwidth
in data transport as well, so it would surely help if you could share information more
quickly and efficiently, while maintaining your privacy "firewall."

My current operation is quite similar. I have built a very efficient network for our many
regional locations to communicate. Diversified Centers builds and manages strip mall
shopping centers for Tom Thumb grocery stores. Our network enables each regional office to stay in touch via email and shared drives through our WAN, as well as to utilize
the Sprint ION network for real-time communications of high-bandwidth development
plans, similar to your use of golf course designs.

It appears that my accomplishments with Diversified Centers is in line with your MIS
needs at GB. I will give you a call next week to set up a meeting to talk further.

Looking forward to meeting you.

David Hines

P.S. Gerald told me that you are quite close with Mr. Nicklaus. Please congratulate him
on his fine Masters showing!

CAROLYN KELLENBURGER

5534 College Parkway, Cape Coral, FL 33410 (941) 555-9753

March 15, 1997

Ms. Kimberly Houston
Paramount Pictures
4800 Hollywood Boulevard
Santa Monica, CA, 90211

Dear Ms. Houston:

Jim Talley at Touchstone recently informed me that you are overseeing costumes and makeup for the new film, *The Nutty Professor*. Jim shared with me some of the effects that you are planning to use to transform the lead character between the thin professor and the very overweight professor. In order to pull this off, you will undoubtedly need artists skilled in this field.

I have experience with plastics, makeup, special wraps and the various maskings, which take a great deal of skill to apply in a way that is not transparent to the viewer. I know; I was the lead artist for several movies and clips, including Michael Jackson's *Thriller* video, *Halloween H20*, and in several *Tales from the Crypt* episodes.

My experience is very consistent with what you will need for your upcoming film. Please review my attached resume for the specifics of my film credits. You will see that I would be a good fit for helping you with all of the makeup and related preparations for the demanding transformation scenes. I will call you next Tuesday and set up a time to stop by the studio to meet you.

Sincerely,

Carolyn Kellenburger

Attachment

MISTI DeORNELLAS

45227 Michigan Avenue, Chicago, IL 24197 (312) 555-3125

March 9, 1999

Ms. Maria Lane, Executive Vice President
Hyde and Smithson Public Relations, Inc.
1800 Scenic Way
Mountain View, VT 19877

Dear Ms. Lane:

Over the last few months I've noticed your firm moving into consulting with several healthcare firms. After speaking with Tom Aimee, I am aware that you are bidding on the upcoming opening of two new Columbia hospitals. You will no doubt need significant healthcare industry expertise to drive this account. Healthcare can really get complicated when trying to balance aggressive marketing and sales techniques along with a more public entity image.

The two new locations in Portsmouth and Springfield will be delicate openings given the amount of bad press Columbia has received in the last year or two. Columbia has been in trouble with both the IRS and FBI for tampering with federal aid and overbilling to Medicare. They will undoubtably need good advice on how to position their openings to get off on the right foot.

I have been working in marketing and public relations for nine years, most recently with Humana in Florida. We successfully opened 11 new hospitals over the last six years, and even experienced a storm when we opened the one in Orlando. That one opened in the midst of a major citywide controversy regarding the for-profit nature of Humana versus the for-the good-of-the-people persona hospitals have maintained. Under my direction, Humana successfully overcame that encounter, and now that hospital is one of the most successful in the region.

My skills are very much in line with the needs of both your firm and your clients:

- 15 years in public relations
- 15 years in the healthcare industry
- Expertise in new launches and crisis management
- Key contacts within the industry

Please expect my telephone call in the next week so that we might be able to set a time to meet and discuss employment possibilities that would serve our mutual interests.

Sincerely,

Misti DeOrnellas

BEN CHANG

125 Torrey Pines Drive
Del Mar, CA 92103
(310) 555-5330

September 21, 1996

Ms. Diane King, Sales Coordinator
TJ Cellular Corp.
2300 La Jolla Blvd., Suite 400
La Jolla, CA 92164

Dear Ms. King:

A mutual acquaintance, Mr. Roger Smith, recommended that I contact you regarding a possible sales opportunity with TJ Cellular Corp. I have taken the liberty of enclosing my resume for your review. Thank you in advance for your consideration.

I now realize that I have been missing my calling. *I love sales, but have not been selling the products and services that I love.* I am a strong sales professional with solid technical skills, but have not been selling technical products. As Sales Manager for PDC (please refer to resume), I must have sent two dozen people to your company to purchase cellular phones (and they bought!), after they saw the slick phone I use that I purchased from you!

Now here's the irony—I get more excited promoting your phones than I have ever gotten from promoting anything I've ever sold—and I've been successful in all my sales endeavors! This is why I would like to pursue a sales position with TJ Cellular. I have over 20 years of successful sales experience. I offer you the following:

⇒ **A strong closer; excellent cold-canvassing and market development skills**
⇒ **A professional demeanor**
⇒ **A strong network of contacts in place**
⇒ **Enthusiasm and high energy**

Though my resume is quite detailed, it cannot fully profile the manner in which I have been successful. This can only be accomplished in a face-to-face meeting where we can exchange information and examine whether there might be mutual interest. I will call you in the coming week to arrange an interview. Again, I thank you for your time and review. I look forward to meeting with you soon.

Sincerely,

Ben Chang

Enclosure: Resume

PATRICIA CAPIZZI

1031 Rainbow Lane
Irvine, CA 92720
(714) 555-1791

January 15, 1996

Marianne Cox, Director of Human Resources
Medical Products, Inc.
124 Grant Avenue
Irvine, CA 92720

Dear Ms. Cox:

I noticed your advertisement for Sales Manager in the June edition of the *Medical Messenger*. I am very interested in pursuing this opportunity and have enclosed my resume for your review.

YOUR REQUIREMENTS	MY QUALIFICATIONS
1. Minimum of 5 years' management medical sales.	1. I have 8 years' experience in experience in medical sales.
2. Extensive training and coaching experience.	2. Received "Trainer of the Year" award, Bristol, Inc., 1994–95.
3. Proven ability to adapt sales programs to meet environmental and economic changes.	3. Increased territorial market share 32% per year over past 8 years.
4. A solid professional who is respected industrywide.	4. Member and past president, CA Medical Sales Association.

I recently read in a local newspaper that Medical Products, Inc. is streamlining its operations and is positioning itself to expand into the international arena. In addition to meeting the criteria you outlined in the above-mentioned ad, I speak four languages fluently and can be an asset in the area of international sales.

I will take the liberty of calling you early next week to discuss the possibility of arranging a face-to-face meeting to explore a number of ways that I feel I can contribute to Medical Products, Inc. Have a great day, and I look forward to speaking with you next week. Thank you.

Sincerely,

Patricia Capizzi

Encl: Resume

Monica Joseph

1117 Aaron Lane, Reidsville, GA 30453 (912) 555-4337

March 9, 1996

Ms. Andrea Kazen, RN, Head Nurse
Thompson Medical Complex
230 Medical Way
Reidsville, GA 30453

Dear Ms. Kazen:

I have returned home! After 25 years of living in Florida, I have returned home to spend the second half of my life where it all began. I am presently exploring nursing positions at Thompson Medical Complex and have enclosed my updated resume for your review.

I worked here in the 1960s. I left on great terms, have outstanding references, and would love to come back and conclude my career where I started.

As you see from my resume, I have not formally worked in the past 24 months. I have spent time with my children and grandchildren, traveled a bit with my semiretired husband, and have taken advantage of my free time to take a number of continuing education courses to improve my skills for twenty-first-century America—including computer courses, Advanced Nursing Techniques (JFK Medical Center), and other personal development-related workshops and seminars.

Now back in Georgia, I am seeking part-time employment. I am flexible as to the shifts and days I can work, and would like to find a position that would allow me to work about 24 hours per week. I can work three 8-hour shifts or two 12-hour ones. I have excellent letters of reference from my years in Florida, in addition to the fine reputation I left behind when I left Georgia some 25 years ago.

I will stop by your office next Tuesday between 2 p.m. and 3 p.m. to fill out your formal application. If you can take a few moments to see me at that time, I would be very grateful. I will call you on Monday to see if this can be arranged.

Thank you for your attention. I am excited about the possibility of returning to Thompson Medical Complex.

Sincerely,

Monica Joseph

Joe Siebert

1497 Dale Mabry Boulevard • Tampa, Florida 33587 • (813) 555-6684

February 8, 1996

Mr. Mike Cline
Director Sales and Marketing
PCS Wireless
3333 Westwood One
Tampa, FL 33587

Dear Mr. Cline:

I would like to thank you for meeting with me last week to discuss PCS Wireless and the possibility of my joining your team. I've been working in the wireless industry with Bell Atlantic since college, and becoming part of a start-up operation is a very exciting prospect.

I have learned a great deal about the wireless industry over the last two years. Between the cellular incumbents, the new PCS licensees, resellers, and future C-Band entrants, your market is sure to be very competitive. Obviously, pricing will become more competitive, but to become the market leader will require positioning beyond just price.

PCS Wireless has the opportunity to change this local market, one of the largest in the country. With new services and a better quality product, you have a great opportunity to make your operation the new standard in Central Florida. Mike, I am very interested in becoming part of this team and building this customer base.

The marketing role I have at Bell Atlantic is a great foundation for working in a business development capacity with you. I have conducted market research, target market segmentation analysis, and competitive analysis, and I have prepared various business planning presentations. This kind of market research and wireless experience would be a key added value to your staff.

Thanks again for staying in touch over this. There are few opportunities one gets to work in a dynamic organization, and I'd like to be a part of this one. I would like to be involved in the sales or promotions part of your team, where I can be of the greatest value. I will talk to you more as you near your launch.

Sincerely,

Joe Siebert

Fred Morey

1477 SW 40th Court, Coral Springs, Florida (954) 555-6583

September 12, 1996

Ms. Lori Harding
Robert Half International, Inc.
1450 E. Las Olas
Fort Lauderdale, FL 33444

Dear Ms. Harding:

If you are in need of a senior-level engineering manager for one of your executive searches, you may want to give serious consideration to my background.
Highlights of my experience are:

- M.S. Mechanical Engineering, University of Florida
- B.S. Electrical Engineering, Georgia Tech
- 16 years' Engineering and Management experience with:

  - Pratt & Whitney; V.P. Engineering (aircraft division), 4 years
  - IBM; Director of Project Engineering (software interface), 7 years
  - Boeing Corporation; Project Engineer, 5 years

In my current capacity as Vice President for Pratt & Whitney, I manage an engineering group of 450 responsible for aircraft motor design in three facilities in the country. This includes engineering design through to process design of manufacturing.

I have established a strong reputation for the quality and quantity of capital project work completed in my department. I have a solid reputation as a demanding and fair leader. The work performed under my direction has come in at or below budget, and we always meet project deadlines.

I have chosen to leave Pratt for personal reasons; they are unaware of my decision. My current compensation is about $130,000. Should you be interested, please contact me at home at (954) 555-6583.

Sincerely,

Fred Morey

Carolyn Fornataro
846 Blue Ridge Circle
Miami, FL 33335
(305) 555-7893

June 3, 1996

Mr. John Loureiro
TTS Personnel
420 Lexington Avenue
New York, NY 10170

Dear Mr. Loureiro:

Several of my associates in the communications industry here in South Florida have mentioned you as someone experienced with similar firms in the New York area. We should talk soon.

My experience with sales and distribution of wireless communications products in this market is certainly one of success:

— After I became Regional Sales Manager for Pactel in 1988, we improved our sales by 55% in one year. The sales staff was demoralized, and we improved their training and replaced other staff members. Our market share is up to 22% in just three years.

— We created a selling program locally that resulted in an 18% higher closing rate, and that program was taken on the road to train all other Pactel sales reps.

Unfortunately, all this hard work has caused the company to be acquired. The new brass have indicated a desire to sell off the division I manage. This is a great opportunity for me to return to New York. I will call you next week to discuss possible opportunities in the "Big Apple."

Sincerely,

Carolyn Fornataro

11

Tips to Get You Hired

25 UNCONVENTIONAL TECHNIQUES FOR UNCOVERING AND SECURING NEW OPPORTUNITIES

1. If you see a classified ad that sounds really good for you but only lists a fax number and no company name, try to figure out the company by trying similar numbers. For example, if the fax number is 555-4589, try 555-4500 or 555-4000, get the company name and contact person so you can send a more personalized letter and resume.

2. Send your resume in a Priority Mail envelope for the serious prospects. It costs only $3, but the envelope will stand out and get you noticed.

3. Check the targeted company's Web site; it may have postings there that others without computer access haven't seen.

4. If you see a classified ad for a good prospective company but a different position, contact the company anyway. If it is new in town (or even if it is not), it may have other nonadvertised openings.

5. Always have a personalized card with you just in case you meet a good networking or employment prospect.

6. Always have a quick personal briefing rehearsed so you can speak to someone.

7. Network in nonwork environments, such as a happy-hour bar (a great opportunity to network) or an airport.

8. Network with your college alumni office. Many college graduates list their current employers with that office, and they may be a good source of leads, even out of state.

9. Most newspapers list all the new companies that have applied for business licenses. Check that section and contact the ones that appear appealing to you.

10. Call your attorney and accountant and ask them if they can refer you to any companies or business contacts; perhaps they have good business relationships that may be good for you to leverage.

11. Contact the Chamber of Commerce for information on new companies moving into the local area.

12. Don't give up if you've had just one rejection from a company you are targeting. You shouldn't feel that you have truly contacted that company until you have contacted at least three different people there.

13. Join networking clubs and associations that will expose you to new business contacts.

14. Ask stockbrokers for tips on which companies they identify as fast growing and good companies to grow with.

15. Make a list of everyone you know, and use that list as a network source.

16. Put an endorsement portfolio together and mail it out with targeted resumes.

17. Employ the hiring proposal strategy (see another of our books: *101 Best Cover Letters*).

18. Post your resume on the Internet, selecting newsgroups and bulletin boards that will readily accept it and match your industry and discipline.

19. Don't forget to demonstrate passion and enthusiasm when you are meeting with people, interviewing with them, and networking through them.

20. Look in your industry's trade journals. Nearly all industries and disciplines have multiple ones, and most have an advertising section in the back that lists potential openings with companies and recruiters. This is a great resource in today's low-unemployment environment.

21. Visit a job fair. Although there won't be recruitment for managerial positions, there will be many companies present, and you may discover a hot lead. If they are recruiting in general, you should contact them directly for a possible fit.

22. Don't overlook employment agencies. They may seem like a weak possibility, but that may uncover a hidden opportunity or serve as a source to network through.

23. Look for companies that are promoting their products using a lot of advertising. Sales are probably going well, and they may be good hiring targets for you.

24. Call a prospective company and simply ask who its recruiting firm is. If it has one, the person will tell you, and then you can contact that firm to get in the door.

25. Contact every recruiter in town. Befriend them, and use them as networking sources if possible. Always thank them, to the point of sending them a small gift for helping you out. This will pay off in dividends in the future. Recruiters are always good contacts.

25 TIPS FOR USING THE INTERNET IN YOUR JOB SEARCH

1. When preparing your resume with the intent of emailing, make sure it is in an ASCII format.

2. Use keywords heavily in the introduction of the resume, not at the end.

3. Keywords are almost always nouns related to skills, such as financial analysis, marketing, accounting, and Web design.

4. When sending your resume via email in an ASCII format, attach (if you can) a nicely formatted one in case it does go through and the reader would like to see your creativity and preferred layout. If you do attach it, use a common program like MS Word.

5. Don't focus on an objective in the introduction of the resume, but rather accomplishments using keywords to describe them.

6. Don't post your resume to your own Web site unless it is a very slick page. A poorly executed Web page is more damaging than none at all.

7. Before you email your resume, experiment sending it to yourself and to a friend as a test drive.

8. Look at the Web site of the company you are targeting to get recent news about new products, etc., and look for its job posting for new information.

9. Before your interview or verbal contact, research the company's Web site.

10. Use a font size between 10 and 14 points, make it all the same font for an ASCII format resume, and don't create your resume for emailing with lines exceeding 65 characters.

11. In case your resume is scanned, use white paper with no borders and no creative fonts.

12. Include your email address on your resume and cover letter.

13. Don't email from your current employer's Internet Protocol network.

14. Don't circulate your work email address for job search purposes.

15. In the "Subject" area of your email heading, put something more creative than "Resume Enclosed." Try "Resume showing 8 years in telecommunications industry" (if that is your chosen industry), for example.

16. For additional sources of online job searching, do a "search" on the Web for jobs, your target company, and your specific discipline.

17. Be careful of your spelling on the Net. You will notice more spelling errors on email exchanges than you will ever see in mailed letter exchanges.

18. Try to make sure your resume is scannable. This means that it is in a simple font, with no borders, no creative lining, no boldface, no underlining, no italics, and limited if any columning. Though the practice of scanning is overestimated, it should still be a consideration.

19. Purchase or obtain from a library an Internet directory listing the many links to job opportunities out there. There are thousands.

20. If you are using the email as your cover letter, keep it brief. If the reader is reading on screen, the tolerance for reading long information is reduced dramatically.

21. Always back up what you can on a disk.

22. If you post your resume to a newsgroup, make sure that is an acceptable practice, to avoid any problems with other participants.

23. Remember that tabs and spaces are the only formatting you can do in ASCII.

24. Make sure that you check your email every day. If you are communicating via the Net, people may expect a prompt return.

25. Don't send multiple emails to ensure that one gets through. Try to end it with a confirmation of receipt, or keep a lookout for a notice from your Internet service provider that the message didn't go through.

25 TIPS FOR JOB SEARCHING WHILE STILL EMPLOYED

1. Do not let your current employer find out about your intent to look around. This means no loose resume left on the copy machine, no mailing from the office, and no signal that could jeopardize your current position.

2. Get organized and commit to the process. Without the immediate pressure of unemployment to motivate you to look for a job, you may run the risk of being sporadic in your job search efforts. You must schedule time for the search and stick to it.

3. Don't feel guilty about looking around while employed. You owe it to yourself to make the most of your career, especially in today's environment of companies looking out for their own financial health.

4. Get a voice mail pager so that you can quickly return calls, or get a reliable answering machine at home.

5. Do not circulate your work number for new employment purposes.

6. Do not send your resume or any other correspondence on current employer stationery.

7. Take advantage of different time zones to make calls, if this applies to you. This enables you to make calls early in the morning or after work.

8. Use a nearby fax (if you don't have one at home) for correspondence (but not the one at work).

9. Do not use any resources of your current employer.

10. Commit to 10 to 12 hours per week for your job search, and schedule your activities for the week on the weekend.

11. Utilize executive recruiters and employment agencies. In some cases they will be able to cut down on your leg work significantly.

12. Schedule direct-mail efforts on the weekends. Though the success rate may be lower than sending them out during the week, it won't cause you to be overworked on busy weekdays.

13. Make use of lunchtime during the week to schedule phone calls and interviews.

14. Network through your family and friends.

15. Use electronic means to speed up your search, including surfing the Net for job listings and company information.

16. Try to schedule interviews and other meetings before the workday (e.g., breakfast meetings) and after 5 p.m. You'll be shocked at how many recruiters will try to accommodate this, and they'll appreciate your work ethics.

17. Though the hit rate may not be great, you may consider identifying a direct-mail company to help you contact many companies. It could even direct fax for you, and the rates aren't usually too high.

18. Network off hours and through a few professional contacts, using caution and good judgment as to whom should be contacted.

19. If you are concerned about your current employer's finding out about your search, leave it off your resume, and note such in your cover letter.

20. Consider using a broadcast letter in lieu of a resume (see Chapter 9).

21. In confidence, utilize vendors, customers, and other people associated with your current position, especially if you want to remain in your industry.

22. Contact your stockbroker for ideas of growing companies.

23. Create a business/calling card with your name and personal contact information. Hand them out in sync with your one- to two-minute prepared pitch about yourself.

24. Do not be critical of your current employer.

25. Read your newspaper cover to cover to determine which companies are growing, not who's advertising for jobs.

25 TIPS FOR WRITING COVER LETTERS

1. Use customized stationery with your name, address, and phone number on top. Matching your stationery to that of your resume shows class and professionalism.

2. Customize the cover letter. Address it to a specific individual. Be sure that you have the proper spelling of the person's name, title, and the company name.

3. If you don't wish to customize each letter and prefer to use a form letter, use the salutation "Dear Hiring Manager." (Do not use "Dear Sir." The hiring manager may be a woman.)

4. The cover letter is more informal than the resume and must begin to build rapport. Be enthusiastic, energetic, and motivating.

5. The cover letter must introduce you and your value to a potential employer.

6. Be sure to date the cover letter.

7. An effective cover letter should be easy to read, have larger typeface than the resume (12-point type is a good size), and be kept short—four to five short paragraphs will usually do the job.

8. Keep the cover letter to one page. If you are compelled to use two pages, be sure that your name appears on the second page.

9. The first paragraph should ignite interest in your candidacy and spark enthusiasm from the reader. Why is the reader reading this letter? What can you do for that person?

10. The second paragraph must promote your value. What are your skills, abilities, qualifications, and credentials that would meet the reader's needs and job requirements?

11. The third paragraph notes specific accomplishments, achievements, and educational experience that would expressly support the second paragraph. Quantify these accomplishments if possible.

12. The fourth paragraph must generate future action. Ask for an interview or tell the reader that you will be calling in a week or so to follow up.

13. The fifth paragraph should be a short one, closing the letter and showing appreciation.

14. Demonstrate specific problem-solving skills in the letter, supported by specific examples.

15. Unless asked to do so, don't discuss salary in a cover letter.

16. If salary history or requirements are asked for, provide a modest window (low-to-mid thirties, for example) and mention that it is negotiable (if it is).

17. Be sure that the letter has a professional appearance.

18. Be sure that there are no spelling, typographical, or grammatical errors.

19. Be sure to keep the letter short and to the point. Don't ramble on and on.

20. Do not lie or exaggerate. Everything you say in a cover letter and resume must be supported in the eventual interview.

21. Be careful not to use the pronoun "I" excessively. Tie together what the company is doing and what its needs might be. To come full circle, explain how you fit into its strategy and can close potential gaps in meeting its objectives.

22. Avoid negative and controversial subject matter. The purpose of a cover letter and resume is to put your best foot forward. This material (job hopping, prior termination, etc.) can be tactfully addressed in the interview.

23. If you are faxing the cover letter and resume, you need not send a fax transmittal form so long as your fax number is included in the heading along with your telephone number.

24. To close the letter, use "Sincerely," "Sincerely yours," "Respectfully," or "Very truly yours."

25. Be sure to sign the letter.

25 NETWORKING TIPS

1. Two-thirds of all jobs are secured via the networking process. Networking is a systematic approach to cultivating formal and informal contacts for the purpose of gaining information, enhancing visibility in the market, and obtaining referrals.

2. Effective networking requires self-confidence, poise, and personal conviction.

3. You must first know the companies and organizations you wish to work for. That will determine the type of network you will develop and nurture.

4. Focus on meeting the right people. This takes planning and preparation.

5. Target close friends, family members, neighbors, social acquaintances, social and religious group members, business contacts, teachers, and community leaders.

6. Include employment professionals as an important part of your network. This includes headhunters and personnel agency executives. They have a wealth of knowledge about job and market conditions.

7. Remember, networking is a numbers game. Once you have a network of people in place, prioritize the listing so you have separated top-priority contacts from lower-priority ones.

8. Sometimes you may have to pay for advice and information. Paying consultants or professionals or investing in Internet services is part of the job search process today, as long as it's legal and ethical.

9. Know what you want from your contacts. If you don't know what you want, neither will your network of people. Specific questions will get specific answers.

10. Ask for advice, not for a job. You cannot contact someone asking if they know of any job openings. The answer will invariably be no, especially at higher levels. You need to ask for things like industry advice, advice on geographic areas, etc. The job insights will follow but will be almost incidental. This positioning will build value for you and make the contact person more comfortable about helping you.

11. Watch your attitude and demeanor at all times. Everyone you come in contact with is a potential member of your network. Demonstrate enthusiasm and professionalism at all times.

12. Keep a file on each member of your network and maintain good records at all times. A well-organized network filing system or database will yield superior results.

13. Get comfortable on the telephone. Good telephone communication skills are critical.

14. Travel the information highway. Networking is more effective if you have email, fax, and computer capabilities.

15. Be well prepared for your conversation, whether in person or over the phone. You should have a script in your mind of how to answer questions, what to ask, and what you're trying to accomplish.

16. Do not fear rejection. If a contact cannot help you, move on to the next contact. Do not take rejection personally—it's just part of the process.

17. Flatter the people in your network. It's been said that the only two types of people who can be flattered are men and women. Use tact, courtesy, and flattery.

18. If a person in your network cannot personally help, advise, or direct you, ask for referrals.

19. Keep in touch with the major contacts in your network on a monthly basis. Remember, out of sight, out of mind.

20. Don't abuse the process. Networking is a two-way street. Be honest and brief, and offer your contacts something in return for their time, advice, and information. This can be as simple as a lunch or offering your professional services in return for their cooperation.

21. Show an interest in your contacts. Cavette Robert, one of the founders of the National Speakers Association, said, "People don't care how much you know, until they know how much you care." Show how much you care. It will get you anywhere.

22. Send thank-you notes following each networking contact.

23. Seek out key networking contacts in professional and trade associations.

24. Carry calling cards with you at all times to hand out to anyone and everyone you come in contact with. Include your name, address, phone number, areas of expertise, and/or specific skill areas.

25. Socialize and get out more than ever before. Networking requires dedication and massive amounts of energy. Consistently work on expanding your network.

25 "WHAT DO I DO NOW THAT I HAVE MY RESUME?" TIPS

1. Develop a team of people who will be your board of directors, advisers, and mentors. The quality of the people you surround yourself with will determine the quality of your results.

2. Plan a marketing strategy. Determine how many hours a week you will work, how you'll divide your time, and how you'll measure your progress. Job searching is a business in itself—and a marketing strategy is your business plan.

3. Identify 25 (50 would be better) companies or organizations that you would like to work for.

4. Contact the companies, or do some research, to identify hiring authorities.

5. Define your network (see Networking Tips). Make a list of everyone you know, including relatives, friends, acquaintances, family doctors, attorneys, CPAs, the cleaning person, and the mail carrier. Virtually everyone is a possible networking contact.

6. Prioritize your list of contacts into three categories: (1) strong, approachable contacts, (2) good contacts or those who must be approached more formally, and (3) those whom you'd like to contact but can't without an introduction by another party.

7. Set up a filing system or database to organize and manage your contacts.

8. Develop a script or letter for the purpose of contacting the key people in your network, asking for advice, information, and assistance. Then start contacting them.

9. Attempt to find a person, or persons, in your network who can make an introduction into one of the 25 or 50 companies you've noted in tip 3.

10. Spend 65 to 70 percent of your time, energy, and resources networking, because 65 to 70 percent of all jobs are secured by this method.

11. Consider contacting executive recruiters or employment agencies to assist in your job search.

12. If you are a recent college graduate, seek out assistance from the campus career center.

13. Scout the classified advertisements every Sunday. Respond to ads that interest you, and look at other ads as well. A company may be advertising for a position that does not fit your background, but say in the ad that they are "expanding in the area," etc. You have just identified a growing company.

14. Seek out advertisements and job opportunities in specific trade journals and magazines.

15. Attend as many social and professional functions as you can. The more people you meet, the better are your chances of securing a position quickly.

16. Send out resumes with customized cover letters to targeted companies or organizations. Address the cover letter to a specific person. Then follow up.

17. Target small- to medium-sized companies. Most of the opportunities are coming from these organizations, not large corporations.

18. Consider contacting temporary agencies. Almost 40 percent of all temporary personnel are offered permanent positions. Today, a greater percentage of middle and upper management, as well as professionals, are working in temporary positions.

19. Use online services. America Online, Prodigy, and CompuServe have career services, employment databases, bulletin boards, and online discussion and support groups, as well as access to the Internet. This is the wave of the future.

20. If you are working from home, be sure the room you are working from is inspiring, organized, and private. This is your space, and it must motivate you!

21. If your plan is not working, meet with members of your support team and change the plan. You must remain flexible and adaptable to change.

22. Read and observe. Read magazines and newspapers and listen to CNBC, CNN, and so on. Notice which companies and organizations are on the move and contact them.

23. Set small, attainable weekly goals. Keep a weekly progress report on all of your activities. Try to do a little more each week than the week before.

24. Stay active. Exercise and practice good nutrition. A job search requires energy. You must remain in superior physical and mental condition.

25. Volunteer. Help those less fortunate than you. What goes around comes around.

25 INTERVIEWING TIPS

1. Relax. The employment interview is just a meeting. And although you should not treat this meeting lightly, don't forget that the organization interviewing you is in need of your services as much as, or perhaps more than, you are of theirs.

2. The key to successful interviewing is rapport building. Most people spend their time preparing for interviews by memorizing canned responses to anticipated questions. Successful interviewers spend most of their time practicing the art of rapport building through the use of powerfully effective communication techniques.

3. Prepare a manila folder that you will bring to the interview. Include in the folder:
   - Company information (annual reports, sales material, etc.)
   - Extra resumes (6–12) and your letters of reference
   - 15 questions you've prepared based on your research and analysis of the company
   - A blank legal pad, pen, and anything else you consider helpful (e.g., college transcripts)

4. Dress appropriately. Determine the dress code and meet it. If the dress is business casual, you still need to be dressed in business professional. Practice proper grooming and hygiene.

5. Shoes, of course, must be polished.

6. Wear limited jewelry.

7. Call the day before and confirm the appointment. This call will set you apart.

8. Be certain that you know exactly where you're going. Arrive in plenty of time. You should be at the receptionist's desk 10 to 12 minutes before the scheduled interview.

9. Prior to meeting the receptionist, check your appearance. Check your hair, clothing, and general image. Test your smile.

10. Secretaries, administrative assistants, and receptionists often have a say in the hiring process. Make a strong first impression with them.

11. Look around the office and search for artifacts that disclose the personality and culture of the company—and possibly the interviewer. This information will be helpful in breaking the ice, when you first begin discussions.

12. Be aware of your body language. Sit erect, with confidence. When standing and walking, move with confidence!

13. Your handshake should be firm, made with a wide-open hand, fingers stretched wide apart. Women should feel comfortable offering their hands and a firm and friendly handshake. A power handshake and great smile will get you off to a great start.

14. Eye contact is one of the most powerful forms of communicating. It demonstrates confidence, trust, and power.

15. During the interview, lean forward toward the interviewer. Show enthusiasm and sincere interest.

16. Take notes during the interview. You may want to refer to them later in the interview. If you are uncomfortable with this, ask permission first.

17. Be prepared for all questions, especially uncomfortable ones. Before the interview, script out a one-page response for each question that poses a problem for you, and practice repeating it until you're comfortable with it.

18. Communicate your skills, qualifications, and credentials to the hiring manager. Describe your market value and the benefits you offer. Demonstrate how you will contribute to the bottom line. Show how you can (1) improve sales, (2) reduce costs, (3) improve productivity, or (4) solve organizational problems.

19. Key in on specific accomplishments. Accomplishments determine hireability. They separate the winners from the runners-up.

20. Listening skills are priceless! Job offers are made to those who listen well, find hidden meanings, and answer questions in a brief but effective manner.

21. Let the interviewer bring up salary first. The purpose of an interview is to determine whether there is a match. Once that is determined, salary should then be negotiated.

22. There is no substitute for planning and preparation, practice and rehearsing—absolutely none.

23. Practice interviewing techniques using video technology. A minimum of five hours of video practice, preferably more, guarantees a stellar performance.

24. Close the sale. If you find that you want the position, ask for it. Ask directly, "Is there anything that would prevent you from offering me this position now?" or "Do you have any reservations or concerns?" (if you sense that). At the very least, this should flush out any objections and give you the opportunity to turn them into positives.

25. Always send a thank-you note within 24 hours of every employment meeting.

25 SALARY NEGOTIATING TIPS

1. From the moment you make initial contact with any company or organization that you wish to work with, you are in negotiation. You may not be discussing money openly, but you are making a permanent imprint on the mind of the hiring authorities.

2. Delay all discussions of salary until there is an offer on the table.

3. You are in the strongest negotiating position as soon as the offer is made.

4. Know your value. You must know how you can contribute to the organization. Establish this in the mind of the hiring manager.

5. Get employers enthusiastic about your candidacy, and they will become more generous.

6. There is no substitute for preparation. If you are well prepared, you'll be confident, self-assured, and poised for success.

7. Prior to going into employment negotiations, you must know the average salary paid for similar positions with other organizations in your geographical area.

8. Before going into employment negotiations, you must know, as best you can, the salary range that the company you're interviewing with will pay, or what former employees were earning.

9. Prior to going into employment negotiations, you must know your personal needs and requirements, and how they relate to tips 7 and 8 above.

10. Remember, fringes and perks, such as vacation time, flex time, health benefits, pension plans, and so on, have value. Consider the *total* salary package.

11. Salary negotiations must be win-win negotiations. If they're not, everybody loses in the end.

12. Be flexible; don't get hung up on trivial issues, and always seek compromise when possible.

13. Listen carefully and pay close attention. Your goals will most likely be different from the goals of the employer. For instance, the firm's main focus might be base salary. Yours might be total earning potential. So a win-win solution might be to negotiate a lower base salary but a higher commission or bonus structure.

14. Anticipate objections and prepare effective answers to these objections.

15. Try to understand the employer's point of view. Then plan a strategy to meet both the employer's concerns and your needs.

16. Don't be afraid to negotiate out of fear of losing the offer. Most employers expect you to negotiate, as long as you negotiate in a fair and reasonable manner.

17. Always negotiate in a way that reflects your personality, character, and work ethic. Remain within your comfort zone.

18. Never lose control. Remain enthusiastic and upbeat, even if the negotiations get a little hot. This might be your first test under fire.

19. Play hardball only if you're willing to walk away from, or lose, the deal.

20. What you lose in the negotiations will most likely never be recouped. Don't be careless in preparing for or conducting the negotiation.

21. Be sure to get the offer and final agreement in writing.

22. You should feel comfortable asking the employer for 24 to 48 hours to think about the deal if you need time to think it over.

23. Never link salary to personal needs or problems. Compensation should always be linked to your value.

24. Understand your leverage. Know if you are in a position of strength or weakness and negotiate intelligently based on your personal situation.

25. End salary negotiations on a friendly and cheerful note.

12

101 Career Design Resumes That Will Get You Hired!

1—ACCOUNTANT

Lorraine Bent

lbent@earthlink.org - 191 Sutter Street, San Francisco, CA 94104 - **415-555-1212**

Professional Profile

- Controller with more than 10 years of progressive experience in high-tech, including six years of successful financial leadership for a pre-IPO Internet service provider.

- Astute financial planning and analysis, identifying big-picture trends through close attention to the smallest of details. Proven expertise in SEC reporting, executive/board reports, design and implementation of revenue processes, forecasting and budget development.

- Exceptional skills in Great Plains Dynamics (eEnterprise), Excel, Lotus SmartSuite, SAP Accounting, and Oracle, as well as Microsoft Office, Microsoft Project, and Internet research. Experienced in selection, procurement, and implementation of new accounting software.

- Highly productive and results-focused, effectively managing multiple projects and day-to-day accounting operations. Solid staff recruiting, development, and motivation.

- Recognized by executive leadership for keen insight and business judgment in the rapidly evolving Internet economy.

Experience

San Francisco Internet   1994-Present

Internet Service Provider
Controller ~ Assistant Controller

Hired to create and manage general accounting functions to support company's rapid growth and preparation for initial public offering. Develop and implement accounting controls and procedures, consulting extensively with technical and business groups.

Prepare and present financial statements, forecasts, and executive reports at monthly management meetings and executive board meetings. Direct audit and tax processes. Manage key vendor and bank relations.

Accomplishments:

- Ensured sufficient cash flow during early months of operation by negotiating ample lines of credit with several key vendors and two commercial lending institutions.

- Researched and recommended a new accounting system, upgrading from QuickBooks Pro to a customized SAP Accounting system. Planned and directed implementation of system in conjunction with technical support team and vendor consultants, ensuring seamless data conversion and go-live. Provided system training for the accounting and sales departments.

- Co-designed and implemented the revenue process, including accounts receivable, reconciliation, and collections.

- Performed due diligence in the acquisition of two privately held Bay Area ISPs.

- Prepared company financials for IPO, ensuring compliance to all SEC reporting and auditing requirements.

Continued on Page 2

Lorraine Bent

Page 2 - 415-555-1212

Experience

Continued

Sun Microsystems   1992-1994
Staff Accountant, World Wide Sales (WWS) Financial Planning & Analysis Group

Developed and presented financial analyses and reporting. Maintained and reported WWS metrics. Performed impact analyses of multiple sales programs, projects and initiatives on sales cost and ROI.

Accomplishments:

- Designed several new financial planning models which were subsequently adopted company-wide. Credited with positively impacting earnings for the second and third quarters of 1994.

- Recognized with corporate award for incorporating extensive knowledge of economic, industry and competitive trends in a mission-critical ad-hoc reporting project.

Big Six Accounting Firm   1988-1990
Audit Supervisor ~ Auditor

Provided audit leadership for clients throughout Silicon Valley, including independent software vendors, PC hardware distributors, and systems integrators.

Managed all facets of audit projects, including client briefings, audit planning, delegation of assignments, staff motivation and advising, pre-partner review, client review, and preparation of representation letter and auditor's standard report. Directly managed critical audit procedures for key clients.

Accomplishments:

- Received letter of recognition from the firm's partner for swift resolution of a difficult audit for a major client.

- Promoted within one year of hire to become the firm's youngest audit supervisor.

Education & Professional Affiliations

Master of Business Administration (MBA), **Finance,** Stanford Graduate School of Business, Stanford, CA

Bachelor of Science (BS), **Accounting,** Minor in Information Systems, Stanford University, Stanford, CA

Charter Member, San Francisco E-Commerce Accounting Association

Certified Public Accountant

Professional Development: Studies in e-commerce and global economics, as well as technical overviews of SAP Accounting, GL, and Financial modules.

2—ADMINISTRATIVE ASSISTANT

Kathleen Young

12 Cherry Street • New City, New York 10956 • (914) 555-5555 • kiy@isp.com

Profile

A results-oriented **Administrative Assistant** with ability in assuring consistently high levels of productivity and customer satisfaction. Proven ability in developing and administering budgets, analyzing opportunities to increase productivity and efficiency while reducing expenses with Internet related projects. Proactive troubleshooter with superior interpersonal skills to develop and maintain rapport with clients and management on all levels. Solid administration, organization and supervisory capabilities with background encompassing knowledge of employee training and team development. Software expertise includes Java, HTML, Microsoft Office, Lotus cc:mail and Lotus Notes and an extensive knowledge of the Internet. Core Competencies Include:

- Contracts and Negotiations
- Account Development
- Strategic Buying and Leasing
- Administrative Management
- Customer Service
- Systems Projects

Professional Experience

Net Source – White Plains, New York • 1997/Present
SENIOR ADMINISTRATIVE ASSISTANT
Rapidly promoted through positions of responsibility for this $3 million Internet business solutions provider. Provide product management inventory business plan support to large organizations. Administer contracts and supplier programs. Develop resource planning and determine field availability.
- Assisted team in reaching company goal of $195,000 in monthly revenues.

Telespectrum Worldwide Inc. - White Plains, New York • 1996/1997
CUSTOMER ASSISTANCE REPRESENTATIVE
Initiate leasing sales for this business equipment lending organization. Responsible for providing rate and leasing information and support to IBM staff and Industry Re-marketers.

The Traynor Group Ltd.- White Plains, New York • 1995/1996
ADMINISTRATIVE SPECIALIST
Deliver administrative support for this independent insurance broker. Responsible for expediting client inquiries and delivering certificates of insurance.
- Reduced office supply costs through development of spreadsheet inventory accounting system.
- Increased appointment flow through implementation of new business tracking system.
- Enhanced internal communication through sign-off procedure for minutes of staff meetings.

Education/Certifications

- Pace University - White Plains, New York
Bachelor of Science • Communications

3—ADVERTISING DIRECTOR

Michael Desa

| Creative layout and font works for advertising discipline. | e-mail@e-mailaddress.com
1725 K Street NW
Washington, DC 20006

202-555-1725 |

Advertising Director

- Creative, Web-savvy Marketing & Advertising Executive with unparalleled ability to build advertising revenues in the Internet publishing market.
- Exceptional skills in business development, including market definition, campaign design and implementation, and development of online services.
- Key strengths in identifying and managing opportunities for strategic alliances, spotting trends in consumer markets, and anticipating emerging technologies.
- Dynamic, inspirational leadership style, eliciting the best from creative contributors and sales support teams while meeting publication standards and deadlines.
- Credited by executive management team for outstanding results in forecasting, budgeting, executive reporting, and project management.

Experience

iWORLD (www.iworld.com) Mecklermedia's Daily Internet Newspaper
Advertising Director, Eastern Region, 1995-Present

- Manage an advertising operations support team of eight with a sales budget of $58 million.
- Create and continually improve a market-sensitive menu of strategic advertising options serving the diverse needs of e-commerce businesses across multiple industries.
- Foster strong business relationships with Fortune 100 clients. Act as advertising consultant to up-and-coming Web and technology companies.
- Facilitate innovative, interactive territory meetings on a weekly basis. Set and measured progress toward team and individual objectives.

   Accomplishments:

- Ranked #1 among iWORLD's six global regions, 1997, 1998, and 1999. Grew key account base by 75% in first year, representing new revenues of $27 million.
- Promotion was recognized by executive leadership in a press release: "Michael has consistently achieved major gains in advertising revenues by positioning iWORLD as the #1 Internet news destination for executives." - James Jamison, VP of Marketing for iWORLD

Advertising Account Manager, Mecklermedia, 1992-1995

Education

Bachelor of Arts, Communications, with emphases in Electronic and Print Media.
State University of New York, Albany, NY

Grace Holmes
e-mail@e-mailaddress.com • 5155 72nd Avenue, Denver, CO 80030 • 303-555-5155

Affiliate Program Manager ~ Web Marketing Specialist with eight years of marketing leadership, including four years of success in attracting and retaining worldwide affiliates.

- ❑ Expert design and launch of winning affiliate programs, increasing market share and profitability.

- ❑ Demonstrated results in planning, executing, and validating multiple projects and campaigns simultaneously, achieving all time, budget, and growth objectives.

- ❑ Strong analytical skills, creating methods to define, measure, and immediately impact program effectiveness.

- ❑ Persuasive, high-profile presentation skills, acting as liaison among executive leadership, sales and marketing teams to integrate business initiatives.

- ❑ Motivated, energetic, and results-focused, with an entrepreneurial spirit, guaranteeing optimal performance in fast-paced, start-up environments.

- ❑ Technical proficiencies include Microsoft Office (Word, Excel, Access, and PowerPoint), and Microsoft Project. Basic knowledge of Dreamweaver and Adobe PhotoShop.

Experience

ScienceWise.com, Gaithersburg, MD   1996-Present
The Web's Leading Source of Science and Education Information
Affiliate Program Manager

- ❑ Develop, measure, and grow the affiliate partnership program, presenting goals and results to the Director of Business Development and Senior VP of Marketing.

- ❑ Create, implement, and manage contracts, promotions, programs, and relationship-building activities. Support and integrate strategic efforts among sales and marketing teams, coordinating marketing tactics and tracking program success. Assist with product development processes.

- ❑ Oversee calculation and distribution of affiliates' monthly commission checks. Provide individual strategies for affiliates interested in boosting sales and commission amounts. Analyze key account metrics to evaluate return on investment (ROI); prepare monthly reports on performance actuals.

- ❑ Forecast, formulate, and manage market development budgets. Recommend pricing, promotions, and programs to meet sell-through and ROI goals.

- ❑ Conduct competitive analysis activities to differentiate ScienceWise's features, benefits, and business practices from similar sites.

- ❑ Design and launch innovative and efficient affiliate recruitment campaigns, collaborating with technical, content, and marketing teams on all facets of implementation.

- ❑ Recruit, train, and manage an Affiliate Care Team of four. Develop and implement scripts for affiliate frequently asked questions (FAQs) and procedures for the Affiliate Care Team; publish and update FAQs on Web site.

- ❑ **Credited with quadrupling affiliate base from 300 to over 1200 active affiliates in three years' time.**

Experience continued

The Metropolitan State College of Denver   1992-1996
Marketing Specialist, Science Program Communications

- Coordinated, implemented, and managed marketing communications and promotions for the Metropolitan State College of Denver (MSCD) Science Program.

- Developed accurate, marketing-oriented descriptions of degree programs and individual courses. Wrote faculty profiles and program overviews to differentiate MSCD's Science Program from other regional undergraduate programs.

- Published marketing content on MSCD's Web site as well as school newspapers, marketing brochures, annual catalogs, and semester course offering publications.

- Designed, tested, and refined graphics and tools to be used for marketing content on the Web site.

- Wrote and distributed marketing copy for e-mail newsletter promotions.

- Coordinated all facets of an annual "Science Career Day," orchestrating among officials and student representatives of area high schools as well as the campus events departments.

- Prepared and presented ongoing reports for the marketing director, science program chair, and the dean of academic affairs.

- Orchestrated internal and external resources, budgets, and schedules to ensure performance to all departmental objectives.

Education

Bachelor of Arts, Communications, Summa Cum Laude, 1992,
Metropolitan State College of Denver

JACK ANNADEL

50 Cathedral Lane
Saratoga, California 95070
(408) 555-7473 / jacknnd@home.com

Conventional resume utilizing effective "Executive Summary" and "Technical Expertise" sections.

EXECUTIVE SUMMARY

Analyst and Method Specialist with more than ten years' successful consulting/IT experience in multiple industries including government, financial (banking and insurance), manufacturing, mining, petroleum, property management, travel, publishing, and pharmaceuticals.

- Proven ability to integrate projects with quality methodologies to achieve solid, comprehensive solutions that come in on-time and on-budget.
- Strong communication, negotiation and leadership skills, success in leveraging situations to achieve predictable, reality-appropriate outcomes that significantly benefit project goals and team morale. Bring consensus to the decision-making and reorganization process.
- Effectively implement tools to support environments, work flow, planning, defect tracking and assist in achieving technology deliverables.
- Ability to predict and respond to both time and cost-containment considerations to achieve software development and delivery with issues of cost containment, time, and quality addressed within the methodology.
- Strong familiarity with the unique environment/demands within Silicon Valley technology industries. Actively attend VC briefings, conferences, and quality/software development forums.

TECHNICAL EXPERTISE

Packages:	PMS, TRIPS, PMAS
Applications:	Accounting & Financial Management Systems, Insurance (General, Life, Pensions), Travel Reservation, Water Monitoring, Sales Analysis
Non-Application Specific:	
	Metrication, Documentation Standards, Application conversion between platforms
Languages:	Assembly, RPG, RPGII, Cobol
Platforms:	Mainframes, System 3, AS/400, Client Server

EXPERIENCE

1989 to present   **Waterford Consulting,** Ottawa, Ontario, Canada (headquarters)
DIRECTOR and SENIOR CONSULTANT, Redwood City office, California

Client projects include:

Harrold Teledigital

Y2K Due Diligence Manager
- Designed and established the methods to be followed for all Y2K Projects (574). Developed standard WBS and walkthrough processes. Managed a team of seven walkthrough moderators ensuring due diligence of all Y2K projects.

Project Manager
- Project manager working with a team of three for the rollout of a work-flow tool (Remedy) to manage the flow of change requests between the business and the new prime vendor. Implemented the new processes and supporting tool throughout Optus and the prime vendor.

Methodologist
- Designed a RAD (Rapid Application Development) methodology for the Concept, Requirements, and Preliminary Analysis phases of the development life cycle.

- continued -

Jack Annadel
Page 2

Wells Cody Bank, Australia

Business Analyst to EDS Prime Vendor
- Member of the GST Program Team developing the requirements to support the new Federal Government Goods & Services Tax on all relevant bank fees.

Northpoint Financial Services (Subsidiary of Northpoint Bank, Australia)

Measurement Program Manager
- Sourced an appropriate measurement tool to support the WFS Measurement Strategy and then assisted in its implementation. Educated staff in Function Point Analysis and supported staff throughout the year in reviewing their counts.

Application Cost Analyst
- Participated in an executive review of the various Superannuation Applications the organization maintained to rationalize six applications into one. This involved Function Point counting the applications, selecting the most cost-efficient one and then designing a strategy for the transfer of functionality from six applications into one. Presented findings to the Board.

Stahlwatt Engineering

SAP Change Manager
- Took over as Change Manager one month prior to the implementation of nine modules of SAP R/4. Trained the 24 staff trainers and managed a staff of five in the delivery of training to 700 personnel. Facilitated the site organizers' monthly meetings during the length of the project.

Project Manager
- With five direct reports, produced Courseware Documentation for the SAP Project. Managed ongoing production, updating, and distribution of courseware throughout the implementation. This fixed price, fixed time contract was completed on-time and on-budget.

Eastern Star Insurance

Facilitator, Methodologist
- Assisted the CIO in the restructure of the Systems Development department. Facilitated team-building workshops focusing on highlighting team issues, defining what the team did and how to resolve existing problems.

Analyst
- Provided client support for all financial systems including the Financial Management System (FMS) and analyzed enhancements to the Policy Management System (PMS).

ComPlanet Financial

Organizational Change Consultant and Methodologist
- Consultant to the Executive Committee responsible for the restructuring of the IT Department. Prepared, on behalf of senior IS management, a plan for the implementation of Rapid Applications Development (RAD) within ComPlanet.

EDUCATION
> **Diploma** (3-year program), **Business Computer Systems**
> Williams College of Technology, Ottawa, Ontario, Canada

6—APPLICATIONS DEVELOPMENT MANAGER

Neil MacLean

55 North Avenue, San Diego, California 92124 ● 858 555-4561
nmaclean@earthlink.com

PROFILE

Applications Development Manager with considerable diverse experience in design and implementation of Computer Aided Design (CAD) Systems, computer facilities, and software applications. Specific expertise includes a graduate level education in Computer Science, Industrial Engineering, and Business Management. Strengths include programming knowledge and experience in development and enhancing computerized systems to increase productivity and efficiency of industrial manufacturing and MIS operations. Global perspective based upon life, studies, and work in European Countries. Bilingual/Bicultural: Turkish and English, fluent.

EDUCATION

University of California at Los Angeles, Los Angeles, California
   Anderson Graduate School of Management
   Post Graduate Studies, Management

Istanbul Technical University, Istanbul, Turkey
   Master of Science – Computer Science and Industrial Engineering – Cum Laude
   Bachelor of Science – Major: Meteorological Engineering

PROFESSIONAL EXPERIENCE

CHEREEF CONSULTING COMPANY, San Diego, California – 1999 to present

Application Development Manager. Provide custom software development solutions and consulting to the public using knowledge of SDLC, OOD, application servers, programming standards, RDBMS, multi-tiered, UNIX, Java, Web development applications.

Combined finance and accounting MIS systems into a LAN System for Prudential Insurance.

DIS-X-EK COMPUTER SYSTEMS, LTD., Bursa, Turkey – 1996 to 1999

Applications Developer/Systems Engineer. Partner in an international information technology corporation specializing in developing custom software applications and turnkey projects involving time analysis, production, and project planning for new products and new markets. Scope of responsibility included working as an Industrial Applications Engineer on the "Computer Aided Productivity Measurement & Analysis Systems" project for international corporations.

Designed, developed, and implemented LAN and WAN Systems to enhance productivity. Conducted feasibility studies for production plants.

KETOM TECHNICAL SOFTWARE COMPANY, Izmir, Turkey – 1992 to 1996

Industrial Applications Engineer. Specialized in developing custom software applications, e.g., Computer Aided Productivity Measurement and Analysis System. Designed, analyzed, implemented, tested, and evaluated projects. Scope of responsibilities expanded to include software design, feasibility studies, development of local area network applications, production area productivity studies, and time analyses. Developed and managed diverse projects for a variety of international corporations, e.g., Tofas Automobile Plant (a partner of the Fiat Auto Group in Italy) producing 475,000 cars a year, Arcelik Refrigerator & Electrical Oven Plant

(Continued on next page)

Neil MacLean

Resume   55 North Avenue, San Diego, California 92124 ● 858 555-4561   Page Two
nmaclean@earthlink.com

PROFESSIONAL EXPERIENCE *(Continued)*

(a partner of the Boch Company in Germany) producing 1.2 million units each year, and Mako Electrical Devices Plant (a partner of the Fiat Auto Group in Italy).

Designed Local Area Network (LAN) and Wide Area Network (WAN) applications to enhance productivity, improve accuracy, and reduce costs.
Combined finance, accounting, and logistics, Management Information Systems (MIS) into a LAN System to improve accuracy, facilitate retrieval of information, and reduce costs.
Key participant in designing Just-In-Time (JIT) system for Toyota's Adapazari Automobile Plant.
Developed an excellent reputation for completing projects on time and under budget.
Consistently achieved a 65% productivity increase with minimal equipment purchases.

NEEKATAA TECHNICAL COMPANY, Adana, Turkey – 1991 to 1992

Project Planner/Systems Engineer. Reported to the General Manager and CEO of an international corporation specializing in general contracting in chemical and mechanical production plants. Established and coordinated all project planning and management activities. Oversaw all PC and workstation based computer applications.

Designed and implemented a cost-effective Computer Aided Draft System (CAD) for the Technical Drafting Department; achieved a 59% annual reduction in CAD costs.

ISTANBUL TECHNICAL UNIVERSITY, Istanbul, Turkey – 1987 to 1991

Research Assistant. Provided research assistance and clerical support to Professors. Participated in departmental activities and administration.

Taught Computer Programming in FORTRAN IV course at the University.

RENTCA ENGINEERING RESEARCH & CONSULTING COMPANY, Ankara, Turkey – 1986 to 1987

Systems & CAD Engineer. Actively participated in software development applications using the Computer Aided Design and Drafting facility. Managed the company's computer facilities.

Oversaw completion of the Kinali-Sakarya Motorway Project in Ankara, Turkey.

AFFILIATIONS AND MEMBERSHIPS

Institute of Industrial Engineers, Atlanta, Georgia
European Geophysical Society, Strasbourg, France

COMPUTER TECHNOLOGY

Programming Languages: Basic, Fortran, Pascal, C, C++, and Object Oriented Programming
Operating Systems: DOS, Windows 95, 98, NT, and UNIX
Network Protocols: Ethernet Protocol over the TCP-IP connections, Windows NT
Software Applications: Integrated Systems: MS-Office 97. Word Processing Systems: Word and WordPerfect. Spreadsheets: Excel and Lotus. Data Base Management: Access. Graphics: PowerPoint. Project Planning: MS-Schedule and Primavera. CAD Systems: AutoCAD, ME10/20

7—BROADCASTING

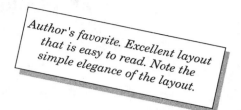

Victoria Holbloth ✳ Television and Video Production

✤ Professional Profile file

Produce daily interview segments airing on Bloomberg Terminals, Bloomberg News, and BIT (Bloomberg Information Television) worldwide Handle live, two-way satellite and remote preproduction, production, post-production, and editing.

Set up and tape live news programming and studio, satellite and remote television interviews with business leaders, heads-of-state, celebrities, and newsmakers.

Professionally committed, focused, responsible, and cool in chaos. Utilize an effective combination of technical abilities, creativity, and good humor to produce excellent interviews and programming in normal or unforeseen situations.

✤ Technical Equipment and Abilities

Switchers	❑ Abekas A34, PDG 418 Videotek
Cameras	❑ Sony BetaCam, Hitachi studio camera
Remote Controls	❑ Fujinon, Radamec advanced robotic cameras
Audio	❑ Mackie 32x8 Audio Console
Routers	❑ BTS Digital CP-300, SYC-3200 Sigma, Codec
Editing	❑ AVID / Video cube, Abekas A34, RM-450, PVE-500
Computers	❑ Audio Video Capture Computer (AVC), PC, Mac

❑ Pre and postproduction and basic editing for live and remote newscasts.
❑ Live production transmission utilizing multimedia computer.
❑ Dubbing and duplication of tapes and tape format changes.
❑ On-air switches and master control duties. Live daily newscast teleprompting.
❑ Remote and studio control cameras. Live and taped.

✤ Employment and Education

Bloomberg, LP, New York, NY   1996 to present
Video Forum Technician and Segment Director
WLNY, Melville, NY   1994 to 1996
Studio Technician and Editor for live daily news show

610 Broadway, Amityville, NY 11701   ❑   516-555-5555   ❑   alexz@aol.com

8—C++ PROGRAMMER

KIMBERLY SRADER
675 East 14th Street • New York, New York 10021 • (212) 555-5555
ksrader@milly.net

SOFTWARE APPLICATION DEVELOPER
C++... JAVA

A dynamic, innovative computer programming professional with demonstrated expertise in developing and implementing highly technical, user friendly programs in C++ and JavaScript. **Core competencies include:**

- **C/C++ and JAVA NT**
- **UNIX and LINUX**
- **Installshield, Microsoft Developer Studio, CVS**
- **GUI Design, Object Oriented Design and Design Patterns**

- **POSIX thread API, Sentinel License Manager and IRIS Performer.**
- **WIN32(with Internals), Motif, OpenGL, FOX(Open Source),**

PROFESSIONAL EXPERIENCE

1997 – Present   **Software Engineer, BLG Research Corporation,** Washington, DC

- *Database Object Library*: Designed an Object Library for in-house **D**ata **T**ransfer **F**acility **(DTF)**. Implemented in C++, using Object Oriented principles.
- *License Manager*: Designed and implemented a license manager with Graphical User Interface for all related software on all the UNIX platforms and Windows, using the SDK provided by Rainbow Tech, POSIX thread API and WIN32 SDK; implemented in C++.
- *Database Management System*: Worked as part of a software development team to retrieve, input, and store data. It was developed in C++, using Object Oriented Design principles. All applications featured a GUI.
- *Software Packaging*: Solely responsible for packaging all flagship products using Installshield.
- *WIN32 Programming*: Developed a variety of utilities using **WIN32 SDK**.
- *Visualization*: Responsible for developing modules for data visualization with interfaces using in-house Object Oriented widget library, along with OpenGL; implemented in C++.
- *Porting*: Responsible for all software/tools to all the UNIX and WIN32 platforms.
- *Filament Grid Generator*: Designed and implemented a grid generation tool for thin filamentlike stuctures (like microprocessor pins, etc.) ; implemented in C++, using Object Oriented Design principles.
- *Grid Adaptation tool*: Worked as a team member, in the development of a Grid Adaptation tool, which adapts grid using user defined criterion; implemented in C++, using Object Oriented Design principles.

(Continued)

KIMBERLY SRADER

ADDITIONAL EXPERIENCE

1996 – 1997   **Programmer, Aeronautical Development Agency**, Bombay, India
- Successfully completed a Surface grid generation tool utilizing C++, X/Motif, and OpenGL.

1995 – 1996   **Lecturer, Regional Engineering College**, Surathkal, India
- Taught AutoCAD and Basic ME courses for undergraduate Mechanical Engineering students.
- Conducted undergraduate Engineering Labs.

EDUCATION

- **Bachelor of Science • Mechanical Engineering**
  Gogte Institute of Technology, Belgaum, INDIA • August 1995

9—CALL CENTER MANAGER

Becky Hiebert

5699 Glen Trail • Austin, Texas 78127 • 512.555.5555 • bh@austin.rr.com

CALL CENTER MANAGER • CUSTOMER SERVICE MANAGER

Highly experienced Call Center Manager with over 20 years' experience in Customer Service Program Development, Call Center Management, and Quality Improvement. Excellent success in managing and improving large call centers. Resourceful problem solver with proven record of achievement in operational turnaround of lagging ventures, successful shaping of new programs, and improvement of productivity in established departments. Positive individual able to build and motivate telemarketing and sales teams to self-improvement. Highly ethical professional, able to improve revenues without sacrificing values.

Highlights of Performance

Instituted program improvements that resulted in "Call Center of the Year Award" by Telemarketing Magazine for the Harte Hanks Response Management - Austin Call Center in 1998

Managed Telemarketing Department to achievement of 3.86 out of 4.0 rating on Price-Waterhouse telemarketing audit, effecting an increase of .76 points

Reduced TSR agent turnover rate of 77% to 14%

Increased productivity by 90% through implementation of improved technology

Boosted sales by 25% for Q1 1998 through establishment of sales goals and quotas

Elevated appointment hold rate from 25% to better than 90% through electronic transfer of appointment data

Areas of Expertise

Program Improvement

Established performance measurement metrics and internal/external processes standards for Call Center to achieve COPC-2000 Certification
Formulated improved screening and hiring processes for telemarketing agents to improve productivity and quality of service
Set communications procedures to improve interdepartmental communications and build common goals among branch offices geographically separated
Developed Disaster Recovery Plan that set a global standard for Response Management
Masterminded Career Advancement Program that significantly impacted agent turnover rate and improved depth of training of employees
Spearheaded formation of Performance Initiative Team for improvement of service and performance award selections
Created Quality Control procedures and set benchmarks for quality goals achievement

Technology

Developed standardized, online account tracking application that allowed secure documentation tracking, quality measurements, and auto-generated reports resulting in reduced processing/billing errors
Designed "pop up" technology for quality control of appointment confirmation using proprietary Unix-based software
Migrated operating environments from Unix to NT based platforms
Improved overall technology environment through workstation upgrades and integration of cutting edge support peripherals for information sharing
Trained Tech Support Agents on SAP, PeopleSoft, MediLife, Dialogic, and other applications for various high tech accounts

(Continued)

Professional Experience

PC.com
INFORMATION TECHNOLOGY MANAGER   1999-2000

SecuritySystems.com
QUALITY CONTROL SYSTEMS MANAGER   1999

Harte Hanks
QUALITY IMPROVEMENT COORDINATOR   1996-1997
TELEMARKETING MANAGER OF TRAINING   1995-1996
TELEMARKETING PRODUCT TECH SUPPORT REPRESENTATIVE   1994

1973-1994
*Career history in Sales, Business Development, and Entrepreneurial endeavors developing multimillion-dollar
revenue generating ventures and growing successful Sales/Marketing divisions
Details happily provided in an interview situation*

Technical Skills

Windows NT Server	UnixWare	MS Access
Novell NetWare	HP-UX	MS Office Suite 95/97
Ethernet	Solaris	Executone ACD
Token Ring	Visual Basic	ACT!
LAN Manager	Visual FoxPro	GoldMine
LAN Server	AlphaFour	Netscape
NetDirector of Unix	Lotus Notes	Communicator
System Management	Lotus 123	Internet Explorer
Server	FoxBASE	NFS
Enterprise/Solver	FoxPRO	

Protocols and Processes:

SMTP	IPX/SPX	PPP
IMAP	TCP/IP	DNS
IP	Telnet	ZIP
SNMP	TFTP	FTP
IPSec	POP3	

Military Service

United States Navy • Honorable Discharge • 1971

Education

Associates Bachelor of Arts – Business and Marketing
Richland College • Dallas, Texas

10—CEO

Michael J. Greene

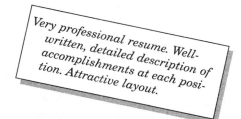
Very professional resume. Well-written, detailed description of accomplishments at each position. Attractive layout.

---

91 Elm Circle • San Jose, California 00000 • (555) 555-5555 • mjgreene@aol.com

Executive Summary

Telecommunications executive with over 30 years successful industry experience in Executive Leadership, Product/Process Development, Strategic Marketing/Sales, and Operations. Strong leader with extensive knowledge of wireless communications and cutting edge network technologies. Proven record of building revenues, increasing profitability, building strong customer relationships, and establishment of solid operations in the wireless communications industry. Visionary leader, able to bring organization, creative thinking and innovative problem solving to bear on business operations. Inspirational manager of talent teams.

Professional Experience

FUTUREWEB, INC.
WWW.FUTUREWEB.COM

High tech start-up company meeting special market for B2B wireless broadband IP network services using advanced platforms to bridge the "first mile" bandwidth bottleneck.
San Carlos, California

CHIEF EXECUTIVE OFFICER/PRESIDENT
1999 – PRESENT

Founder and operational leader of company aimed at developing market for fixed broadband wireless access for small to medium businesses. Performed all financial planning and raised seed funding from Kaiser and supporting founding team members. Defined vertical markets and constructed strategic marketing overview for market penetration. Modeled complete network infrastructure market by market. Applied depth of professional experience to creation of trial system and establishment of initial agreements with service providers and equipment vendors. Negotiated with Cisco Systems, Exodus, PacBell, First Virtual Corporation, CoSine, and local ISPs for proprietary equipment, leased lines and services. Recruited and positioned highly talented professionals in key roles for corporate start-up success.

> **Negotiated with Kaiser Permanente for seed funding and physical asset contributions to launch** start-up phase of FutureWeb.

> **Built unique trial system consisting of broadband connectivity structure, VPN, and ClicktoMeet™ video services plus complete network model for all markets.**

> **Successfully negotiated with multiple entities to secure key services and access to communications backbone ensuring model success.**

> **Played key role in negotiation of corporate acquisition of privately held company (Western Multiplex) by Glendale Corporation.**

> **Smoothed transition from private to public company while continuing to achieve revenue and profitability growth, increased levels of production, and customer satisfaction.**

(Continued)

Michael J. Greene   Page 2

EDMONTON WIRELESS INTERCONNECT (FORMERLY EASTERN MULTIPLEX, INC.)

Leading worldwide supplier of digital microwave radios utilizing Direct Sequence Spread Spectrum technology for industrial telecommunications.
Sunnyvale, California

PRESIDENT/GENERAL MANAGER
1995-1998

Led self-contained Wireless Interconnect division of Edmonton, Inc. with gross annual run rate of $45 million. Shouldered complete Profit and Loss answerability, reporting directly to corporate CEO at national level. Applied practical technical experience to strategic decision making for profitability and increase in market share. Led market launch of cutting edge wireless communication device (CATZ RF radio) that resulted in great expansion of revenues and dominant market share. Spearheaded all operations including Sales/Marketing, Finance, Customer Service, MIS, and Manufacturing activities. Administered 8 Senior Managers in turn supervising over 150 employees in the United States and Canada.

More than doubled revenues from $17 million to $45 million within 3 years.

Brought to market the family of CATZ brand radios that operated in the ISM band of frequencies for unlicensed, end-user applications using cutting edge DSSS technology.

Successfully brought division through several periods of expansion and contraction without loss of profitability and with zero reduction in labor force.

CHIEF OPERATIONS OFFICER
1991-1995

Managed complete operation of Eastern Multiplex prior to acquisition by Edmonton, Inc. achieving completely internally financed, profitable record. Led development and introduction of CATZ DSSS radio product and readied for market launch, applying for patent in 1993. Devised corporate strategies and held complete P&L responsibility. Member of Board of Directors.

Grew revenues from $2 million to $17 million and positioned for profitable buyout.

Introduced completely new and innovative product concept/application to the telecommunications industry.

Built highly successful management team that played pivotal role in company's acquisition, providing talent base that was strong issue for negotiation of buyout price.

Worked with Federal Communications Commission on certification of CATZ radios to bring into regulatory compliance and ready for market launch.

Active participant in FCC rule-making process regarding unlicensed band regulations playing instrumental role in setting industry standards for wireless communications.

Education and Training

Bachelor of Science – Business Administration
Notre Dame College, 1982

11—CHIEF FINANCIAL OFFICER

Lorraine Bent, C.P.A.

(904) 555-7654 • 1770 Arron Road • DeLand, Florida 32720

CAREER PROFILE

CHIEF FINANCIAL OFFICER with 18 years' experience in corporate accounting and 10 years' experience in multicorporation accounting operations in the medical field. Areas of expertise include:

- Financial Administration/Reporting
- Operations Management
- Telecommunications Integration
- Multicorporation/Partnership Taxes
- Acquisitions/Joint Ventures
- Credit Lines/Administration
- Accounting Systems Design/Implementation

- Financial Planning/Analysis
- Acquisition Negotiations
- Premium Rate Strategies
- Equipment Leasing/Portfolio
- Multisite Retail Purchasing/Negotiations
- Strategic Planning/Budgeting
- Central Accounting Administration

PROFESSIONAL EXPERIENCE

Chief Financial Officer   1991–Present
FOREST HOME MEDICAL CENTER, Orlando, Florida

Florida-based group of affiliated home health care and pharmacy companies headquartered in Orlando, Florida.

- Design, implement, and manage all centralized accounting, management information systems, and internal control policies and procedures for 11 corporations.
- Manage accounting department consisting of controller and accounting staff.
- Prepare all federal and state tax requirements including corporate, partnership, payroll, and property tax returns.
- Formulate appraisals and negotiate purchases of all group and company acquisitions.
- Negotiate contracts and purchasing commitments with manufacturers for buying group.
- Coordinate all financing and external reporting with financial institutions for the group.
- Spearhead groups to assess value of potential acquisition targets: observe and critique operations, determine feasibility and asset valuations.
- Instrumental in the negotiation and acquisition of $3 million home care and retail pharmacy stores; negotiated a $14 million contract for pharmaceuticals resulting in a savings of 1.5–3% on cost of goods for each retail store.
- Prepare and administer operating and cash budgets for each retail profit center.

Achievements:

- Instrumental in the research and coordination to integrate voice, data, and fax over data lines which will save $ 100–200k in long distance charges annually.
- Installed and manage a 10-node Novell Netware LAN, Solomon Accounting software, MicroSoft Office, and Excel.
- Instrumental in instituting MestaMed billing software, resulting in a reduction of workforce and savings of $189k annually.
- Centralized subsidiary's previously subcontracted accounting functions to headquarters saving $89–90k annually.
- Increased credit lines from $1.5 million to $2.9 million in credit in three years, resulting in a savings of .5 point on interest, or $14k per year.
- Saved $87k in annual corporate management salaries through comprehensive management of the financial programs and credit administration of the group.
- Negotiated the purchase of an acquisition holding a market value of $2–3 million for less than $1.1 million.

(Continued)

95

Chief Operating Officer   1985–1991
BEST MEDICAL RENTAL SUPPLY INC., Albany, Georgia

A Georgia-based home health care company.

- Managed daily operations in conjunction with Regional Managers.
- Negotiated contracts and purchasing commitments with manufacturers for buying group consisting of 34 retail locations.
- Managed accounting department consisting of controller, billing auditor, and accounting staff.
- Prepared all federal and state tax requirements including corporate, partnership, individual, and pension plan returns.
- Formulated appraisals and negotiated purchase of all acquisitions.
- Prepared and administered operating budgets for all retail locations.
- Received, secured, and disbursed all corporate funds concerning company operation in conjunction with the President and CEO.

Achievements:
- Designed, implemented, and managed all accounting and management reporting systems.

Partner / CPA   1976–1985
MARTIN AND MARTIN COMPANY, P.C., Albany, Georgia

Public accounting firm.

- Coordinated and managed the firm's automated write-up practices, which interfaced between accounting, data processing, and financial reporting functions.
- Prepared clients' tax requirements.
- Assisted with certified audits of municipalities, banks, and construction and retail clients.

EDUCATION

Certified Public Accountant—Florida State Board of Accountancy—1991

Certified Public Accountant—Georgia State Board of Accountancy—1983

Bachelor of Science Degree in Business Administration—1979
Valdosta State College, Valdosta, Georgia

PROFESSIONAL AFFILIATIONS

American Institute of Certified Public Accountants
Georgia Society of Certified Public Accountants
Florida Institute of Certified Public Accountants
Rotary Club—Board Member
Chamber of Commerce—Steering Committee

JOHN K. WICKER

3053 Dyersome Road • West Palm Beach, Florida 33405
(561) 555-1212 • Email@email.com

CFO / SENIOR TREASURY MANAGER

10 Years' High-Tech Financial Leadership Experience in Enhancing Bottom-Line Performance

- Increasing Productivity
- Lowering the Cost of Funds
- Providing a Better Work Product
- Automation/High-Tech Integration

A seasoned professional with extensive leadership skills and experience over a broad range of financial operations and management functions. A solution-focused, analytical team player with a consistent record for successfully increasing annual operational productivity by 15 percent.

A solution-driven analytical individual who strives to implement appropriate technologies successfully to increase operational productivity.

Core Professional Strengths

Expert in financial markets/products	Financial forecasting
Financial reporting	Cash management
Start-up and turnaround management	Expense/cost control
Management and staff empowerment	Complex problem solving

Professional Experience

DST FINANCIAL CORP., West Palm Beach, Florida   1993 to Current
CFO—Treasury and Bank Operations
(DST is a $3.3 billion specialty finance-holding company of DST Federal Bank, FSB, which primarily acquires, manages, and resolves troubled real estate loans.)

Direct Treasury and Bank Operations function including daily cash and funds management, forecasting, budget and P/L, and management reporting. Acquisition and pricing of funds through the Money Desk and Warehouse Lines to include covenant compliance and collateral management through securitization. Transact business on behalf of the Bank with various counterparties including brokers, investment bankers, DTC, FRB, FHLB, BONY, and BOA. Management of back office operations comprised of wire transfer operations, securities settlement, cashletter, Fed adjustments, and check processing. Administration of Branch Operations and personnel to include policies and procedures, FDICIA, and contingency planning.

- Implemented a Treasury Management System saving $2.2 million by creating operating efficiencies.
- Automated various business units' pipeline reporting functions to enable Treasury proactively to manage funding requirements.
- Reduced interest expense by 20 basis points per annum by implementing a "sell-side strategy" that forced competition between counterparties.
- Raised $8 billion in retail, wholesale, and brokered deposits.
- Negotiated and closed in excess of $1 billion in one-off-term financing and warehouse lines of credit.
- Successfully negotiated pricing on correspondent banking services including Lockbox processing for Loan Servicing business.
- Improved Treasury work product re: cash positions, counterparty exposures, and management reporting.

(DST continued on page two)

John K. Wicker
(Page two)

Professional Experience (Continued)

DST FINANCIAL CORP. (Continued)

Treasury Operations

- Daily cash and short-term liquidity management of $200–$500 million via various funding alternatives such as Repurchase Agreements, Fed Funds, Advances, Credit Facilities, and Money Desk deposits.
- Created and produced running three-month Cash Flow Forecasting with a two-year forecast adjusted monthly.
- Managed warehouse lines of credit including covenant compliance and collateral management.
- Responsible for wire transfer operations, securities settlement, short-term investments, and check processing.
- Systems literate on Treasury platforms, Quantum, and Bank of America Direct—Bloomberg, A5400/Fiserv, Access, and Excel.

Bank Operations

- Managed Money Desk, which raised $8 billion in retail, wholesale, and brokered deposits.
- Established weekly liability pricing for Money Desk and Branch Operations.
- Managed bank back office operations and operational processing. Average monthly cashletter of approximately 600,000 items.
- Administration of Bank policies and procedures, as well as reporting requirements.

M.J. WAITINGS LP, Miami, Florida   1990 to 1993
Principal—NASD Series 24 & 27
(Founded in 1974 by veteran value investor Martin J. Whitman, the company is a full-service brokerage firm that adheres to a disciplined value approach to investing.)

Recruited to assist in the start-up of a satellite office. Successfully built the business from the ground up that included site location, build-out, and recruiting/training staff. As the General Securities Principal, supervised the company's corporate securities business and as the Financial and Operations Principal, was responsible for financial rules, record keeping requirements, as well as NASD filings.

- *Grew office production to $4.5 million.*
- *Automated portfolio management to provide cash flow and pay down projections to institutional accounts.*

Professional Experience (Prior to 1990)

Campbell and Associates, Palm Beach Gardens, Florida   1988 to 1990
CFO

President Country Club, West Palm Beach, Florida   1981 to 1988
CFO

Education

TRINITY COLLEGE, Hartford, Connecticut
Bachelor of Science: Finance, 1981

NASD licenses—Series 7,24,47,63

Languages: Fluent in English, French, and Spanish

References Furnished on Request

13—CHIEF TECHNOLOGY OFFICER

Robert C. Hensley

333 West Road • Fremont, California 90805 • (555) 555-5555 • rchensley@yahoo.com

Chief Technical Officer

Web Based Development • E-Commerce • Client-Server • Software Development

Executive Summary

Senior executive experienced in leading technology advancements for Fortune 1000 company resulting in multimillion-dollar revenue increases and strategic industry positioning. Visionary leader of cutting edge technology innovations that significantly impact business operations and profitability. Keen insight into Web technology innovations, e-commerce direction, and future trends. 30 years' experience in software development, project management, national program rollouts, and research and development. Expert in modern application development tools including Cold Fusion, ASP, and Java.

Areas of Expertise:

Corporate Technology Strategies • Leading Edge Software Development
Web-based Client/Server Development in Cold Fusion
Program Leadership • System Innovation

Professional Experience

CHIEF TECHNICAL OFFICER

ASSISTANT VICE PRESIDENT OF R & D

VIS.com
Orange, California • 1968 – present

Directed cutting edge software development projects for over 12 years as Assistant VP of Research and Development for one of nation's leading information services firms. Served as CTO since 1999, directing new technological developments toward Web-based future. Successfully managed rapidly evolving technological environment, acting as key player in corporate strategies and direction toward Web-based developments.

Technology Leadership

Played pivotal role in corporate advancement of technology to Web-based client server applications development in Cold Fusion. Spearheaded cutting edge research and development and led company to forefront of technology advancement.

Successfully led multiple technology projects that resulted in multiple hundred million dollar contracts and revenues for VIS with Fortune 100 companies and governmental agencies. Earned reputation as strong leader able to motivate managers to meet aggressive deadlines while creating new, innovative technologies and applications.

(Continued)

13—CHIEF TECHNOLOGY OFFICER (CONT.)

Research and Development Accomplishments

Directed conversion of VIS's proprietary in-house resume retrieval recruiting tool to a completely Web-based client-server technology utilizing Virtual Private Network, Internet, and intranet capabilities for information sharing. Planned and directed national project including evaluation and selection of technology. Key player in VIS's advancement into Web-based technologies used for information sharing, management, and HR sourcing. Played crucial role in diagnosing system software/hardware/Operating System/LAN problems and needs, and recommending changes/improvements.

Broke new ground with development of first ever computer-direct-to-plate system that achieved production. Managed full life cycle of multimillion-dollar project from conception to support, successfully delivering system to 2 European companies and 1 U.S. daily newspaper. Personally authored all documentation and performed design reviews. Designed innovative system that deployed on mainframe system and utilized specialized terminals.

Invented compression schemes for fonts, and graphics for rapid information sharing of graphic material in the printing process of Yellow Page directories. Created system for Yellow Page pagination that is used by majority of directory publishers today, 10 years after initial application rollout. Created other software systems related to Yellow Page pagination that are still in use today, 20 years later.

STARTED CAREER WITH ALPHANUMERIC PUBLICATION SYSTEMS (ACQUIRED BY VIS IN 1971) IN 1968 AS A FIELD ENGINEER AND HAVE PROGRESSED THROUGH THE RANKS TO CURRENT POSITION. THROUGHOUT 30 YEARS IN THE TECHNOLOGY INDUSTRY, SUCCESSFULLY STAYED AT THE CUTTING EDGE OF SOFTWARE AND SYSTEM DEVELOPMENT, APPLYING OUTSTANDING MANAGERIAL, TEAM BUILDING, AND TECHNICAL EXPERTISE TO CONTRIBUTE TO EVOLUTION OF COMPANY INTO A LEADER IN TECHNOLOGY.

Positions held with Volt Information Services include:

BRANCH MANAGER – SOFTWARE DEVELOPMENT
PROJECT MANAGER – SOFTWARE DEVELOPMENT
DATA CENTER MANAGER – OPERATIONS AND PRODUCTION
FIELD ENGINEER

Technical Expertise

Web Development Tools

Cold Fusion	VBScript	HomeSite
HTML	FrontPage	Visual Studio
DHTML	IE4.0/5.0 Document Object	Visual InterDev
Java	Model	ASP
JavaScript	Cold Fusion Studio	ADO

Languages and Applications

C	SQL	SQL Server
Borland C++	Visual C/C++	**SQL Base for Windows**
Turbo Pascal 5.5	DB2	Pascal
Delphi, Delphi 32	MS Access	PL/1

Network and Client Server

Ethernet	LANtastic	System Management Server
Token Ring	Novell Netware	Windows 2000
LAN Server	Windows NT Server	
Multiple Protocols		

RICHARD D. LLOYD

1168 Jason Way
Los Angeles, California 90223
Home: (213) 555-2121 I Cell: (213) 555-6565
Email: email@email.com

INDUSTRY LEADER—TECHNOLOGY EXECUTIVE / CONSULTANT
CIO / CTO / INFORMATION TECHNOLOGIST

Orchestrating Explosive Growth in Volatile and Down DOT COM Markets

Expanding and Reengineering Organizations / Start-Up Management Expert
Organizational / IS Leadership of Public and Private Enterprises

---

High-profile career spanning 25 years spearheading the development, commercialization, and implementation of emerging technologies across key industry sectors including Internet, healthcare, and high-tech environments.

CORE PROFESSIONAL STRENGTHS

Strategic Visioning / Planning
Corporate / Business Development
System Integration / IT Infrastructure
Building Strategic Alliances and Partnerships

Management / IT Team Development
Product Development / Enhancement
Project Management / Leadership
New Technology Development / Transfer

PROFESSIONAL EXPERIENCE

COURT-LAND, INC., Boca Raton, Florida — 1998 to Current
Chief Technology Officer
- Spearheaded team to develop an Internet healthcare plan that became the basis for Cybear's vision.
- Core management team member that took this developmental-stage Internet company public.
- Designed and implemented Court-Land's HIPAA-ready national ISP network and Network Operations Center (NOC).
- Drafted initial specifications and developed "Dr. Cybear Internet Portal."
- Integrated strategic business partner's applications into the product.

CYBERMATRIX CORP., West Palm Beach, Florida — 1995 to 1998
Chief Information Officer
- Directed IT strategic planning and implementations in preparing PhyMatrix for its IP.
- Built a national network to support corporate medical practice management, managed care, and data warehousing systems.
- Worked with the top management to identify, evaluate, and integrate organizations into PhyMatrix's core business systems.

PALM BEACH COUNTY HEALTH CARE DISTRICT, West Palm Beach, Florida — 1991 to 1995
Chief Technology Officer
- Reengineered the internal infrastructure and implemented a new managed care system.
- Developed team to plan countywide managed healthcare network.
- Managed internal and consulting resources during this effort; project was on time and under budget.

DIGITAL OFFICE SYSTEMS INTERNATIONAL, West Palm Beach, Florida — 1986 to 1990
Chief Technology Officer
- Developed the first Cable TV (CATV) facilities resource management system for integration into the advance Geographic Information System (GIS) and Cable TV Engineering software.
- Headed the development team responsible for the D-tain House Arrest System. Developed all facets of the system: hardware, systems software, imbedded microprocessor software, unit fabrication, and manufacturing. Product deployed nationally in 1987.
- Founded and managed DOSI operations and development teams.

EDUCATION & TRAINING

Bachelor of Science: Analytical Chemistry — University of Florida — 1985
Associate Faculty Member — College of Engineering — 1990–Current

Comprehensive Resume, Specific Achievements, and References Furnished Upon Request

Appealing one-page resume.

DAVID HAUS
92 Common Drive · Teaneck, New Jersey 07662
Tel: (201) 555-7234 · Email: email@email.com

CAREER OBJECTIVE:

EXPERIENCED computer professional seeks a position with advancement opportunities that will utilize educational training and acquired skills to contribute to organizational development. Areas of interest include:

NETWORK ADMINISTRATION · DESKTOP SUPPORT · HELP DESK

CERTIFICATION:

Microsoft Certified Product Specialist in Windows NT4

COMPUTER PROFICIENCY:

Hardware: All PC related hardware
Software: Windows, Windows NT · Web browsers · various utilities · numerous software applications

EDUCATION AND TRAINING:

MS Education Center / TrackOn · Paramus, New Jersey	1994
Bergen Community College · Paramus, New Jersey	1994

- Administration Windows NT4
- Supporting Windows NT4 Core Technologies
- Introduction to Networking
- Setup, Installation, and troubleshooting of Hardware and Software

Teaneck High School · Teaneck, New Jersey	1990

- Graduated in top 10% of class

SKILLS:

- Installing and configuring software/hardware
- Troubleshooting computer problems
- Instructing users in various computer topics
- Supporting end users

TECHNICAL EMPLOYMENT:

IBM   **Bridgewater, New Jersey**
Help Desk Technician   *2000 - Present*

Contracted by EDP Contract Services and brought onboard to install, maintain, and service LANs, computers, and printers. Interface with end users in computer workstation, network, and e-mail set-up; assist with training and ongoing technical support for an average of 2,000 staff.
♦ **Improved staff productivity/efficiency by identifying and resolving end-user problems.**

THE SOUNDING BOARD   **East Rutherford, New Jersey**
Installer / Sales Associate   *1995 - 2000*
Assisted departmental employees with resolution of computer-related problems. Demonstrated, sold and installed high-end audio and video equipment to customer throughout the New York/New Jersey metropolitan area. Performed custom installations including remote-controlled complex audio/video systems.

16—COMPUTER PROGRAMMER

Frank Benuscak

15 North Mill Street - Nyack, New York 10960 - (914) 555-3160

Note use of specific skills under "Software • Hardware / OS" that provides keywords to shorten the time it takes a reader to understand this person's skills.

Profile

A results-oriented **COMPUTER PROGRAMMER** with extensive experience in all stages of design, coding, and testing for multi-user systems.   Background encompasses extensive experience in software analysis and development in demanding hi-tech environments.   Demonstrated ability in providing end-user training and developing on-line Help documentation and user manuals.

Software • Hardware/OS

Assembly (16 Bit) - Liberty Basic - Visual Basic 4.0, 5.0 - VBA - MS TSQL - MS Access - MS SQL Server 6.5 - Crystal Reports - C - C++ - DOS - UNIX - FORTRAN - COBOL - Microsoft Office
IBM -PC's and Compatibles -Windows NT, 95, & 3.1

Professional Experience

Institute of Energetic Researches of Academy of Sciences - Washington, DC - 1990/Present
Programmer/Analyst - 1995/Present
Directed all stages of design, coding, and testing of the Environmental Management System (EMS) project concerning the ecological safety of power plants.
*   Designed multiple forms allowing employees to enter research resulting and forecasting
         information into the EMS Database.
*   Developed on-line Help documentation and user manuals as a result of gathering information
         from client interaction.

Programmer - 1990/1995
Participated in the development and implementation of the Coolant Flow Regimes Calculating System (CFRCS) for the needs of the physics and hydrodynamics laboratories of the power plants.
*   Utilized numerous scientific formulas and created Assembly Language (16 bit) with later
         transition to Liberty Basic for Windows.

Scientific Research Center for the Atomic Power Engineering - Moscow, Russia - 1987/1990
Engineer

Scientific Research Institute for the Nuclear Power Stations - Moscow, Russia - 1979/1987
Engineer

Education

NRI Schools - McGraw-Hill Companies - Washington, DC
Programming Training

Moscow Physics Engineering University - Moscow, Russia
Bachelor of Science - Physics and Engineering

17—CONTENT DEVELOPER

Maria Lane

907 Main Street
Rochelle Park, NJ 07662
(201) 555-5555 ▪ email@email.com

WEB CONTENT DEVELOPER
▪ ▪ ▪
ON-LINE WRITER

New Media Writing & Editing

Web Site Content Development

Project Planning & Management

Research & Journalistic Writing

Production Coordination

Digital Copyright Issues

HTML Coding & Visual Design

Overview

Professional writer offering 7+ years' experience coupling expertise in leading-edge technologies with powerful on-line content development skills.

Blend in-depth understanding of e-commerce issues with powerful writing skills to create compelling, original content that reflects e-business missions and strategies.

Demonstrated talent for transforming abstract ideas into high-quality written communications. Concise writing style proven effective in capturing and holding Web browsers' attention.

Strong team player with consistent record of contribution in collaborative efforts with interface designers, HTML editors, marketing specialists, and strategists.

Detail-focused and organized; proven time management and multitasking skills in coordinating the completion of complex research and writing assignments.

Professional Experience

Senior Content Developer – Omnipoint.com, New York, NY   1997 – Present

Meet daily production deadlines, planning and developing on-line content designed to build community for this dot.com company. Confer with management to brainstorm and crystallize content ideas. Define specifications, scope, and resources, and coordinate a team of associate writers. Write, edit, and disseminate Web content and articles targeting a high-tech audience.

Selected Achievements:

Developed creative, timely, and relevant content that was instrumental in generating 76% expansion in readership and a 30% increase in average time spent at the site.

Wrote intriguing introductions to site channels that increased click-throughs 45% and fostered a sense of community by doubling reader participation in on-line discussions.

Conceptualized and wrote hundreds of well-received articles including 2 national award-winning pieces that produced widespread publicity and a 15% increase in site traffic.

Journalist/Editor – New Media Communications, Rutherford, NJ   1993 – 1997

Authored 200+ journalistic and editorial articles focusing exclusively on technological advancements and societal impacts. Served as top feature writer and assisted with editing the weekly publication distributed to government and social service agencies.

Education

B.A., Communications and Journalism – Magna Cum Laude
Fairleigh Dickinson University, Rutherford, NJ – 1993

Trained and experienced with most Windows-based applications including MS Office Suite (Word, Excel, Access, PowerPoint), WordPerfect, and Lotus Notes. Skilled in Web page development with MS FrontPage and Macromedia Dreamweaver.

VAL KRUPP, C.P.A.
7 Fair Way
Bergona, New Jersey 07823
(201) 555-9277
email@email.com

CONTROLLER

E-Commerce / Dot.Com Business

A precise highly professional individual with comprehensive experience in the management of financial operations for dot.com companies · Self-directed and motivated with the capability to consistently achieve objectives · An effective leader with a proven talent for developing syner-gist teams for greatest profitability · Experienced in aiding e-commerce business in meeting their organizational and financial objectives.

STRENGTHS:

E-COMMERCE	**ACCOUNTING RESEARCH**	**FINANCE**
SYSTEMS KNOWLEDGE	**PROJECT LEADERSHIP**	**FINANCIAL CONTROLS**
STAFF MANAGEMENT	**STRATEGIC PLANNING**	**INTERPERSONAL SKILLS**

AREAS of EXPERTISE:

- Interact with other senior financial managers; direct and supervise analysts and finance staff in all financial/accounting procedures.
- Strong financial reporting experience - expert in the preparation of quarterly/monthly/year ends, cash flow, SEC 10-Q - 10K, Federal Reserve, and other related reports.
- Strong systems background; conversions, designing security profiles, developing procedural controls and resolving operational difficulties.
- Prepare long- and short-term projections and develop strategic plans based on models; provide projections on the sale/acquisition of divisions and debt financing.
- Maintain full responsibility for intersubsidiary accounting (domestic and worldwide); experienced in the conversion of domestic results into international standards.

MAJOR PROJECTS & ACCOMPLISHMENTS:

- **At Spirit Craft.Com, installed a 4-user local area network for the finance areas which utilizes Novell Netware 3.12.**
- **Created new monthly reporting procedures that resulted in consistent on-time reporting.**
- **Completed a comprehensive (20+ hours) Netware Administrator training program.**

- **At Ross Cherry, facilitated over $100K in corporate savings by developing corrective procedures for royalty reporting; uncovered numerous instances of misreporting and recovered funds.**
- **Reduced monthly reporting preparation time by several days by developing new procedures affecting inter-departmental communication.**
- **Implemented the use of monthly commentaries to improve management communication/reporting.**

- **At CITY CORP., implemented FASB 95 "Statement of Cash Flow."**

(Continued)

VAL KRUPP, C.P.A.   (201) 555-9277   -Page Two-

PROFESSIONAL EXPERIENCE:

SPIRITCRAFT. COM - Bergenfield, New Jersey   20xx-Present
A distributor to U.S. mass merchandisers, chains, and specialty stores. Annual revenue exceeds $71 million.

Controller

Oversee financial operations including monthly reporting, cash management analysis, accounts payable, payroll for 100 employees, general ledger, and 401k/Profit Sharing Plan administration.

ROSS CHERRY - Oakland, New Jersey   19xx-19xx
A $250 million publicly held international importer of plush toys and gifts.

Assistant Corporate Controller

Maintained responsibility for all monthly closings and internal reporting activities. Supervised 9 staff members in SEC reporting, the preparation of commentary on operating results, budget variance analysis, and the development of financial statements.

THE CITY CORP. - Livingston, New Jersey   19xx-19xx
An asset-based financing group; $1 billion interest and fee income.

Supervisor of Corporate Reporting · 19xx-19xx
Supervisor of Systems Accounting · 19xx-19xx
Supervisor of Payroll Accounting · 19xx-19xx

ERNST & YOUNG/ARTHUR YOUNG & CO. - Metro Park/Newark, New Jersey   19xx-19xx

Staff Accountant

EDUCATION:

· **FAIRLEIGH DICKINSON UNIVERSITY** - Teaneck, NJ
M.B.A. in Accounting · G.P.A. 3.4

· **STATE UNIVERSITY OF NEW YORK AT BUFFALO** - Buffalo, NY
B.A. in Psychology ◆ G.P.A. 3.6

Additional Training:
C.P.E. Courses in Financial Statements, Analysis, SEC Reporting & FASB Updates

PROFESSIONAL AFFILIATION:

Member of the New Jersey State Society of CPAs

19—COPY EDITOR

Jim Allen

jallen@emailaddress.com

2298 Shadowlawn Drive
Plymouth, Michigan 48170
Residence: 734.555.4550

COPY EDITOR/WRITER – *e-Commerce*

Enthusiastic, conscientious, and keen writer who is eager to advance skills to a supervisory level. Self-motivated and disciplined at managing multidimensional, complex projects. Highly analytical abilities, recognizing problems/concerns to evaluate alternatives and implement solutions. Experience with traditional copy editing, and an eye for detail.

Qualifications include::

- Extensive experience on the Internet
- Clear understanding of media relations
- Excellent command of English grammar
- Logo development, typeface management
- Familiar with Chicago and AP style manuals
- Advanced computer skills
- Experience writing headlines
- Project management expertise
- Web preparation & publication
- Technical writing, story boarding
- Experience with a variety of voices and styles (technical, sales focused, humorous)

EXPERIENCE

CLASSIFIED VENTURES   Chicago, Illinois
ONLINE COPY WRITER/EDITOR, 1998-current

Oversee the online editorial content for classified real estate Websites for Chicago's largest Internet and e-Commerce company, with national Websites including Apartments.com, Cars.com, Auctions.com, MovingCenter.com, NewHomeNetwork.com, and HomeHunter.com.

- Responsible for assembling and editing all editorial content for real estate Websites, including editing, headline writing, and daily posting of articles.
- Provide original reporting, including coverage of breaking news, trend stories, and producing enterprise stories and packages.
- Provide support using HTML and other basic Internet software applications and programs for development of content pages and packages.

FRITO LAY CORPORATION   Plano, Texas
COPY EDITOR, 1995-98

Worked with a group of Website developers, script writers, and Web-based training developers to edit text and style for high-end deliverables for corporate ePublishing sector.

- Proofread and edited copy for Website, promotional materials, and manuals.
- Interacted with editorial and marketing staffs to ensure consistency of style and to achieve a high level of quality in the end product.
- Responsible for developing and maintaining in-house Web style guide and for ensuring consistency between client and portal interfaces.

EDUCATION & TRAINING

WHEATON COLLEGE   Wheaton, Illinois
BACHELOR OF SCIENCE degree in **Communications**, 1995

- Broadcasting major. Performed numerous radio and television broadcasts; wrote scripts.

Computer efficient in Microsoft Office applications (Word, Excel, Access, PowerPoint);
Quark Express, Netscape, Explorer, HTML; PDAs; Internet–intermediate to expert level

Patrick Dudash

Good profile, could be even more detailed to help give the reader a clear picture of the candidate.

pdudash@link.net

39 93rd Street
Encinitas, California 92024
(760) 555-3450

PROFILE

Confident, competent, results-oriented professional offering personal selling skills enhanced through leadership augmented by diversified experience. Global perspective based upon travels throughout Europe and Mexico. Willing to travel and willing to relocate. Positive and personable attitude; professional image and demeanor. Qualifications include skills in:

- Sales & Marketing
- Public Relations
- International Sales

- New Business Development
- Domestic Sales
- Market Trends

- Distributor Relations
- International Markets
- Corporate Accounts

EXPERIENCE

NEVER CONCEDE COMPANY (NCC), Solana Beach, California - 1997 to present

Director of International Sales and Domestic Leaderboard Manager reporting to the Vice President of Sales. Accountable for sales, distributor relations, and service for ex-USA sales territories and top tier sales accounts. Direct and manage international distributor accounts to meet budgeted sales expectations; maximizing international sales while maintaining existing markets; monitoring and maintaining all aspects of international records, contracts, sales trends, and marketing information. Collateral responsibility includes liaison with manufacturing, shipping, USA sales, customer service, accounting, and operations to ensure a coordinated effort and distributor satisfaction. Obtain, analyze, and provide competitive and market intelligence for the international markets and assist in directing, shaping, and monitoring the sales communications programs of third party distributors. Coordinate sales activities between "leaderboard accounts" and outside sales representatives. Acquired and provided competitive and market intelligence to shape sales programs and communications.

- Developed an effective, loyal, and cohesive sales team that increased sales by 139% in 1999.
- Increased Client Satisfaction Ratio from 89% to 99.5% within 9 months.

Customer Service Representative. Primary focus was on introducing the company products by accomplishing sales-related activities, providing customer service, and expanding accounts according to assigned quotas. Duties included telephone sales, ongoing support to the product distribution channel, and coordination with external independent territory sales representatives.

- Increased general revenues by $1.75 million within 12 months using innovative sales techniques.
- Developed 2,175 national accounts within 6 months; promoted to current position.

Customer Service Representative. Primary focus was on building new business by providing excellent customer service. Provided materials, communication, and assistance to customers, accounts, and sales representatives to support sales-related activities. Troubleshot potential and resolved existing problems. Coordinated sales activities with the sales and telemarketing staffs. Fostered and nurtured excellent customer relations and expanded existing client database.

- Expanded telemarketing base to include 3 geographical regions; increased sales $978K.
- Established national client database and sales reporting procedures; promoted within 60 days.

(Continued on next page)

Patrick Dudash

pdudash@link.net

39 93rd Street
Encinitas, California 92024
(760) 555-3450

PROFESSIONAL EXPERIENCE *(Continued)*

DOT.COM SOFTWARE, Southparke, California - 1994 to 1997

Corporate Accounts Manager reporting to the Vice President of Sales. Scope of responsibility included establishing and maintaining corporate accounts through sales and service contracts of Toshiba, Dell, IBM laptop computers, Hewlett Packard printers, and related peripherals. Participated in onsite upgrades of hard drives, memory, and other computer accessories.

- Implemented national sales campaign; increased sales revenues to $45 million in 1996 to 1997.
- Spearheaded increase of regional sales revenues to $35 million in 1995 to 1996.

Customer Service Representative. Provided sales and customer service by selling in-house upgrades and performing repairs of computer systems and related peripherals.

- Selected by management for promotion to Corporate Accounts Manager.
- Increased sales revenues to $25 million in 1994 to 1995.

SONY PICTURES ENTERTAINMENT, Burbank, California - 1992 to 1994
MOTION PICTURE CORPORATION OF AMERICA, Burbank, California - 1992 to 1994

Electrician/Camera Assistant/Reader. Performed a variety of diverse support activities involving setting up lighting and camera equipment for live action films and recommending scripts to producers.

- Read and recommended the script for the hit movie *"Dumber and Dumbest."*
- Developed solid industry relationships working on 1994 low budget film *"Last 100 Yards."*

MANIFOLD AIR FILTER, Hollywood, California - 1990 to 1992

Co-Manager and Account Representative of an independently owned manufacturer of air filters for air conditioning systems. Co-managed daily operations and related activities involved in manufacturing air filters and servicing air filtration systems for established accounts.

- Significantly increased existing accounts base by 39% within 18 months.

COMPUTER TECHNOLOGY

- ACT for Windows
- Crystal Reports
- Domain Management

- E-Commerce Skills
- Great Plains Dynamics
- Internet Proficiency

- Microsoft Office 97
- Web Development
- Word, Excel, & Outlook

EDUCATION

San Diego State University, San Diego, California
Bachelor of Science - Major: **Computer Information Systems**

Appropriate personal and professional references are available.

21—DATABASE ADMINISTRATOR

Alicia Paramo-Dionne

1238 Sum Street, Carlton, California 92008 • (760) 555-2837
apd@aol.com

PROFILE AND STRENGTHS

Competent, conscientious, and detail-oriented Database Administrator and Management Professional with considerable, diverse experience augmented by a formal, graduate level education in Computer Science reinforced by specialized, industry-related training. Specific expertise in Information Systems Technology included financial services, manufacturing, distribution, and retail industries. Global perspective based upon life, work, and studies abroad. Bilingual: Farsi, fluent, and English. Expertise includes skills in:

• Accounting/Finance	• Network Administration	• Strategic Planning
• Computer Technology	• Problem Analysis	• Systems Development
• Cost Controls	• Programming	• Troubleshooting
• Inventory Control	• Staff Development	• Warehouse Distribution

COMPUTER TECHNOLOGY

☑ Hardware: Main Frames, IBM 360/370, Mini Computers, RISC6000, AS400, PCs and peripherals.
☑ Connectivity: Novel NetWare, LAN, WAN, Windows NT, 95, NT's Workstation
☑ Languages: Assembler, C, C++, COBOL, FORTRAN, PL/I, Visual Basic, Basic
☑ Relational DataBase SQL (Relational DataBase), Informix, SQL Server, FOX Pro
☑ Operating Systems: AIX, UNIX, XENIX, DOS, DOS VS, OS, OS VS, LAN, and WAN

PROFESSIONAL EXPERIENCE

U. S. FOODS SERVICES, La Mirada, California - 1997 to present

Database Manager and Director of Information Systems of the Southern California Division. Recruited to assume Director, Information Systems position. Scope of responsibility includes management of all systems. Primary responsibilities involve creating new systems based upon client needs. Ancillary duties involve enhancing, servicing, and maintaining existing systems applications for new customers. Oversee daily activities of a Network Administrator and three Systems Administrators, and seven PC Support, Computer Operators, and Data Processing Clerks. As Chairman, MIS Steering Committee duties involve acting as focal point coordinating inputs from 12 departments. Primary duties include identifying specific needs of each department, determining feasibility and assigning systems administrators to accomplish.

- Achieved $78 million increase in annual sales ($322 to $400 million) by eliminating systems downtime, increasing availability of systems time, and increasing customer computers allowing 24 hours a day usage.
- Led focus group that created systems designed to eliminate an average 3 hours downtime. Monitored and modified systems achieving weekly labor costs savings of $72K.
- Developed a program that monitors systems every 10 minutes to identify "problems" prior to development and allowing preventive action to eliminate downtime.
- Expedited sales orders processing by providing 200+ laptops to sales persons. Implemented direct order entry systems to expedite sales process.
- Developed and implemented an Electronic Data Input (EDI) ordering system for U.S. Navy within 6 weeks. Achieved $25 million annual order from Navy by meeting the established deadline.

UNIX Systems Administrator and INFORMIX Database Administrator, Vista, California - 1995 to 1997.
Acted as an Independent Contractor performing systems and database administration.

- Designed multiple instances on UNIX systems to allow program testing before releasing to production.
- Implemented paperless reporting environment throughout the Division reducing paper usage by 15-20% and achieving significant cost savings ($27K monthly).
- Creating Internet customer link ordering systems to expedite orders and facilitate.

(Continued on next page)

Alicia Paramo-Dionne

1238 Sum Street, Carlton, California 92008 ● (760) 555-2837
apd@aol.com *Page Two*

PROFESSIONAL EXPERIENCE *(Continued)*

SOLE SOURCE COMPUTERS, Cardiff by the Sea, California - 1990 to 1995

Vice President, Application Development. Scope of responsibility included direct supervision of nine programmers, systems analysts, and network administrators. Designed a turnkey system for retail chain stores that included inventory control, accounting, POS, and warehousing distribution. Sold hardware, software, and onsite training of staff throughout an assigned territory covering Arizona, California, Utah, Nevada, Oregon, and Washington.

- Built POS (picture-driven system) that scanned items, indicated current cost, and displayed a product picture to ensure accuracy in sales.
- Implemented Radio Frequency Systems to scan items using the hand-held wireless Telxon scanner system.
- Recipient, 1990 Malcolm Baldridge Award, IBM, in San Diego, California.

COMPUTING POWER INT'L, Lynn Harbor, Michigan - 1987 to 1990

President responsible for bottom-line P&L. Scope of responsibility included operational management of the AVIS Enterprise subsidiary. Designed, implemented, tested, evaluated, and managed a Telemarketing Systems and a complete Local Area Network for Telemarketing companies.

- Increased annual sales to $36 million from $5-6 million.

TRIANGLE SYSTEMS, CORPORATION, Liverworst, California - 1985 to 1987

Application Development Manager. Coordinated and supervised the software department and customer support for the Point Of Sale (POS), Inventory Control, and Accounting Systems. Oversaw daily activities of the 3,600-customer base in the Lumberyard Division.

- Developed computer systems including database, POS, and Inventory Control with remote communication pulling data for updates to expedite and control customer ordering for five stores in New York state area.
- Designed a stand-alone terminal with battery contingency for power failures. System allowed stores to continue selling and automatically updated sales information when power returned to the main system.

EDUCATION

University Southwestern Louisiana, Lafayette, Louisiana
Master of Science in **Computer Science**
Bachelor of Science in **Computer Technology**
Minor: Business Management
Cum Laude Graduate - GPA 3.9

Institute of Technology of Tehran, Tehran, Iran
- **HND** in **Computer Programming** (Associates Equivalent)

PROFESSIONAL DEVELOPMENT

IBM Technical Sales Support Training, San Jose, California

Oracle Seminars and Training Courses, San Diego, California

Novell Seminars and Training Courses, Los Angeles, California

---

Appropriate personal and professional references are available.

22—DATA ENTRY

Linda James

3798 Cedar Wood Path * Baltimore, MD 21045 * 410.555.5124 * LJ@yahoo.com

Objective   **Data Entry Specialist**

Skills
- Enter Data at 11,000 Keystrokes Per Hour (KPH)
- Type 65 Words Per Minute (WPM)
- Operate a ten-key pad
- Accurate Data Entry Skills

Computers   Microsoft Windows NT ♦ Paradox ♦ Lotus 1-2-3 ♦ WordPerfect dBase ♦ Microsoft Publisher ♦ Excel ♦ Lotus Freelance ♦ PageMaker

Education   **AA Degree in Computer Science**
Howard Community College, 1999
** Graduated with Honors

Vocational Training   **Myers Secretarial School**
Completed 240 Hours of Training in Word Processing, Data Entry, and Records Management, 1998
** Received a Certificate in Data Entry Operations

Experience   **Database Assistant**
Sands Software Creations, 2000 to Present
- Detail-oriented Data Entry Specialist with meticulous precision and keystroke accuracy.
- Review, analyze and verify information in the database for accuracy.
- Maintain task lists, calendars, and files. Manage mailing lists. Enter and track orders. Accelerate clerical tasks using spreadsheets. Track data. Meet all mailing and tasking deadlines.

Data Entry Technician
Professional Doctors' Group, 1997 to 2000
Worked for this company for three years while attending community college. Held a part time schedule during the school year and a full time schedule during summer breaks.
- Maintained and updated medical databases and patient schedules. Generated mailing lists. Assisted with billing.

References   *- References, KPH and WPM scores available upon request -*

23—DATA MINING SPECIALIST

Denise Bradford

73 Dearborn Avenue, Chicago, IL 60613 ■ (773) 555-6543 ■ emailaddress@emailaddress.com

Career Summary & Focus

Data Mining Specialist – Developing Solutions for On-line Relationship Marketing

Specialist in developing customer affinity through the design, implementation, and management of data mining solutions for relationship marketing applications. Full life-cycle experience on enterprise-scale data warehousing/mining projects. Strong team leader and results-focused manager. Capabilities include:

Data Warehousing, Mining & Reporting	Mass Marketing Communication Tools
Data Analysis & Knowledge Discovery	Systems Design & Development
CRM Technologies & Tools	Web-Enabled Decision Support Applications

Technical Qualifications

Extensive experience in design and construction of data warehousing and processing systems.
Oracle Certified Professional - DBA; extensive Oracle PL/SQL qualifications.
In-depth understanding of OLAP, data mining, and ad hoc query tools.
Experienced in UNIX/Perl scripting; C and C++ software development abilities.
Highly proficient with most popular reporting tools – Actuate, Crystal Reports, and Cognos.
Advanced skills with data analysis applications – SAS and SPSS.
Deep understanding of CRM tools - E.piphany, Broadbase, and Siebel eConfigurator.
Knowledgeable in strategies for linking data to Web content management platforms.

Professional Experience

Manager of Data Mining, Guardian.com – Chicago, IL, 1997 – Present

Assessed, procured, and implemented the vendors, tools, and technologies that enabled and facilitated data warehousing, mining, and analysis for this start-up dot.com.
Designed and provide ongoing management of the systems allowing one-on-one relationship marketing within an e-commerce space.
Evangelized the role of knowledge sharing within the organization; credited with successful promotion of intimate relationships with consumers.
Initiated real-time processing and presentation of data on the Internet; linked to Web content management platforms to create instantaneous, personalized product offerings.

Data Warehouse Engineer, Norcross, Inc. – New York, NY, 1995 – 1997

Analyzed and specified requirements for scalable databases, data mining, and reporting.
Designed, constructed, maintained, and modified Oracle/UNIX databases to meet needs.
Researched and evaluated emerging data warehouse techniques and tools; recommended cost-effective solutions for data mining and reporting.

Education & Training

M.S., Computer Science
New York Institute of Technology (1995)

B.S., Electrical Engineering
Boston University (1993)

Associations & Memberships

Association of Database Developers, Member (1995 – Present)

Customer Relationship Management Association, Member (1995 – Present)

Unique approach in the text used to describe the candidate's "Experience," particularly in the way it is broken up into sections within each position.

Robert J. Strong

6204 Acorn Lane * Laurel, MD 21054 * 410.555.0812 * RJS@yahoo.com

Data Security Manager

- ⊟ **Data & Application Security Consulting**
- ⊟ **Encryption Key Infrastructures**
- ⊟ **C + +, Java, JB Script**

- ⊟ **SSL / S-HTTP**
- ⊟ **Security Hierarchy**
- ⊟ **Identify Security Risks**

- ⊟ **Windows NT**
- ⊟ **TCP/IP**
- ⊟ **Routers**

🖾 Primary advisor and consultant regarding the implementation of technical principles, practices, and procedures to ensure data security, properly identify risks, monitor security controls, and manage other contingencies. Devise complex security solutions. Cross-platform experience.

🖾 Remarkably fast-tracked career in computer operations, security controls, and program development. Managed unique data security projects in the military.

Experience

The e-Bank Corp., Baltimore, MD   1997 to Present
Data Security Manager
· The e-Bank Corp is a leader in online credit cards and e-banking with cutting-edge Internet technology.

- ❑ Review the development, testing, and implementation of data and application security plans, products, and control techniques to ensure the security of clients' personal and sensitive credit card information being transmitted via the Web. Control access to data and change passwords.

- ❑ Thoroughly investigate and recommend appropriate corrective actions for data and application security incidents. Identify data security risks and report breaches. Lead and direct staff to scan all application and production software environments.

- ❑ Technically proficient with Firewalls, Virus Detection Software and Web site checking platforms. Evaluate and test security and virus detection software. Work closely with the administrator to monitor the system for intrusions.

- ❑ ***Develop Security Tools***
  * Designed and implemented a highly effective data and computer operations security checklist for daily use by computer operators. The result was a decrease in noted security deficiencies of 11% in less than six months.
  * Designed and incorporated a tiered level of access to databases creating a 'hacker-proof/need to know' security measure environment.

- ❑ ***Implement Security Contingency Plans***
  * Drafted an Intrusion Response Plan: Implemented the plan during a real-life security crisis—every computer database was infected with a contagious virus that deleted data files. Directed operators to follow protocol and operations resumed within 3 hours.
  * Drafted a Disaster Recovery Plan: Wrote and implemented a procedures manual to ensure the security of data through off-site storage measures and theft avoidance including contingency plans for natural disasters or terrorist attacks.

(Continued)

Robert J. Strong, Page 2

U.S. Army, USA and Germany (Officer/SECRET Clearance)   1985 to 1997
Computer Specialist
· Knowledge Engineer, Test Control & Training Standards Administrator, Intelligence Analyst

- ❏ Handpicked to design a prototype electronic income-tax-filing program to support a military office. This program, implemented in Object Pascal, was used to file about 1,600 returns for personnel at 10 beta-user sites worldwide. *Incorporated internal security measures in the database to ensure clients' confidentiality.* The users saved $70,000 – and the cost to the Army was $300. Completed the project in record time.

- ❏ Operated various computer systems, installed software, maintained hardware and software, and used secured communications via computer. Assisted computer users and resolved complex automation security problems.

- ❏ Taught intelligence personnel how to leverage the Internet to enhance productivity. Directly supervised the installation of a fiber-optic Local Area Network (LAN). Supervised the installation of a Joint Worldwide Intelligence Video Teleconference System. Constantly monitored and upgraded automation installations and checked for security breaches.

- ❏ Technical authority for high-resolution constructive battle simulations. Technical advisor for nine computer training classrooms. Managed software installation, computer maintenance, and operator training. Conducted troubleshooting for complex problems.

- ❏ Provided imagery subject matter expertise. Mastered the intricacies of researching lucrative intelligence technologies to develop and prototype expert system based imagery analyst exploitation aids. Experimented with parallel programming implementations using Occam 2 and Inmos 800 and 400 series transputers available on the Kodak Imagery Exploitation Workstation (KIEWS).

Education

Bachelor of Science Degree in Computer Studies, 1985, University of Maryland
Major: Computer Studies; Minor: Business Management *(GPA: 3.8)*

Completed thousands of hours of specialized training in computer operations and programming. Attend conferences discussing and presenting the most current technology.

Publications

<u>Intelligence & Database Security</u>, published in the *Military Intelligence Professional Bulletin*

Presented <u>Intelligence & Database Security</u> as the Featured Speaker, Leadership Conference

25—DATA WAREHOUSE MANAGER

> *Author's favorite. Very good style and efficient use of one-page resume.*

deborah neal... data warehouse manager

101 w. 10th avenue, denver, co 80201...e-mail@e-mailaddress.com...303.555.1010

core competencies..

- Data Warehouse Manager offering 10 years of experience and in-depth knowledge of the functional and data needs of e-businesses.

- Data warehouse development experience incorporates skills in programming, analysis, architecture, and project management. Expertise in high-level and detailed system design, requirements gathering, logical and physical data modeling, development, and implementation. Expert knowledge of data modeling in ERP and other major application areas.

- Well-versed in Oracle (Oracle Express, Oracle Reporter, Oracle Financial), Oracle tools, and Erwin products. Data migration experience using Informatica, C++, Java, Corba, multidimensional database, JavaScript, Oracle Web server, and Java. Exceptional use of CASE tools as part of an overall development effort.

- Extensive knowledge of DBMS: Oracle RDBMS, SQL, PL/SQL, STAR Schema Modeling. Experienced in UNIX operating system, Microsoft PC operating systems including NT, desktop productivity software, and client/server system architecture.

- Proven ability to assemble and mobilize project teams, building consensus among multidisciplinary technical and functional teams in the rapid development and implementation of data warehousing solutions. Recognized by managers and colleagues as a strong, positive leader and a sharp strategic thinker.

experience..

amazon.com, Denver, CO
Data Warehouse Manager, 1995-Present

- Drive the strategic vision and realization in the evolution from centralized data warehouse to distributed data marts. Report to divisional IT management with accountability for global processes. Manage a budget of $5.6 million.

- Provide guidance to software development teams on the use and purpose of data warehouses. Direct a team of seven data warehouse developers/analysts in the daily operations of the corporate data warehouse. Oversee all aspects of the warehouses, including data sourcing, data migration, data quality, data warehouse design, and implementation.

- Scope, plan, and prioritize multiple project deliverables, based on data warehousing dependencies and changing business needs. Develop project plans, identify and fill project resource needs, and manage projects to on-time, on-budget completion.

- Influence toolset and business needs assessment. Lead the selection of third-party software; manage vendor relationships. Successfully manage multiple projects in the design and implementation of warehouse functionality and interfaces.

Colorado Department of Revenue, Denver, CO
Data Warehouse Architect, 1990-1996

- Translated an enterprise data model, created dimension, and fact tables to support budgeting, financial planning, analysis and data ware systems, in collaboration with the DBA and Data Steward.

- Determined database/data mart business requirements. Created the logical and physical database/data mart design for Relational and OLAP Data Warehouse environment.

education...

Master of Science, Data Warehouse Management, University of Denver, Denver, CO

Bachelor of Science, Computer Information Systems, University of Colorado, Boulder, CO

26—DISTANCE TRAINING

CAROLYN FORNATARO

5987 Wadleigh Falls Road ▪ Boston, MA 02114
Phone: (617) 555-4536 ▪ Fax: (617) 555-3214 ▪ E-mail: emailaddress@emailaddress.com

---

DISTANCE TRAINER ▪ INSTRUCTIONAL DESIGNER ▪ CURRICULUM DEVELOPER
Computer, Internet, Video, & Telecommunications Technologies

Technically sophisticated professional well qualified by 10+ years' experience for creating and facilitating high-quality, high-impact internal/external educational solutions using innovative technologies. Rare depth and breadth of experience with distance learning tools and proven abilities in applying advanced technologies to enhance adult learning. Skilled in collaborating with subject matter experts to enhance course content and ensure technical accuracy. Extraordinary written and verbal communication skills. M.Ed., Educational Technology.

AREAS OF EXPERTISE

Computer- & Video-Based Training (CBT/VBT)	Instructional Systems Design (ISD) Methods
Web-Based Training Creation	Adult Education Needs & Theories
On-line Course Development & Facilitation	Multimedia Authoring & Visual Design Concepts
Instuctor-Led & Self-Paced Training Delivery	Training Program Evaluation & Quality Standards
Curriculum & Course Materials Development	Project & Program Management

---

EXPERIENCE HIGHLIGHTS

DISTANCE EDUCATOR / ON-LINE COURSE DESIGNER — DXE Internet Training, Inc., New York, NY 1996 — Present

Joined this cutting-edge Internet and Web-based training firm during the start-up phase. Manage training projects from conception through delivery. Develop and design custom technology-based course content, lesson plans, and training materials for diverse customers, including major corporations, small e-business ventures, and government agencies. Teach and facilitate both technical and nontechnical courses using a variety of distance training delivery methods.

Key Achievements:

Combined expertise in instructional design methodologies, adult learning theories, and advanced technologies to create more than 30 on-line courses. Conferred with clients to assess needs and developed distance educational strategies and solutions successful for both internal and external training purposes.

Applied multimedia authoring and Web design tools such as MS FrontPage, PowerPoint, Dreamweaver, and NetObjects Fusion to create dynamic training and workshop materials proven through analysis of evaluation data to increase student learning and retention 24%.

Generated 16 new corporate training accounts valued at more than $1.2 million through referral and add-on business. Built solid client relationships and a reputation for ability to quickly create courses that consistently surpass quality and effectiveness objectives.

Led Web-based training on diverse subjects and utilizing both instructor-led and self-paced delivery methods. Interacted with students in real-time during scheduled on-line meetings. Facilitated self-paced study through e-mail correspondence and coordination of Web activities.

Achieved consistent 99% instructor effectiveness ratings through surveys of students' and educational sponsors' satisfaction. Overachieved goals for students' completion of self-paced study courses, with 92% of students finishing all coursework and examinations.

Introduced the use of Internet telephony as a cost-effective alternative to traditional long-distance student/instructor conference calls. Improved student communication and interaction by implementing and managing Web discussion forums and instructor moderated e-mail distribution lists.

(Continued)

CAROLYN FORNATARO – Page 2

DISTANCE TRAINER/CURRICULUM DEVELOPER – School of Lifelong Learning, San Diego, CA   1991 – 1996

Developed and taught coursework on a vast range of subjects for this accredited correspondence school specializing in home-study certification for adult students located nationwide. Researched and consulted with experts on topics spanning a wide range of industries and professions. Created and implemented curricula and lesson plans, authored course content, and designed training and evaluation materials.

Key Achievements:

Conceptualized and produced critically-acclaimed multimedia computer- and video-based training modules that built student interest and is credited with increasing revenues 18%.

Initiated the use of Web-based technologies that enhanced student/instructor communication while capitalizing on cutting-edge technologies to outpace the competition and establish the school as a pioneer in this area.

Exploited learning opportunities on the Internet by revising coursework to include Web-based activities; dramatically improved students' self-reports of learning and retention at a minimal cost to the school.

Provided guidance to students in completing self-paced training courses; counseled and instructed students needing special assistance and evaluated performance at the completion of each unit. Ranked consistently as the distance trainer generating the highest student satisfaction rate.

SALES TRAINING COORDINATOR, RMS Technology, San Diego, CA   1989 - 1991

Rejuvenated the sales training department of this premier telecommunications equipment manufacturer. Re-engineered educational methodologies and processes, instituted department goals, and established training certification programs. Created a new training methodology that refocused emphasis to build consultative and solution sales competence.

Key Achievements:

Transformed the sales process by empowering the sales force with the knowledge and tools to assess customers' business needs and meet requirements through product solutions. Drove a 112% increase in sales.

Encouraged expansion into emerging telecommunications markets worldwide by creating special monthly workshops that introduced and familiarized the sales team with various industry segments.

Designed and developed a precedent-setting multimedia sales training module that taught the sales force both basic and advanced selling skills. Launched and delivered the module at a national sales conference.

Formulated and deployed an innovative customer training program on a new telecommunications switch. Successfully transferred technical knowledge and played a primary role in establishing top market positioning.

EDUCATION & TRAINING

M.Ed., EDUCATIONAL TECHNOLOGY, cum laude –1995
University of California, San Diego

B.S., BUSINESS ADMINISTRATION, MINOR IN COMPUTER SCIENCE – 1989
University of New Hampshire, Durham

Extensive training and experience with PC applications; advanced user of MS Office Suite (Word, PowerPoint, Excel, Access, Outlook), MS Internet Explorer, and Netscape Communicator. Skilled with multimedia authoring tools such as FrameMaker, Authorware, Director, and Dreamweaver, and Web design tools including HTML, MS FrontPage, NetObjects Fusion, and Lotus Domino Designer.

Member, Distance Education and Training Council

27—DISTRIBUTOR

Notice the "Milestones" listed sections in the "Professional Experience" section category. This is another way of documenting accomplishments, a stronger validation of worth than just listing responsibilities.

Mark J. Smythe

1687 Coral Cavern Court * Laurel, MD 21045 * 410-555-1236 * markjs@hotmail.com

~ DIRECT & INDIRECT INTERNATIONAL DISTRIBUTION CHANNELS ~
~ CUTTING EDGE DOCUMENT IMAGING TECHNOLOGY ~
~ "I believe that a job worth doing is worth doing well" ~

Key Credentials & Technical Proficiencies

P&L ▪ Negotiations & Contracts ▪ Product Positioning ▪ Team Training
Production & Operations ▪ Strategic Business Planning ▪ Key Accounts ▪ Import of Special Items
Budgets & Pricing ▪ Customer Relationship Management

Microsoft Project, Excel & Word, Microsoft Windows 95/98/NT, Lotus Notes v4.5, SQL Backend, VB Web site design, and imaging document software: ViewStar & Kodak. Create Complex PowerPoint Presentations. Develop Extensive Access Databases and Excel Spreadsheets.

Consistently maximize revenue and earning opportunities through cost containment and quality service delivery in highly competitive international markets. Define revenue-generating activities.

Sophisticated knowledge of emerging Document Imaging Technologies and its commercial applications. Implemented successful inventory management software.

Professional & Personal Value Offered

** Demonstrate excellent professional ethics with high integrity ... strive for perfection
** Skilled networker ... maintain industry contacts and vendor listings ... build strong and lasting relationships ... highly customer service oriented
** Assemble and train sales teams and customers on use of Document Imaging Technologies
** Proven communication skills ... write clear and concise reports and deliver effective presentations
** Provide solid leadership, set goals, and motivate sales teams to achieve high performance and profitability ... grow start-up ventures
** Organized and methodical with a keen ability to plan and prioritize key tasks ... and effectively recognize problems as opportunities

Professional Experience

e-IMAGE Technologies, Columbia, MD, 1997 to Present
* e-IMAGE Technologies is a newly restructured subsidiary providing various document management services and products within emerging international markets.

.. **OPERATIONS DIRECTOR** .. Recruited to prepare a long-range, easily implemented strategic business plan to grow distribution operations. Forecasted and implemented an operating budget of $1.2M.

** MILESTONES **

- Challenged to provide vision, strategy, and action to meet with company's objective to increase revenue and earnings growth initiatives, and market positioning. Successfully grew sales and distribution within 18 months increasing revenue from $200,000 to $4.6M.
- Reengineered operations by introducing inventory control models and modern processes for accurate asset reporting, reducing inventory assets by 12%. Established an in-house training program.
- Incorporated a new software inventory/logistics management system (CrunchTime!) ensuring accurate tracking of 105 separate activities within a single enterprisewide inventory distribution system. Direct the distribution management and warehouse control program.
- Skillfully calculate annual product requirements and determine inventory and control planning functions.
- Current knowledge of import/export regulations.

(Continued)

Kodak Inc., Baltimore MD, 1987 to 1997
* Kodak is a $13B company and the world's largest manufacturer and marketer of imaging products—with one of the most recognized and respected brand names.

.. **LOGISTICS DIRECTOR** .. Expanded marketing channels in Eastern Europe and maintained distributor relationships. Supervised supervisors in six major warehouses in America and Europe.

** MILESTONES **

- Inventoried and shipped the single biggest order of microfilming equipment for Kodak Document Imaging in 1997.
- Drafted a proposal to fully automate distribution activities—consequently installed, managed, and monitored a new inventory management software system that supported multiple currencies and bar coding—ensuring accurate product tracking across an eight-week delivery cycle. Analyzed reports that tied together 200 plus customers, thousands of products, purchases, reconciliations, storage warehouses, and vendors. The result was a decrease in late deliveries by 36% and an increase in inventory accountability, saving the company nearly $900,000 in inventory discrepancies.
- Tracked and managed logistics functions and shipments to channel distributions. Finalized, approved, and officiated channel pricing tools. Adjusted competitive pricing.
- Ordered inventory from stateside and international vendors. Expanded vendor sourcing and identified low-cost/quality suppliers. Validated prices, reconciled discrepancies and verified contracts.
- Interfaced directly with users, providing regular reports, suggesting substitutions for out-of-stock items, and general information regarding shipments.
- Established and published guidelines for mail processing functions and created a database for tracking all outgoing shipments.
- Significantly improved the overall customer satisfaction index to meet corporate objectives and targets. Interfaced with clients to discuss and solve distribution problems and concerns.

Other:

.. **DISTRIBUTION MANAGER** .. Radio House Stores, 1983 to 1987
* Directed warehouse distribution activities for a national retail electronics chain with over 400 retail outlets. Monitored activities and inventory in three major warehouse/distribution points with merchandise worth over $65M. Coordinated shipment of inventory via truck and rail.

Education, Languages, Affiliations

- MBA, George Washington University, Washington DC, 1987
- BS in Electronics Engineering, Kansas State University, KS, 1983

- Read, Write, and Speak Fluent German and French Learning Czech.

- Institution of Electrical and Electronics Engineers (IEEE)
- Association for Information and Image Management (AIIM)
- Association of Records Managers and Administrators (ARMA)

Notable Award

- Received the Prize for Distribution Management Excellence, awarded by Kodak – Greater Europe Region, 1997

~ **Please inquire as to how my distribution management experience will increase your profits** ~

> *Title and summary at top work well. Good job description within the "Business Experience" section.*

Katherine C. O'Connor

9876 South Street   Farmington, CT 06034   emailaddress@emailaddress.com   860-555-6789

BUSINESS DEVELOPMENT / SALES / MARKETING
Internet / E-Business / Business-to-Business

- Dynamic and creative marketing professional with fifteen years of experience in hospitality industry and specialization in Internet and B2B.
- Unique blend of customer needs assessment, product knowledge, and technology producing verifiable success in e-commerce.
- Strong written communication skills; capable developer of online marketing content.
- Proven ability to overcome resistance to Internet marketing and sales; able to identify and communicate with key decision makers.

BUSINESS EXPERIENCE

Farmington Technologies, Ltd., Farmington, CT   3/99 - Present
Subsidiary of Wholesale Vacations Company, a leading national wholesale vacation provider
Business Development Manager

Manage / maintain interactive Website, providing updates, adding new sales promotions, and developing features for co-brands and new partnerships. Define and develop new target markets. Conduct ongoing marketing research and report results of indicators including page view requests, gross/net sales, and special offer bookings. Create, distribute and coordinate all permission marketing, including e-mail campaigns, to members of branded Websites. Coordinate with vendors to develop Website content: Negotiate contracts and confidentiality agreements and monitor integration time lines. Supervise interactive features such as chat rooms, lists, and forums. Assist in development of intranet content for key customers including major wholesalers and home products companies, featuring co-brand vacation packages for members/employees.

- Establish and nurture online partnerships, co-branding opportunities and revenue sharing grants with major customer sites, search engines, and booking engines.
- Developed and maintain public and partner Websites for online vacation providers. Increased from 26 to 100+ partners in the past twelve months.

BuyALot.com, Hartford, CT   1/98 - 1/99
General Manager / Vice President of Marketing
Corporation Secretary / Member, Board of Directors / Registered Agent

Managed the day-to-day operations of a private Internet retailer with $1 million annual sales. Refined marketing strategies, budgets, and P & L statements for 23 online retail stores with combined annual revenues of $5 million. Interacted with legal and accounting professionals to prepare documentation for memoranda, corporate prospectus, and IPO strategy. Served as liaison among shareholders, Board of Directors, and senior corporate management. Managed private investments; issued stock certificates; prepared / presented quarterly reports. Directed 15+ sales / marketing staff, from job development to pay scale and benefits packages. Provided yield management results and cost-benefit analysis to determine demographics for marketing efforts and rollout of new products.

- Negotiated contracts with major portals.

(Continued

National Wholesale Floral Services Company, Columbus, OH   9/95 - 12/97
Marketing Manager / Project Manager
Coordinated customer database of over 25,000 florists. Created, developed, and promoted marketing programs for florists nationwide. Coordinated industry conventions, from logistics to entertainment and from onsite preparation to celebrity appearances. Designed and created instructional materials and follow-up for attendees. Developed and analyzed seasonal promotions to enhance marketing efforts and improve profitability.

- Successfully coordinated all aspects of major national convention for 8,500 member florists.

Motivation & Education Company, Lexington, KY   7/93 - 9/95
Marketing Coordinator / Training Analyst
Created and delivered ATrain the Trainer@ instructional seminars for hospitality and retail industry audiences nationwide. Produced promotional materials; wrote press releases and media displays.

EDUCATION / CERTIFICATION

B.S. Business Management, Pennsylvania State University, University Park, PA
   Minors: Psychology, Human Resources and Hospitality Management

Travel Consultant Certification

AFFILIATIONS

Meeting Planners International
Association of Marketing Professionals
World Flower Council

29—E-BUSINESS/INTERNET EXECUTIVE

HANS BAASCH

408 China Camp • Sausalito, California 94965 • 415-555-6678 • E-mail: habaa@home.com

PROFILE Innovative, resourceful E-BUSINESS and INTERNET EXECUTIVE. Recognize critical junctures in international business, marketing, and technology and lead actions to capitalize on them. Advanced expertise in leading technologies and security issues.

- **Develop and apply high-level, long-term IT and processing solutions that integrate the demands of complex business procedures, personnel, and cultures** into streamlined networks and products that are fast, stable, and secure.
- **Broad-based knowledge of the global marketplace, current technologies and future trends;** successfully build on convergence-models and achieve sustainable systems.

HIGHLIGHTS of ACCOMPLISHMENTS

- **Substantially contributed to converting perception of company** from an industry "dinosaur" **to one of the most innovative business leaders in the industry** as direct report and consultant to CEO on future trends, technologies, and integrity assurance for a Danish company.
  - **Significantly contributed to strategic vision and implementation of Internet security structure and guidelines based on proactive solutions** instead of reactive "fixes" resulting in robust networks with effective, tightly integrated protection over international intranets and VPNs.
  - **Established global routing for Internet resources that allowed diversified access and the fastest response times possible in a secure, stable environment.** Initiated the acquisition of server space at five locations around the world and installed system to provide several services to include Name Services, Directory Services, Mail Services, and Web Access.
- As a member of Danish Executive Board, representing technology advances, **spearheaded the first industry association Website in the country** that integrated secure e-commerce solutions into travel industry forums, increasing competitiveness and catapulting Danish services to the forefront of the global market.
- As technology/business consultant to a leading Danish association, was a **primary player in the introduction of the first online Danish-based forum,** revolutionizing this country's outreach and communications. Established framework to generate traffic through content development and exchange services to create a virtual community. Ensured ongoing success of the venture through intensive training of client company staff.

EXPERIENCE

1996 to present	**Owner-Operator, Convergence ISP** Founded this Internet service provider in Marin. Established two locations to create a stable, robust platform. Partnered with Visa to use this business-to-business ISP as a beta site to test and verify e-commerce security strategies and ensure reliability under all conditions.
1995 to present	**Consultant, E-Commerce Security and Technology to the Travel Industry** Addressing the specialized high-tech needs of the travel industry, work with agencies and international companies in the use, implementation, and strategic developments related to current technologies including: connectivity, communication, database access, security, and emerging technologies.
1991-95	**Managing Director/Owner, Bagheera Consulting** Projects have included testing and proofing of systems including sophisticated travel-related back-office software, reservation, and online systems. Author for computer and CRS-subjects in the Danish Tourism Industry. Solution provider for Microsoft; certified Microsoft reseller; certified consultant for Novell. Consultant for computerization and travel technology for the Danish tourism industry. Section-sysop for six years in Compuserve. Trainer for networking, OS, and standard applications for Novell and Microsoft.

PREVIOUS EXPERIENCE

PC-Consulting, Marketing Communication and Training, Travel Indio, London, England, 1991

Travel Industry Manufacturers Representative - Germany, 1981-91

- continued -

Hans Baasch
Page 2

EDUCATION

M.B.A. studies, Harvard University (currently enrolled)
Focus: Strategies for Change
Graduate, Kant Gymnasium Bergen, Norway
(**U.S. Bachelor of Science** equivalent per INS standards)

TECHNICAL QUALIFICATIONS

Technologies

- IPX
- Netbios
- TCP/IP
- Routing
- Switching
- Internet Security
- DNS/DHCP/Bind
- SNMP
- SMTP
- ISDN
- Digital Certificates
- X.500/X.509
- HTML
- XML
- CGI/Perl
- Streaming Media
- Real-time Messaging
- LAN/WAN
- LDAP
- Intra-/Extranets
- VPN
- PKI

Operating Systems

- Windows 95/98
- Windows NT 3.51,4.0
- Novell 3.1X, 4.1X, 5.X
- Linux
- Solaris

Hardware

- Standard PC Hardware
- Cisco Router
- CSU/DSU
- Firewalls

Internet Applications

- Netscape Enterprise Server
- Netscape Fasttrack Server
- Netscape Messaging Server
- Netscape Directory Server
- Netscape Certificate Server
- MS Internet Information Server
- Listserv
- Majordomo
- Lyris
- MS Exchange
- MS FTP Service
- Metainfo DNS/DHCP
- Checkpoint Firewall-1

Certifications

- Microsoft Certified Trainer
- Microsoft Certified Product Specialist
- Certified Novell Instructor
- Check Point Certified System Engineer (Firewall-1 4.0)
- Netscape Solution Provider
- Cisco Certified Network Associate
- Certified Novell Administrator

CONFERENCES

- Speaker on technology and online security issues for the travel industry:
  - ASR World Conference, Antalya, Turkey
  - ACTE World Conference, Berlin, Germany
  - AFFITT International Technology Forum, Berlin, Germany
  - ITB Technology Congress, Berlin, Germany

LANGUAGES

Internationally traveled and multilingual:
Fluent in English, Danish, and German; speak conversational French; understand basic Spanish.

Unique approach of batching all accomplishments into one section and listing employers more as supporting information. This works if you have stayed in the same industry and discipline.

LANCE HODGES

187 Millbrook Court
Redmond, WA 98052
Phone: (425) 555-9076 • Mobile: (425) 555-0154 • E-mail: email@emailaddress.com

E-BUSINESS SPECIALIST / DIGITAL BUSINESS STRATEGIST
Creating & Driving Winning Digital Business Strategies for the New Economy

Recognized e-business expert offering fresh insight and a passion for innovation; proven track record in planning, building, and launching successful, high-profile dot.com and e-commerce businesses. Powerful strategist able to map creative business vision, transforming and empowering organizations with the tools, technologies, and strategies to bridge the digital business gap.

Dynamic leader and mentor, able to build team cohesion and inspire individuals to strive toward ever higher levels of achievement.   Exceptional client relationship and management skills; relate and interface easily at the top executive levels. Keen, in-depth understanding of Internet tools, technologies, companies, trends, and revenue models. Solid background and qualifications in all core business functions – finance, marketing, and operations.

AREAS OF EXPERTISE

Strategic Planning & Execution	Large-Scale Project Management
Management Consulting	High-Profile Client Relations
Team Building & Leadership	Strategic Partnership & Alliance Building
E-business / E-commerce Technologies	Business Development & Negotiations
Interactive Industry Dynamics	Business Process Re-engineering

ACHIEVEMENT HIGHLIGHTS

Profiled in *Digital Business Trends* magazine as a "Top 10" leader in the field, based on established record of accomplishment in strategically positioning both start-up and mature businesses to achieve e-business objectives in the new economy.

Formulated strategies and action plans that have driven the launch of 10 start-up dot.coms; performed strategic comparisons; benchmarked and leveraged industry best practices for maximum impact. Guided 4 companies through highly visible and successful IPOs.

Supported entrepreneurs in developing viable plans and e-business models; raised more than $45 million in funding for several ventures, establishing and maintaining relationships with angel investors, venture capitalists, and strategic partners.

Inventoried existing initiatives for major corporate clients, both domestic and global; re-invented business strategies, processes, and systems for the digital economy, achieving increased competitiveness, heightened market valuation, and revenue gains up to $65 million.

Facilitated the successful $54 million acquisition of a start-up dot.com company just 11 months into operations by a well-known e-tailer seeking expansion.

Identified opportunities and built lucrative strategic partnerships and alliances, establishing cost-effective opportunities for win-win co-marketing and revenue growth.

Pioneered and promoted a revolutionary new e-commerce business model that enables explosive lateral growth through partnerships.

(Continued)

LANCE HODGES
Page 2

PROFESSIONAL EXPERIENCE

Intelogis Management Consulting, Inc. – San Francisco, CA, 1998 – Present
SENIOR E-BUSINESS STRATEGIST

Senior consultant managing large-scale, high-profile strategy engagements for diverse clients in a broad range of industries. Facilitate the formulation and execution of e-business strategies and plans, creating on-line businesses that meet clients' unique needs in an increasingly competitive global marketplace. Lead, motivate, and coach teams comprised of talented strategists, technologists, and creatives. Partner at the highest level of clients' organizations and play a key role in business development and negotiations.

Prestige Consulting, Inc. – Los Angeles, CA, 1997 - 1998
DIGITAL BUSINESS STRATEGIST

Consulted on a series of leading-edge engagements, working in collaboration with clients ranging from Global 1000 companies to dot.com start-ups. Developed strategies and tactical plans to assist clients in rapidly deploying innovative digital businesses to achieve aggressive business objectives. Reshaped existing business strategies to drive successful, prosperous transition to the new digital economy.

Vilante International – Washington D.C., 1993 – 1997
PRESIDENT

Turned around this privately held manufacturer of consumer telecommunications products. Surpassed goals, invigorating sales and profits to record levels after just one year and transitioning the company from the brink of bankruptcy in 1993 to profitability in 1994. Led development of e-business strategies and initiated creation of an e-retail division in 1996 that has delivered consistent growth in sales and profits every year since. Doubled sales of top-line, high-margin products through e-marketing initiatives.

Citizens USA Bank – Washington D.C., 1990 – 1993
VICE PRESIDENT, IT (1991 – 1993) / MANAGER OF TECHNOLOGY (1990 – 1991)

Developed the organizational vision and conceptual direction to accelerate development of sophisticated technology tools to meet emerging business needs and corporate objectives. Managed a unique set of responsibilities that blended customer service concerns with technology infrastructure development. Interfaced closely with internal customers and led a staff of senior level managers. Established robust dialogue and cooperative effort between the business and technology divisions.

EDUCATION & TRAINING

M.B.A., Information Technology
California Institute of Technology, Pasadena – 1998

B.S., Business Administration / Computer Science
Georgetown University, Washington, D.C. – 1990

Recent Continuing Education

Business Process Improvement • Executive Development • Team Building
Business Case Development • Project Management • Leadership Alignment
Technology Planning • Transitional Leadership • Risk & Contingency Planning

31—E-COMMERCE APPLICATION SPECIALIST

Robin Claterbough

23794 Indianwood ◆ Clarkston, Michigan 48348 ◆ 248.555.2332
emailaddress@emailaddress.com

eCommerce Application Specialist

Experienced in architecting Web-based business solutions. Provide leadership and expertise by developing intellectual capital, setting standards, assisting with sales efforts, providing skills transfer, and delivering technology leadership on the most complex and high profile engagements.

Qualifications

Experience in relational database development and systems integration
Substantial knowledge of and experience with database-driven applications
Process development and project management abilities
Understanding of DHTML and JavaScript functionality
Advanced PC skills utilizing Microsoft tools
Leadership and facilitation skills
Understands eCommerce and the Internet

Experience

GENERAL ELECTRIC COMPANY - GE Supply; Rochester Hills, Michigan
eCommerce Web Application Specialist 1989 - Current

Design, develop, and maintain GE Supply's Web-based configurator tools as part of Web application team. Assess customer needs, translate concepts into viable technology solutions. Analyze product data and selling knowledge; recommend product data architecture. Work on eCommerce Systems.

Manage creation/editing of HTML product configuration and display templates. Execute technical design and development of application data templates. Develop CTQs and measurement systems for all processes and systems (specify limits for application performance, efficiency, etc.).

Develop/document all processes relevant to development and maintenance of data models and applications. Provide recommendations for product functionality enhancements. Interact with creative teams and developers of other GES.com features and functionalities to create integrated applications.

Education / Training

MBA @ Wayne State University; Detroit, Michigan, 1988
BS @ Michigan State University; East Lansing, Michigan, 1986

Courses/Classes/Workshops & Ongoing Education:
Network Computing, Asynchronous Communications, Synchronous Network Design,
Synchronous Applications Development, Web Development Strategies,
Quality Management, PC-based Time Management, Target Account Marketing,

---

Certified at Expert Level 2000 @ SUN Systems
Certified in the Competency 2000 Program for Excelleration
Enterprise Computing Certification
Workgroup Computing Certification
IBM Hardware Certification
Graphics/Internet, PhotoShop, Web Publishing, WWW Dreamweaver, HTML

32—FORUM MANAGER

Jack C. Spears

7000 N. Mopac • Austin, Texas 78749 • 512.555.5555 • jack@bigfoot.com

EXECUTIVE SUMMARY

Dynamic Internet Technology executive with over 12 years experience in Webcasting, broadcasting, online community development, and Internet Engineering for major online, telecommunications, and software organizations. Recognized pioneer in emerging Internet technologies and applications for B2B and B2C content marketing strategies. Visionary developer of corporate online strategies and portal alliances. Highly skilled in functional and technical aspects of online venture creation and launch. Excellent communicator able to achieve goals and motivate team members.

CAREER HIGHLIGHTS

- ❑ **Industry pioneer in Internet Virtual Community Development and Strategic Online Alliances**
- ❑ **Co-developer of "simulchat" concept combining radio and online communications**
- ❑ **Nationally recognized expert on Online Health and Self-Help portal services**
- ❑ **Key player in start-up and initial public offering stages of .com and software organizations**
- ❑ **Astute multimedia producer with strong knowledge of program development, strategic planning, alliance creation, and online marketing**

INTERNET ENTERPRISE EXPERIENCE

drkoop.com, Inc.   Austin, Texas
DIRECTOR OF FORUM COMMUNITIES   1998-2000

Played key role as creator of most diverse set of online health communities on the Internet during enterprise start-up and launch. Coordinated with Web designers, content developers, public relations specialists, and sales representatives to create award winning health content communities. Negotiated and settled contracts with key health and media organizations for development and delivery of content-rich, customized online health portal services. Produced special events that included special guest chat events, audio/video simulcasts, and cause-based programs. Designed effective incentive programs and managed departmental budget of over $1 million. Instrumental in achieving success in broadband positioning. Managed department of over 80 employees, successfully maintaining morale and motivation despite insecure corporate direction.

America Online, Inc.   Vienna, Virginia
FORUM MANAGER   1993-1998

Managed the National Public Radio and Online Psychology forums for AOL. Originated and deployed content using proprietary AOL publishing software. Directed all events and managed both forums as independent business units. Produced special online events and coordinated with NPR and mental health organizations to produce value-rich content delivery. Broke new ground through launch of simulchat effort, successfully integrating radio and online communications. Initiated thrust for AOL health focus.

HealthDesk, Corp. • elasticMEDIA, Inc.   Berkeley and Walnut Creek, California
ONLINE STRATEGY DIRECTOR/WEBMASTER   1995-1996

Masterminded corporate Internet strategies for both organizations — companies involved in design and deployment of healthcare industry software. Defined e-business strategies from scratch during the infancy stages of the Internet and ecommerce. Led online marketing program and convinced corporate leadership of importance of having online presence.

(Continued)

ONLINE SERVICES CONSULTING

Provided expert consulting and expertise on start-up phases of online healthcare-oriented communities and services for several entities. Spearheaded and defined online strategies and outlined marketing plans for content/service deliverables. Advised on market conditions and consulted during online launch phases of sites and portals.

RadioDigest.com, Inc.	1999-present
MediaLinx Interactive, Inc. • Healthyway.ca	1996
Kaiser Permanente Interactive Technology Group	1996
AT&T Personal Online Services Division	1996

TECHNICAL EXPERIENCE

Exodus Communications, Inc.   Seattle, Washington
NETWORK ENGINEER   1997-1998

Built and managed Network Operations Centers for outsourced network services, serving top 50% of Internet traffic sites. Troubleshot servers and connectivity as Tech Support Specialist and won promotion to Lead Engineer due to work performance. Planned, built, and managed new $20 million data center in Seattle. Supervised installation of servers, creation of security procedures, and built out of infrastructure. Wrote procedures, hired engineers, and trained on operations to provide 24x7 support.

CORE Communications, Inc.   Fremont, California
CATV ENGINEER   1989-1995

Engineered cable television connectivity and planning of services. Managed daily operations of main office and coordinated with offices in DC, Chicago, and the Bay Area on service provision.

NOTED AWARDS AND ACTIVITIES

National Speaker
HealthFinder.gov Launch Department of Health and Human Services, Washington, D.C. • 1997

National Speaker
Online Consumer Health Conference Fred Mutchinson Cancer Research Center, Seattle, Washington • 1996

Distinguished Achievement Award – Online Health • 1996

Cited as Internet health community pioneer by:

Health Online	*MSNBC*
The Self-Help Sourcebook	*The New York Times*
eHealth Strategy & Trends	*USA Today*

EDUCATION AND TRAINING

Bachelor of Science – Broadcast Engineering
University of California, Berkeley, California

Training:
Cisco Router Training • America Online Forum Management • TV Production – TCI Cablevision

Complete Technical Skills Addendum Attached

Patty Burns

21 East 39 Street, Apt. #3   212-555-5555
New York, NY 10016   BurnsP@aol. corn

Senior-Level General Manager   **Modular Manufacturing Processes**

Executive Profile

- Over 10 years of senior-level experience in astute business analysis and profitable management of $20 million custom manufacturer. Forecast sales trends, enhance revenue streams, turn around troubled operations, and achieve profitability in downtrending markets. Administer all manufacturing, marketing, and environmental control functions. Supervise staff of up to 25 direct and indirect reports.

- A hands-on manager and critical thinker who can learn quickly, develop expertise, and produce immediate contributions in systems, analysis, business operations, and motivational team management. Possess a valuable blending of leadership, creative, and analytical abilities that combine efficiency with imagination to produce bottom-line results.

Proven Areas of Knowledge

business planning / development	operations management	operational troubleshooting
revenues and margins	multiple project management	task analysis
modular manufacturing architecture	facilities management	capital / consumable purchasing
trend and competitive analysis	crisis management	high-expectation client relations
joint venture formation	environmental management	training and development

---

Executive Highlights

- Produced exceptional company growth, increased gross margin, enhanced productivity, and set new quality standards through the proactive design of innovative programs, sales techniques, and manufacturing methodologies, as well as the imaginative use of unique suppliers.

- Doubled company's accounts and quadrupled sales by design and implementation of profitable value-added services. Division generated unit sales per employee that were 1.5 times that of the industry's largest independent service bureau. Produced division turnaround time of 10 to 12 weeks vs. industry average of 13 to 18 weeks.

- Created an innovative in-house service bureau, the only one of its kind in the industry. Produced new revenue streams representing 12.5 percent of sales through proactive marketing of new service bureau as a quasi-independent operation that gained new crossindustry, nonprinting accounts.

- Avoided purchase of multimillion-dollar computer graphics system through inventive utilization of offset and reprographic service bureaus, reducing expenses even further by scheduling projects in bureaus' downtimes.

- Designed and directed company's strategy to prevent major losses from 40 percent erosion of customer base during late 80s recession. Spearheaded production of proprietary nationally distributed wallcovering collections, advertising, and collateral materials. Developed manufacturing relationships with large furniture producers and cosmetics firms. Marketed color separation and film services to competitors.

- Prevented massive disruption in service by assuming immediate control of all manufacturing operations in crisis response to key administrators' mismanagement and subsequent departure.

(Continued)

Patty Burns

page two

Employment History

Distinction Printing, Ltd., Long Island City, NY 1980 to present

Company manufactures custom wallcoverings, decorative laminates, large-scale graphics, and point-of-purchase specialties, with a peak sales volume of $20 million and a number-two ranking in this specialized industry of 20 contract wallcovering printers in the United States.

Vice President and General Manager 1995 to present

Assumed control of all manufacturing operations following departure of two key managers. Situation required immediate action to position company to recover from mismanagement. Downsized staff, slashed overhead, crosstrained personnel, instituted strict housekeeping controls to curtail waste, and reduced inventory—all with no reduction in quality.

Increased margins by 60 percent on four existing customer collections, signed with two new national distributors, and developed high-margin accounts. Increased business without increasing expenses through the use of vendors' sales people as a de facto sales force to market company's services to noncompeting screen-print industries.

Manage facility operation and safety / environmental coordination. Supervise all facility functions including hiring of contractors for maintenance and renovations. Administer vital hazardous materials program for entire corporation, including training, compliance, documentation, and reporting. Directed all repairs, contractors, and insurance affairs after partial roof collapse and flooding in 1996.

Sales and Operations Manager 1987 to 1995

Held full P&L responsibility. Increased division sales by 30 percent between 1987 and 1990 and steered company through the recession of the late 80s / early 90s when fully 40 percent of the industry's customer base was lost through consolidation and bankruptcy. Researched and developed new markets, created new opportunities as outsourced producer for competitors' small runs, and positioned company as fast-turnaround specialist.

Pre-Press Manager 1980 to 1987

Planned production, scheduled, procured consumables, capital equipment, and outsourced services. Created value-added services that directly contributed to doubling of company's account base and quadrupling of sales from 1980 to 1987. Ran division turnaround times typically 30 percent less than industry standard, with no decline in quality.

Education and Development

Master of Business Administration, New York University, New York, NY, 1990

Bachelor of Arts in Business Administration, State University of New York at Stony Brook, 1979

Technology

Use PC word processing, database, and spreadsheet software (MS Office), the Internet, and E-mail.

Easily learn specific industry systems and software. Familiar with Mac, especially graphic arts software.

Creative approach, particularly on page 2. Graphics included also tell a story of both qualifications and creativity of this candidate.

Everett Morris
50 Trouble Drive
Fairview Heights, Illinois 62208-2332
(618) 555-8228

Graphic/Visual Arts Specialist

Seventeen years' experience managing and coordinating visual arts projects from concept to completion. Accustomed to working on multiple projects with short notice, little or no instruction, and total creative judgment for quality and details of finished product.

- Well-rounded business management skills, with proven ability to match customer needs with a wide variety of graphics, visual arts tools, and approaches.

- Effective at communicating ideas and capturing the interest of the intended audience.

Professional Experience

Visual Information Specialist   1989-Present
(self-employment under contract to the Defense Information Technology Contracting Office, a full-service telecommunications and information systems procurement office with 400+ employees supporting the entire DoD and 56 non-DoD organizations)

Managed all operations of a $100,000 business supporting telecommunications, information systems, administrative, financial, and management staff. Responsibilities included record keeping, accounting, budgeting, and inventory control.

- Prioritized customer requirements and assigned workload to meet changing contract specifications and customer deadlines.

- Provided detailed instructions to employees for new, difficult, or unusual requirements. Ensured quality of completed products prior to delivery to customers.

- Served as a concept consultant to assist and advise customers on colors, content, and size of finished products.

Additional Experience (1979-1989): Held the same title of **Visual Information Specialist** as a contract employee without the business management responsibilities.

Education

Graphique Commercial Art School, 1978-1979
St. Louis, Missouri

General Coursework, Belleville Area College, 1976-1978
Belleville, Illinois

(Continued)

Everett Morris - Page 2

Creative and Technical Skills

Paste-Up

Designed and produced paste-ups and artwork for illustrative slides, viewgraphs, and charts used in formal presentations, static displays, cover brochures, and posters used for briefings to senior military and civilian personnel, static displays at trade shows, and various reports.

Engraving/Signmaking

Designed and produced plastic and metal engraved signs and plates used for organizational awards, plaques, and other recognitions. Designed and produced vinyl/plastic signs for badges, nameplates, name tags, cubical identification, and hallway directories.

Audiovisual Displays

Maintained audiovisual equipment library including the distribution, setup, and operation of video and still cameras, audio recorders, overhead transparency, 16mm and 35mm projectors for presentations and training sessions.

Computer/Graphic Design

Designed and produced slides, charts, and graphs for weekly staff meetings and formal presentations using various software packages such as Harvard Graphics, Freelance Graphics, and PowerPoint. Manipulated color and size of clip art with software packages such as Arts and Letters. Produced forms, flyers, and publications using PageMaker and Corel Draw software.

Presentation Planning

Provided expert consulting service to assist customers in presentation planning for the various types of media used to market, publicize, and document the organization's goal and services. Used Harvard Graphics and Microsoft PowerPoint extensively.

35—GRAPHIC DESIGNER

Good layout and summary up front.

KRISTEN MCCORMICK
445 5th Avenue Apt 57P New York, New York 10960 (212) 555-5555 • km@email.com

A seasoned *Graphic Designer* with the abiltiy to interpret clients' needs and develope effective designs for logos and collateral materials for use in Web site and point-of-purchase displays. Background encompasses exposure to variety of industries and demonstrated skills in concept creation. Strengths include the ability to develop rapport with individuals at all levels, analyze needs, and implement appropriate procedures. Computer expertise includes Adobe Illustrator, Adobe Photoshop, and QuarkXPress.

PROFESSIONAL EXPERIENCE

McDesign – New York, New York • 1987/Present
President/Senior Design Consultant
Direct day-to-day operations of this graphic design firm with 12 designers specializing in corporate projects handling both short and long term projects for numerous clients including Reckitt & Coleman, Inc, Marcal Paper Mills, M. Kamenstein, Inc., Minwax Corporation, Mem Company, and Russ Berrie and Company, Inc.
- ❖ Consult with Art Directors, Marketing Managers and Product Managers on all facets of print and Internet projects.
- ❖ Coordinate details of designs from initial concepts through productions with clients and direct freelance designers, illustrators and photographers.
- ❖ Evaluate competitive marketplaces to establish basis for creative efforts.
- ❖ Schedule and prioritize all jobs for completion on a timely basis and present concept and design recommendations to clients.

Morgan Whitney, Inc. - Greenwich, Connecticut 1985/1987
Lead Designer
Created concepts and designed collateral materials for this sales promotion and packaging design firm. Developed on-pack promotions and interfaced with outside vendors. Worked on project for this firm's largest account, Chesebrough-Pond's, Inc.

Shannon Design - White Plains, New York 1983/1985
Graphic Designer
Developed layouts through mechanicals for promotional materials including comps and marker renderings for this sales promotion firm.

EDUCATION

- ❖ **Parsons School of Design** - New York, New York
- ❖ **University of Bridgeport** - Bridgeport, Connecticut
  Bachelor of Fine Arts • *Design*
  Rider College - Lawrenceville, New Jersey
  Art History

PROFESSIONAL AFFILIATIONS

- ❖ **Manhattan Chamber of Commerce** • *Board Member*
- ❖ **New York Business Association** • *Member*
- ❖ **The Partnership of Women Entrepreneurs** • *Member*
- ❖ **S.W.A.N. (Self-Employed Writers and Artist Network)** • *Member*

Conventional resume utilizing an "Executive Profile" section.

ELMERINE LARSON

654 Silver Street
Pensacola, FL 32504
H: (850) 555-5555 ◆ O: (850) 555-5555 ◆ E-mail: emailaddress@emailaddress.com

---

EXECUTIVE PROFILE

GRAPHIC USER INTERFACE (GUI) DESIGNER

Dynamic career designing interactive user interfaces in the fast-paced Internet and software development industries. Apply rigor and creativity, combining expertise in usability research, human-computer interaction, and graphic design to solve diverse GUI design issues. Excel in team collaboration and solution brainstorming. Exceptionally strong sense of aesthetics and attention to detail.

**Usability Engineering / Interface Solutions & Design / Web & Multimedia UI Design
Project Management / HTML & Graphic Design / Team Leadership & Collaboration**

PROFESSIONAL EXPERIENCE

1999 - Present

Millennium Ventures – Pensacola, FL

GUI WEB DESIGNER

Manage all phases of graphic user interface design projects for a wide range of clients requiring interactive, transactional e-commerce sites. Assess client needs and develop specifications; plan and implement projects from initial conceptual design through coding, final delivery, and client approval.

> Direct conceptual, strategic, and tactical creation of robust, integrated GUI Web site and Web application solutions using HTML, DHTML, and JavaScript.

> Manage multiple simultaneous projects, successfully meeting all budgets and timeframes. Drove 6 technically complex, large-scale projects from conceptual stages to delivery in less than 8 months.

> Design and optimize original site graphics and navigational elements that have been formally praised by clients for accurately reflecting marketing messages while clearly and logically guiding site users.

> Perform usability testing and synthesize data into concrete GUI design proposals; present design ideas using flowcharts, prototypes, and mock-ups. Played a key role in closing contracts valued at more than $.5 million.

> Lead and coordinate a cross-functional design team; maintain a goal-oriented environment while facilitating boundary questioning and creative thinking.

1990 – 1999

Spengler Software Corporation – New York, NY

LEAD USABILITY ENGINEER, INTERNET PRODUCTS (1997 - 1999)

Coordinated usability research and teamed in design of user interface screens for high profile Web sites and Internet applications. Challenged with research and design issues involving electronic transaction processing, Web productivity and utility, and consumers' expectations.

> Defined users' cognitive framework and expectations by applying formative research methodologies such as participatory design and cluster analysis.

> Assessed quality of interaction and usability goodness of design alternatives with iterative design and usability evaluation of low-fidelity prototypes.

(continued)

ELMERINE LARSON

PROFESSIONAL EXPERIENCE CONTINUED

LEAD USABILITY ENGINEER, Spengler Software, continued

Partnered in user interface design; contributed to content, layout, navigation, interaction flow, and terminology. Collaborated on white-boarding, storyboarding, paper prototyping, specifications, and graphical design.

Initiated focus groups, design reviews, surveys, and site visits to identify the needs and expectations of users. Created strategies and tactics that successfully leveraged research contact as sales and marketing opportunities.

Revisited design assumptions, prioritized features, and realigned development efforts based on research findings. Utilized data to redesign critical aspects of the user interfaces to better map with operator needs and expectations.

USABILITY ENGINEER, CONSUMER PRODUCTS (1990 - 1997)

Built expertise in a wide range of software products and consumer behaviors as a pioneer of the usability engineering industry discipline. Worked on diverse v.1 and v.2 software projects, gaining a broad perspective of user populations and requiring adaptation to contrasting product development processes.

Ensured software product ease-of-use, engagement, and user satisfaction by designing, implementing, and synthesizing research that influenced design of consumer products.

Innovated unique strategies, tools, and methodologies later adopted organization-wide, that streamlined and focused usability research while upholding rigorous research standards.

Collaborated with cross-functional product teams, 3rd party design houses, and business partners to devise usability research plans for diverse groups.

1988 - 1990   **AIM Graphic Designers, Inc., New York - NY**

ASSOCIATE DESIGNER

Designed visual materials and interpreted and created promotional graphics for diverse business customers. Conferred with customers and assisted in transforming intangible concepts to finished products. Worked closely with marketing specialists, photographers, copywriters, editors, and print houses.

EDUCATION   **B.F.A., Communications Design** – University of Illinois, Chicago, 1988
A.S., Computer Science - University of Maryland, College Park, 1985

Additional training in Project Management, Graphic Design Principles, HTML Design, Usability Research Methodologies, and Team Building.

TECHNICAL SUMMARY

Extensive experience with HTML, DHTML, and JavaScript to design interactive Web user interfaces. Proficient working with HomeSite, Dreamweaver, and FrontPage. Highly skilled with PhotoShop, Paint Shop Pro, and Illustrator. Familiar with implementation strategies using Java, server-side Java, and SQL.

37—GSM ENGINEER

Ian M. O'Shea

1234 Green Street NW • Washington, DC 20008
555.555.5555 • cell: 123.456.7890
io@yahoo.com

Objective

Telecommunications Engineer with in-depth knowledge of **GSM communications** and software systems. Seeking full-time position with global telecommunications entity. Eager to bring extensive product and technology knowledge to benefit emerging wireless communications industry.

Technical Knowledge

GSM	Solaris
SS7 Networks	SQL
ETSI standards	Unix
ITU-T Standards	Axe Platforms
ISUP	TDMA
Intelligent Networks	FDMA
Assembler	Common Channel Signaling

Professional Experience

IRISH SATELLITE GROUP – IS, INC.

GSM SATELLITE SUPPORT ENGINEER

Falls Church, Virginia • 1999-present

Team Leader of consulting group serving Hughes Network Systems engaged in deployment of large satellite/wireless access network in the Middle East. Working directly with HNS engineers, advised on product specifications of Global System for Mobile Communications (GSM) node interfaces. Provided expertise on network operations and implementations for 200,000-subscriber switch in the United Arab Emirates that will extend coverage to Africa, the Middle East, Asia, and Eastern Europe. Delivered and tested all software on the switch in anticipation of a go-live in 2001. Performed acceptance testing and documented findings/results. Performed internal planning and carried out process definition and implementation.

- **Consistently met all deadlines and performance benchmarks through dedicated work over an extended period**
- **Fostered positive, productive relationships with customer engineers and involved entities through singular effort in communication and cooperation**
- **Singled out for promotion to Verification Manager for Fairfax location**

(Continued)

37—GSM ENGINEER (CONT.)

INTELLIGENT NETWORKS GLOBAL CUSTOMIZATION COORDINATOR

Dublin, Ireland • 1999

Teamed on development of complete customization process from scratch, initiating existence of Global Customization department for Irish Satellite. Authored documentation and procedures for implementation of a customization process for all IS mobile IN services. Dedicated extensive man-hours over a 4-month period to establish functional entity and participated in several IN service customization prestudies.

SUPPLY AND SUPPORT TEAM LEADER • IRISH SATELLITE PREPAID LITE SOLUTION

Dublin, Ireland • 1998-1999

Led team of up to 3 engineers in supply and support of Irish Satellite prepaid lite solutions. Planned and executed functional system testing of product at customer sites. Assisted Marketing Department through provision of numbers series, tariff structures, and other data for strategic positioning against competing service providers. Trained local companies and colleagues on implementation, features, and functionality as part of technology transfer. Traveled extensively to customer sites in Turkey, Macao, Uganda, Azerbaijan, Serbia, and Zanzibar to provide troubleshooting and implementation of simple and efficient solutions.

- **Successfully implemented product for customers in six different global markets. Carried out an implementation in Serbia, working largely alone under wartime conditions. Completed implementation in location with less than adequate infrastructure and local support. Met all implementation deadlines and benchmarks.**

ISUP CERTIFICATION TEAM LEADER

Tel Aviv, Israel • 1997-1998

Led team involved in Integrated Services Digital Network User Part (ISUP) testing and certification of system software for Public Telephone and Telegraph (PTT – Israeli publicly owned telco). Troubleshot software and wrote corrections in Assembler. Coordinated and documented software testing.

- **Played key role in contract award for Irish Satellite to supply network hardware and software for Israel's first GSM system. Beat competitors Siemens and Nortel Networks to certification finish line despite need to adjust platform to interface with Israeli protocols.**

ENGINEER IN TRAINING

Dublin, Ireland • 1996-1998

Education and Training

Bachelor of Science – Electronic Engineering
University College – Galway, Ireland
Graduated with Honors - 1996

Irish Satellite Engineering Training – 1996-1998

PROFESSIONAL QUALIFICATIONS
OF
Torsten Wayne
3000 Easy Street #25
Some City, California 90000
(714) 555-1212 - email@email.com

Human Resources/Candidate Development/Industrial Relations/ Management Specialist

Gained experience in the corporate environment as the owner/manager of direct/indirect and contingency personnel agencies and outplacement services. As a result of these experiences, have demonstrated the following capabilities:

Department Management
- Coordinate, implement, and supervise maintenance of all personnel related records, finances, and systems.
- Manage and develop recruiters of varying skill levels.
- Administer exempt/nonexempt salary, benefit, bonus, profit-sharing and termination packages. Monitor worker's compensation claims.
- Negotiate union/nonunion contracts and participate in grievance procedures.

Operations
- Consult with corporate planners determining staffing/replacement/redundancy issues.
- Work effectively as a problem solver, team player with managers, union/nonunion labor.
- Establish personnel policies and procedures and formal job descriptions according to company goals while meeting legal requirements.
- Recruit, test, and evaluate administrative, management, technology, and sales applicants.
- Utilize fully-integrated customized data management system.

Personal
- Entrepreneurial in spirit as well as in results, able to set and achieve high personal goals.
- Represent corporation at community and professional activities.
- Long-time member of PC&MA, PHIRA, and Brea Chamber of Commerce and Rotary Club.

MAJOR ACCOMPLISHMENTS

- Authored and administered a no-fault absenteeism program for Branch Management.
- Successfully negotiated union/management agreements to include concessions, health benefits, and 2-tiered wage structures.
- Trained all levels of corporate employees in areas of safety, employee assessment and performance evaluations, 401K plans, and sexual harassment issues.
- Grew successful company in the highly competitive employment industry by securing and maintaining solid business relationships with small/medium-sized and Fortune 500 companies in the Southern California marketplace.

(continued)

Torsten Wayne   *QUALIFICATIONS - 2/2*

CAREER HISTORY

DIGITAL PERSONNEL/THE TECH PLACE
Some City, CA (1988-Present)

7/91-Present **Account Manager** - Develop new and retain existing recruiting business and assist in the recruitment and placement of direct, indirect, and contingency personnel. With a focus on high technology industry needs, develop and implement recruiting strategies that will identify candidate pools. Consult with in-house recruiters and hiring managers to build and implement candidate sourcing plans. Upgrade recruiter knowledge of candidate libraries, databases, target schools, alumni programs, and specialized sites and publications. Monitor industry trends and competitors for referrals for specific candidates. Hire, train, and supervise recruitment staff as needed to fill job orders.

1/88-7/91 **Vice President/General Manager** - Initiated business specializing in light industrial, office, and management placements. Grew company from 2 to 5 office and placement staff. Sold company to Digital Personnel.

APSMANNING, Newport Beach, CA

1/87-1/88 **General Manager** - Managed operations and sales for employee background screening division. Efforts included telemarketing, outside sales, and community networking. Clients included Nordstrom, Pacificare, and other large corporations.

GTE (Sylvania Lighting Services), Pomona, CA

5/84-12/86 **Western Regional Human Resources Manager** - Managed all HR functions for regional office and 16 branch operations West of the Mississippi. Negotiated union/nonunion contracts.

CBS, Inc. (NY/CA)

10/80-5/84 **Assistant Director, Personnel -** As a generalist, implemented management hiring, terminating, and evaluating techniques for a Fortune 100 company undergoing major financial and management restructuring.

Prior to 1980 Gained valuable experience in positions including Personnel Coordinator, Employee Investment Fund, Administrative Assistant and Accounting Assistant.

EDUCATION

Workshops and seminars, PIHRA North Orange County
Master of Arts, Human Resources Management, Univ. of Redlands
Bachelor of Arts, Psychology/Sociology, Mt. St. Mary's College, Maryland

Layout very clean and easy to read. Title at top followed by keywords tells a quick and effective story to the reader.

SHANNON E. BENUSCAK, PHR

12 Your Street, Any Town, New York • (845) 708-5555 • e-mailaddress@internetserviceprovider.com

---

HUMAN RESOURCES MANAGEMENT • IT RECRUITMENT

A seasoned HR manager with extensive expertise in recruiting high-level information technology professionals. Demonstrated skill in organizational development, change management and strategic design of marketing, and recruiting efforts. Strong background in management planning, budgeting, staffing, and facilities designed to enhance productivity and profitability. Core competencies include:

➤ Program Development
➤ Benefits Administration
➤ Preventative Labor Strategies
➤ HR Policy Design & Administration

➤ Succession Planning
➤ Union Negotiations & Mediations
➤ Employee & Labor Law
➤ Compensation & Benefits Design

PROFESSIONAL EXPERIENCE

FAB Associates, LLC – New York, New York   1991 - Present
SENIOR HUMAN RESOURCES CONSULTANT

➤ Recruited as Lead Consultant to standardize organizational structure for an IT Department with 500 employees of an e-commerce company with a subsequent rollout to 6,000 employees nationwide.
➤ Led team in analysis of existing operations and development of an action plan.
➤ Worked with Senior Management to gain support of new strategic design proposals.
➤ Created cost justification of a $2.5 million budget based on savings from retention and retraining expenses.
➤ Examined market and recruiting efforts, role and level descriptions as well as lines of communication.
➤ Developed a standardized organizational model, which clarified authority, relationships, and responsibilities within the department.

Manhattan University Hospital – New York, New York   1983 – 1991
HUMAN RESOURCES MANAGEMENT • 1987 – 1991

➤ Responsible for union contract interpretation, grievances, regulatory compliance, personnel files, performance appraisal system and management of worker's compensation programs for the 6,500 employees.
➤ Supervised direct staff, development of policy recommendations, preparation of implementing procedures, and served on numerous operating committees.
➤ Served as the key player for the institutional authority on state and federal regulatory requirements.
➤ Managed numerous complex worker's compensation program with a high volume of claims, including hearings and litigation on challenged decisions.
➤ Reorganized problem departments, established stability, and installed procedures and systems to maintain quality of operations.
➤ Established improved relationships with the ten unions which reduced adversarial attitudes and labor stoppage threats.
➤ Substantially reduced worker's compensation costs and subsequent litigation.

(Continued)

SHANNON E. BENUSCAK, PHR • PAGE TWO
12 Your Street, Any Town, New York • (845) 708-5555 • e-mailaddress@internetserviceprovider.com

---

TRAINING AND DEVELOPMENT MANAGER   1983 – 1987

➢ Supervised human resource functions for designated units and chaired Institutional Committee for development of employee policy and procedure manuals.
➢ Prepared budgets and coordinated planning with other department managers. Programs included: Compliance with Americans with Disabilities Act, Sexual Harassment Prevention, Labor Relations, Management Development Training, Workplace Literacy, and New Employee Orientation. Additionally, the department selected and installed specialized software systems for tracking training.
➢ Managed JCAHO accreditation process in areas of Orientation, Training, and Education
➢ Appointed to Strategic Design team to participate in broadening Quality Management programs throughout the hospital.

Swiss-American Insurance Group – New York, New York   1980 – 1993
CAREER DEVELOPMENT SPECIALIST

➢ Managed training programs, career database system, and career development promotional programs.
➢ Developed, published, and managed wide-ranging programs to promote professional growth of current employees.
➢ Designed career planning concepts, analyzed data on career mobility, and managed departmental administrative operations.
➢ Developed the Company's first video promotion and multimedia career planning programs, participated in customization of career planning software package and served as Internal Consultant to the Company's ten operating divisions.
➢ Joined the company as Senior Supervisor, managed training for the U.S. Headquarters and national staff. Chaired Corporate Committee for Career Development, organized high-level review courses for the American Society of Actuaries certification examinations, and led curriculum development for the Roosevelt University inauguration of an Insurance degree major.

EDUCATION

➢ **National College of Education**
   MASTER OF ART • EDUCATION AND TRAINING CONCENTRATION
➢ **University of Wisconsin**
   BACHELOR OF ART • HISTORY

PROFESSIONAL AFFILIATIONS

➢ **Member of the American Society of Training and Development (ASTD)**
➢ **Member of the Society of Human Resources Management (SHRM)**
➢ **Advisor in the Chicago Chapter ASTD Human Resources Development Institute**

40—INFORMATION ARCHITECT 1

Detailed "Technical Skills" is excellent summary.

JANICE L. VEY

221 Hermitage Drive • Nashville, Tennessee 37167 • 615-555-5555 • Janice@yahoo.com

- Senior Systems Designer/Information Architect with over 15 years' progressive experience in analysis, design, implementation, and conversions of systems and client/server environments.
- Top-notch professional with proven ability to design solutions, implement new processes and programs, and manage information operations on a large scale.
- Outstanding expertise in systems analysis, program design, system conversions, and software implementation.

_____EXPERIENCE_____

Deloitte & Touche LLP • http://www.dttus.com
Client Service & Information Technology • Hermitage, Tennessee
1990-present

INFORMATION ARCHITECT

Teamed with world-class client service teams in numerous in-house MIS implementation projects, system developments, and training processes. Scoped and planned projects, developed needs assessments, and provided specialized training for implementation teams. Assisted teams through detailed business and functional knowledge application to systems analysis and design. Provided technical guidance to CABS Development Team, Solution 6 software vendor, Financial Control, Firm Accounting, and other teams involved in legacy data conversion and interfaces for CABS. Supervised efforts of 12 implementation team members.

Project Team Lead – SAP Capital Expenditures Implementation
Internal Consultant – CABS Global Practice Management Implementation
Lead Implementation Coordinator – ATSW Client/Server System
Software Implementation Internal Consultant

- ➤ Successfully led implementation of Automated Timesheet System for Windows (ATSW) for 26,000+ users in over 120 sites globally in less than 10 months
- ➤ Teamed on Accounts Receivable System (ARS) development/implementation to successful completion under tight deadlines throughout entire project life cycle resulting in back office implementation in over 85 sites in less than 9 months
- ➤ Led system conversions to migrate DPS6 minicomputer platform to new ATSW and ARS client/server systems (PowerBuilder, ORACLE, and SQL Server) within 11 months, saving Deloitte & Touche over $400,000 annually by eliminating hardware maintenance costs
- ➤ Achieved Lead Analyst position for 3 major systems on Honeywell Bull mainframe, DPS6 minicomputer, and client/server systems

Analysts International Corporation
Contel Information Systems • Washington, D.C.
1990

SENIOR SYSTEMS CONSULTANT

Special Project Consultant retained to lead system conversion from Honeywell Bull mainframe platform to IBM.

- ➤ Investigated corruption of E911 Database through analysis of data received from South Central Bell; designed and developed data comparison system to report all discrepancies for immediate correction
- ➤ Consulted on Customer Billing System revision project with acquisition of new long-distance carriers (AT&T, Sprint, and MCI)

(continued)

Janice L. Vey • (615) 555-5555

_____TECHNICAL SKILLS_____

LANGUAGES

PowerBuilder	COBOL	DML
PowerScript	JCL	
SQL	ECL	

OPERATING SYSTEMS

GCOS6	SR 4020, SR 4500	Novell 4.11
CGOS8	UNIX, AIX	
HVS 6 Plus	Windows 95, 98, NT	

HARDWARE

DPS6+	IBM 3090, 4030	Compaq Proliant
DPS90	IBM RS/6000	
DPS9000	IBM SP2, S70	

SOFTWARE, TOOLS, AND UTILITIES

PowerBuilder	VFORMS	Lotus Notes EPN
PL/SQL Developer	VISION	MS Office Suite
ORACLE SQL*Plus	SCORPEO	MS Project 98
Transact-SQL	FSTE-6	Express
COBOL-74	EDIT 8	Visio Professional
COBOL-85	FRED	Vantive
GCOS Utilities	ACES	SourceSafe
UTL2	FSE	SnagIt
UTL8	EASY-FORM	WinZip
TSS	TOSC1/PFMS	Ultra-Edit 32
MAGNA8	Lotus cc:Mail	
VDAM	Lotus Notes	

DATABASES

MS SQL Server	DMIV-IDSII	TP8
ORACLE	DVIV-TP	MS Access

_____SPECIALIZED TRAINING_____

Deloitte & Touche LLP

MS SQL Server 6.5 & 7.0	Structured Systems Analysis & Design
MS Project 98	ORACLE
PowerBuilder 5.0	SAP R/3 3.0 Business Process
Object-Oriented Systems Design	

_____AFFILIATIONS AND INVOLVEMENTS_____

Nashville ORACLE Users Group
Music City Powersoft Users Group
Association of Information Technology Professionals

Roberta Alexander

4142 W. 108th Street
New York, NY 10022
Emailaddress@emailaddress.com
212-555-5478

> *Title and summary at top work well.*
> *Good job description within the*
> *"Experience" section.*

INFORMATION ARCHITECT

❖ Skilled in the creative design of information architecture, spatial layout, functionality, and site interactivity to increase market exposure, customer service and profitability on the eCommerce frontier.
❖ Expertise in customer needs assessment and client communication.
❖ Experienced in on- and off-line market research and analysis.
❖ B.S. Business Management
❖ Technical skills: Excel / Visio / Dreamweaver / NetObjects Fusion / familiarity with HTML & Java

EXPERIENCE

IMS, Inc., New York, NY   9/99 – Present
Senior Information Architect
Conceptual / organizational / budgetary responsibility for development of **information architecture** within retail eCommerce Websites for key national accounts; overall project budgets range $1-$5 million and above. Facilitate client workshops to introduce Internet marketing trends and concepts and to determine sales / marketing needs. Conduct on- and off-line market research to position clients competitively, applying human factors experience to develop user-friendly solutions. Collaborate with project team, including IAs, graphic designers, and engineers, to create effective and intuitive user experiences.

❖ Key team member in development of a time-saving prototyping process resulting in substantially increased productivity and reduced redundancy.
❖ Implemented proactive merchandising effort that increased sales significantly.
❖ Created a standardized customer sign-off on creative design and site development.
❖ Assigned to taskforce to develop best processes across all functional disciplines.
❖ Selected assist in development of IA training curriculum.

MAJOR CONSULTING COMPANY   5/96 – 8/96; 8/97 – 9/99
Consultant, New York, NY (8/97 – 9/99)
Recruited after successful internship and completion of undergraduate studies. Assessed client needs. Researched solutions; presented findings and suggestions to senior management of client companies.
Projects:
❖ **Implementation of PeopleSoft HRMS at a large International Financial Services Firm, providing solutions for capturing and reporting global HR data.**
  • Interviewed senior clients internationally to determine current practices; analyzed processes and made recommendations to senior management to improve process flow.
  • Defined coding environment for process development. Researched business requirements for various HR interfaces. Designed departmental reports meeting customer specifications.

❖ **Implementation of On-Line Analytical Processing (OLAP) tool at Global Investment Banking Firm to increase efficiency in Human Resources department.**
  • Created detail design and supervised development of data extraction module to produce variable reports quickly and easily.
  • Trained in PeopleSoft Human Resources and Base Benefits, and PeopleTools.

Additionally, established Mentoring Family Program and developed mentoring education materials. Participated in "buddy" program for new-hire analysts. Conducted on-campus recruiting at University.

(Continued)

145

MAJOR CONSULTING COMPANY (continued):
Intern, Chicago, IL (5/96 – 8/96)
  Chosen from nationwide pool of college candidates for one of three intern positions. Researched information on one-to-one marketing; presented findings to senior management. Gained understanding of consumer trends, retailing, and eCommerce within the consumer products industry.

  ❖ Prepared structured case study research.
  ❖ Worked with vendors to coordinate delivery of business-to-customer exhibit messages.

ABC UNIVERSITY, West New York, NY   1995 - 1996
Strategic Planner, University Apple Orchards (8/96 – 12/96)
  Project:
  ❖ Development of improved marketing strategy for orchard produce
    • Conducted extensive market research and quantified information regarding consumer perception, attitudes, and buying behavior. Suggested strategies to increase sales during upcoming season; they were implemented successfully.

Head Teaching Assistant, Marketing   (8/95 – 12/96)
  Assisted professor with lecture, section, and exams. Supervised TA staff; conducted weekly organizational / scheduling meetings. Organized class outline and structure. Proctored and graded exams.

EDUCATION

ABC UNIVERSITY, West New York, NY
  B.S. Business Management, May 1997
    Specialization: Marketing (GPA 3.6)
    Marketing Fellowship; Dean's List

AFFILIATIONS / ACTIVITIES

University Alumni Network   9/97 – Present
  Serve as point of contact, providing information for prospective students and encouraging their attendance.

Member, Alpha Sorority   1/95 – 5/97
  Coordinated philanthropic events to support local community.

42—INFORMATION SYSTEMS MANAGER

MARY O'CONNOR

75 Neperhan Road • Tarrytown, New York 10591 • (914) 524-5555 • moc@isp.com

INFORMATION SYSTEMS MANAGER

Expert in the creation, implementation, and delivery of cost-effective, high-performance technology solutions to meet rigorous business perimeters. Extensive accomplishments in all facets of project development, user training/enhancement, and accounting management. Excellent organizational, leadership, team building, and project management qualifications.

AREAS OF EXPERTISE

System Integration	Staff Development	User Training
Account Management	Cost Reductions	Budget Development
Communications	Productivity Improvements	Department Coordination

TECHNICAL SKILLS

Hardware Platforms:
IBM and compatible PCs, IBM workstations, IBM AS400, IBM System 38, Compaq Prosigna server, IBM RS/6000, PDP 11/70 and Meridian 1 Option 11C.

Operating Systems:
DOS, OS/2 Warp, DG/UX, SCO Unix, Novell Netware, OS/400, and RSTS.

Software:
Windows 3.x, WordPerfect, Excel, Lotus 1-2-3, Paradox, Fastback Plus, cc:Mail, Revive, SDS, Logical Solutions, Inc., EM320, EM5250, Support Net, Infogenesis, Peachtree, Query 400, SDA, Microsoft SQL, NICE recording systems, Win Trak Call Accounting, Meridian Max Release 8, and Windows NT.

Languages:
RPG II and III, RPG400, CL, COBOL, UNIX, DG/UX, and BASIC.

PROFESSIONAL EXPERIENCE

Bee Alive, Inc. – Valley Cottage, New York • 1997 – Present
INFORMATION SYSTEMS SENIOR MANAGER

- ❖ Direct information systems operations for this $15 million herbal health product manufacturer overseeing departmental budgeting, while providing technical support to all departments specifying hardware, software, and monitoring system usage and capacity to optimize performance.
- ❖ Approve procedures and Information System equipment purchases; assist operating and marketing departments to obtain their objectives while coordinating logistical integration.
- ❖ **Implement installation of new programs** and oversee user training to increase productivity.
- ❖ **Reduced costs by 25% by reviewing and enhancing the company's operating procedures.**
- ❖ **Specified, installed, and trained staff on new telecommunication hardware and software.**
- ❖ **Designed, developed and implemented inventory system tracking raw materials to finished products to establish cost of goods.**

(continued)

MARY O'CONNOR

75 Neperhan Road • Tarrytown, New York 10591 • (914) 524-5555 • moc@isp.com

---

❖ **Reviewed and supervised the Company's compliance experience minimal Y2K issues and no effects in the areas of revenue-producing departments.**

❖ **Reduced local and long distance telephone expenses by 50% by renegotiating rates with service providers.**

❖ **Increased productivity by providing recommendations to the Board of Directors on telecommunications protocols for interdepartmental needs and service implementation.**

❖ Supervise operational and maintenance issues involving information and telecommunications systems for both hardwre and software.

Alpha Gulf Coast, Inc. d/b/a Bayou Caddy's Jubilee Casino - Greenville, Mississippi
Bayou Caddy's Jubilation Casino - Lakeshore, Mississippi • 1993 – 1997
DIRECTOR OF INFORMATION SYSTEMS • 1995–1997
MANAGER OF INFORMATION SYSTEMS • 1993–1995

❖ Acted as System Administrator for two casinos and related support facilities handling all departmental budgeting, acquisitions and provided technical support to all departments.

❖ **Relocated two casinos with minimal downtime, while fully complying with stringent State and Federal regulations.**

❖ **Conducted operational analysis and made recommendations resulting in significant monetary savings.**

❖ Supervised operational and maintenance issues involving information systems, hardware, and software. Monitored system usage and capacity to optimize performance.

❖ Implemented and supported online slot reporting, player tracking, casino accounting, financial accounting, payroll, and time and attendance systems.

❖ **Successfully supervised and motivated staff through hiring, training, evaluation, and staff assignments.**

❖ Installed and configured AS400 Model F10, F20, Series 200, terminals, printers, IBM 5394 and 5494 remote controllers and peripherals. Install software upgrade from V2 R3 to V3 R1. Create queries upon request.

❖ Scheduled automated backups and miscellaneous reports. Performed routine I.P.L.'s. Issued user profiles and security authorization.

Alliance Shippers, Inc. – New Orleans, Louisiana and Mobile, Alabama • 1989–1991
ADMINISTRATIVE ASSISTANT

❖ Maintained accounts receivable and accounts payable for Gulf Coast Region performing all computer upgrades, maintenance, and employee training.

❖ Coordinated and monitored transportation needs of customers with respective truck, rail, or seafaring carrier.

EDUCATION

❖ **Tulane University** – New Orleans, Louisiana
   CIS Course • RPG400 Programming

❖ **Pearl River Junior College** – Poplarville , Mississippi
   Associates in Science • Computer Technology

43—INFORMATION TECHNOLOGY SECURITY SPECIALIST

> *Title and summary at top work well.*
> *Good job description within the*
> *"Professional Experience" section.*

Gregory Fantin

123 Dogwood Street
Waterbury, CT 06050

203-555-5555
gfantin@car.com

IT SECURITY SPECIALIST / PKI ENGINEER / ELECTRONIC ANALYST
Experienced in production Public Key Infrastructure (PKI). Skilled in security audit and security analysis; participant in PKI design, development, administration, and maintenance. Comprehensive understanding of computer security, from concept to infrastructure. Competent evaluator of intrusion detection and network vulnerability. Background in network implementation / administration.

Member, X9F Committee: Invited to contribute to development of national standards for biometrics for the American National Standards Institute (ANSI).

OPERATING SYSTEMS/SERVER APPLICATIONS: Windows NT, Windows 95/98, LINUX, DEC VAX VMS, UNIX, NetWare, Microsoft Exchange Server/Outlook, Microsoft SMS.
PROGRAMMING knowledge in C and C++.
NETWORKING/INTERNET: HTTPS/SSL/TLS, LDAP/LDAPS, HTTP/HTML, FTP, Telnet, SLIP/PPP, TCP/IP, IPX/SPX, NetBEUI.
SECURITY APPLICATIONS: PGP (corporate license), Xcert SentryCA/RA, Aventail VPN client, ISS RealSecure.

PROFESSIONAL EXPERIENCE

INSURER, Center City, CT   5/99 – Present
IT Security Specialist, Security Engineering
Recruited to this position. Instrumental in ensuring the confidentiality, security, and privacy of Insurer's proprietary customer information. Verify security from point of origin, through transit, to recipient systems via security audits, security analysis and evaluation of a variety of commercial and proprietary security applications. Ensure compliance with federal security regulations from Health Care Financing Administration (HCFA) and Health Insurance Portability and Accountability Act (HIPAA). Perform ongoing review / upgrades of user certificate enrollment process.

> Research procedures to ensure compliance with federal regulations concerning e-commerce.
> Evaluate intrusion detection and network vulnerability programs including ISS RealSecure, NetProwler and NetRecon [Axent Technologies], and CyberCop Suite [Network Associates].
> Designated PGP Corporate Decryption and Signing Key keyholder.
> Redesigned high-level concept for business connection with Insurer vendor, enabling cheaper, faster, easier, and more secure business-to-business communication.
> Analyzed and verified security of VPN conceptual design.

ROBERT HALF INTERNATIONAL (RHI), Hartford, CT   12/98 – 2/99
Consultant for Financial Management, Inc. (a subsidary of Insurer, Inc.)
> Provided third-level computer support for asset/portfolio managers.   Real-time support for trading floor equipment, including troubleshooting for Bloomberg, Reuters, and other proprietary software.

(Continued)

149

PROFESSIONAL EXPERIENCE (Continued)

SUMMIT TECHNOLOGIES, Hartford, CT   10/97 – 12/98
Senior Consultant/Project Coordinator for Major Pharmaceutical Corporation, Clinical Systems Lotus cc:Mail to
   Microsoft Outlook/Exchange Server 5 migration. Hired for customer relations/communication skills as well as
   technical knowledge. Responsible for individual user application training, help desk support training and
   coordination of migration for resident, regional, and international users.

Senior Consultant to High-Tech Manufacturing Corporation, conducting R&D on backup technology for cutting-edge
   recording equipment for the medical, financial services and legal professions. Provided research,
   compatibility/performance testing, and final recommendations for introduction into product line.

Senior Consultant/Assistant to Project Manager, contracted through UNISYS to Insurer to help coordinate a 3000-
   PC upgrade. Served as Team Leader for up to 16 personnel; trained several junior consultants. Prioritized/scheduled
   work for installers. Assigned to handle special projects and provide customized responses to "fallout." Converted several closets from Token Ring to 10BaseT. Created Ghost images to facilitate uniformity of installations in each department.

HALLMARK TOTALTECH, INC., Rocky Hill, CT   6/97 – 10/97
Customer Support (Level Three), Major Manufacturer: Contracted through DeSai MicroAge and Vanstar
Corporation.
   One of two onsite customer help desk support technicians for over 1300 PCs running Windows 3.1 and
   Workgroups 95, or NT 3.51/4.0. Extensive use of Microsoft SMS Administrator and other NT administration
   tools. Assisted in rollout of new software packages and upgrades, as well as support of all existing software and
   devices. Trained co-worker. Commended by both Major Manufacturer and Vanstar supervisors for exemplary job
   performance.

LOCAL COMMUNITY-TECHNICAL COLLEGE, Center City, CT   9/96 – 5/98
Extension College Instructor *(9/96 – 5/98)*, teaching noncredit continuing education courses:
   Introduction to Networking; Introduction to CadKey for Windows 7.51; CadKey Intermediate; Introduction to the
   Internet.

JLM ENTERPRISES, Center City, CT   10/92 – 10/96
Computer Consultant

EDUCATION

LOCAL COMMUNITY-TECHNICAL COLLEGE, Center City, CT   1/96 – 6/97
   Course work: Programming in C, Computer Graphic Design, Technical Graphic Communication, and CAD.

44—INTERNET MARKETING CONSULTANT

Christine M. Brown

49 Trillium Blvd. - Traverse City, Michigan 49686
Phone: 231.555.4949 - *Facsimile:* 231.555.0049
emailaddress@emailaddress.com

INTERNET MARKET STRATEGIST & CONSULTANT
creative maverick, heady visionary, industry revolutionary

eStrategist and innovator who motivates, inspires, and expresses opinions to advance Internet dynamics. Right brain / left brain strengths in multifaceted roles of strategy development, project management, budget administration, and creative idea generation. Exceptional interpersonal and communication skills to clearly present concepts with pizzazz, while managing client relationships.

Proven track record in managing interactive online projects — concept through launch — with a thorough understanding of emerging technology and how it can be leveraged. Experience using sophisticated Internet tools; excellent computer and project management skills.

Summary of Attributes

- entrepreneurial drive • multitasking strengths
- easily able to shift from high-level strategic thinking to detail-oriented work
- ability to work in a fast-paced, dynamic environment, collaboratively and under critical deadlines
- excellent verbal and written communication skills
- strong tactical and creative abilities

PROFESSIONAL EXPERIENCE

SENIOR eMARKETING STRATEGY DIRECTOR, 1999-current

NOVO — Detroit Michigan

Play the lead role in developing the company's online strategy. Serve as liaison between the IT, sales, and marketing teams. Direct and coordinate all Internet and intranet activities including strategy formulation, strategic plan execution, site design and maintenance, data management, budget forecasting and administration, business development, strategic alliances, and ongoing operations. Drive vision, strategic guidance, and leadership on all online business projects in the automotive channel.

- Develop full understanding of the clients' business goals to develop long-term purpose.
- Integrate all areas of eMarketing (research/strategic planning and media).
- Facilitate integration of the various agency partners (seamlessly to client).
- Explore new and innovative ways to add value to clients' online goals.
- Continually mine for new business opportunities.
- Build relationships within client and partner groups.

Successes:

- Accelerated development of online technology to keep pace with regional and national competition.
- Forged strategic alliance with Sierra Systems to deliver technology innovations corporatewide.

(Continued)

BUSINESS DEVELOPMENT MANAGER, 1998-99

DESTINY, INC. — Chicago, Illinois

Challenged to develop and prequalify new business and obtain an initial high-level managerial audience in order to communicate corporate value for a leading provider of eBusiness solutions to the world's premier financial institutions.

- Negotiated all financial, legal, scope, and engagement timing issues to expand relationships for an extended, mutually beneficial, long-term relationship.

- Maintained a pipeline to accurately represent both current business and the extensions of business as well as future opportunities.

Successes:

- Established Internet presence firmly in the eConsulting market; developed a strong clientele base.

- Generated follow-on business by identifying new opportunities within existing clients.

DISTRICT MANAGER — Agency Marketing, 1985-98

WORLDSPAN — Detroit, Michigan

Scope of responsibility encompassed the management of advanced electronic information in a major market area for the third largest travel information service corporation in the nation. Managed departmental budget and administrated technology life cycle. Set guidelines that ensured profitability and retained customer loyalty.

- Oversaw all marketing strategies for comprehensive computer reservations system/package including LANs, back-office accounting products, and unique functionality.

- Conducted technical and financial negotiations that satisfied customer requirements and met corporate needs.

Successes:

- Achieved 118% of sales goals, and increased overall market share by 5% in 1998.

- Fast-track promoted from Manager — Market Planning and Forecasting (Atlanta, Georgia) responsible for overall planning objectives including market share and revenue forecasting, business planning, analysis of market trends. Managed annual budget of more than $100 million. Prior: Project Manager —Marketing Programs (Atlanta, Georgia).

EDUCATION / PROFESSIONAL DEVELOPMENT

MASTER OF BUSINESS ADMINISTRATION, 1992 — *UNIVERSITY OF DETROIT-MERCY*; Detroit, Michigan

BACHELOR OF SCIENCE DEGREE — Marketing, 1985 B *INDIANA UNIVERSITY*, Bloomington, Indiana

Computer skills/tools/competencies: Web Applications, Resource/Material Tracking Intranets, Contact Management, Distributed Reporting Systems, Web Sites, Computer Based Training, Form Automation, Interactive Benefits, Time Tracking/Timesheets

45—INTERNET SUPPORT

JACOB A. CHRISTIANSON

555 Honey Circle • Girard, Pennsylvania 16417 • (814) 555-5555 • p: (814) 111-1111 • jacob@erie.net

TECHNICAL SKILLS

Platforms and Operating Environments

Windows 95 • Windows NT • Novell • UNIX • Macintosh • Apple

Networking – Applications - Tools

NT User Manager	MS System Management Software
Exchange Administrator	MS Outlook 98
TCP/IP	cc:Mail
UNIX	Mac Manager
SQL Server	MS Office
Syscon	

Mainframe Operations

AS/400	Time Sharing (TSO)
SYS/36	Dispatch
SYS/38	Cullinet Applications Software
IBM 3270/5250 emulation	(CAS)
VAX	JES II
Terminal Productivity Executive	JCL
(TPX)	

Web Design

HTML • Hotdog Pro • MS FrontPage • FTP

TECHNICAL EXPERIENCE

Web Design and E-commerce

Created and launched niche Website serving the employment industry in 1996, considerably ahead of the currently exploding e-commerce push. Designed site that includes Perl-scripted database management, moderated forums, and bulletin board function. Sold advertising and promoted site within niche market. Achieved listing in the best selling book CareerXRoads and has been mentioned in several periodicals including Fortune magazine.

Technical Support

Tier 1, 2, and 3 Tech Support experience working with Desktop and dial-up end-users in corporate and Internet environments. Supported commercial software applications, proprietary packages, and IBM mainframe operations. As part of Tech Support team, worked with as many as 1000 trouble tickets per week achieving an excellent record of efficiently handling calls, providing sound solutions, and meeting quotas.

(continued)

Jacob A. Christianson • (814) 555-5555

Technical Training

Provided training and education to Macintosh Computer Lab users and professional educators in a secondary school. Managed entire computer lab. Teamed with Technology Coordinator on software purchases, hardware selections, and school technology issues. Conducted Professional Development training for use of computer technology in support of the educational curriculum. Troubleshot and maintained all PCs and peripheral devices.

EMPLOYMENT HISTORY

INTERNET SECURITY SPECIALIST

Uunet/Worldcom
2000-present

TECHNICAL SUPPORT SPECIALIST

General Electric Transportation Systems
Erie, Pennsylvania 1998-2000

TECHNICAL SUPPORT SPECIALIST

Erie Net (Internet Service Provider)
Erie, Pennsylvania 1997-1998

COMPUTER LAB AIDE

Northwestern Middle School
Albion, Pennsylvania 1997-1998

TECHNICAL SUPPORT SPECIALIST

Rocky Mountain Internet (Internet Service Provider)
Colorado Springs, Colorado 1996-1997

HELP DESK SUPPORT

Young Life
Colorado Springs, Colorado 1996

EDUCATION

Computer Operations Diploma – concentration in IBM systems
Computer Learning Center • Springfield, Virginia • 520 contact hours

Montgomery College • Rockville, Maryland • Majored in TV/Radio Communications

46—IT CONSULTANT

James O'Neil

88 Brown Cow Lane • Vacaville, California 95687 • 707-555-9394 • 88joneil88@aol.com

PROFILE

Resourceful, solution-oriented IT Consultant / Executive with in-depth knowledge and successful experience in global enterprise systems development, deployment, and project management. Balanced strengths in strategic and technical analysis, systems management, and team leadership. Proven ability to deliver.

- **Create loyal, productive teams.** Maximize potential of existing personnel; identify / draw out talent and provide mentorship and opportunities for growth.
- **Recognized for strong communication, negotiation, and client relation management skills.**
- **Key strength in evaluating and forecasting current and nearly available technologies** to streamline and augment current business processes.

ACCOMPLISHMENTS

- **Key contributor to $10-million, 5-year project for a major automobile manufacturer's international customer service operations** as a consultant with ZEON. One of 7-member team with a one-year assignment responsible for infrastructure to consolidate eight call centers throughout the country to a single location. Team managed all estimating, network infrastructure design, installation, and operational support for data and voice technologies for the new call center.

  — Successfully developed and implemented regional shutdown and call re-rerouting to achieve zero downtime. Anticipated and forecasted volume capacity issues, working closely with client architecture network team to achieve compatible network bandwidth solutions with existing network infrastructure.
  — Established security / accessibility criteria and vendor evaluation for Internet connectivity.
  — Determined and fulfilled operational requirements for technical and human resources, examining current standards and eliminating outmoded standards. Established and implemented new hardware requirements.

> *Note detailed "Accomplishments" section. Employers want individuals who can accomplish tasks.*

  Directed fast-track Internet assignment to provide a turnkey solution fulfilling several functions for national corporate F&B theme franchise, through ZEON. Identified project requirements, contacted vendor sources, established team members, and developed a viable / flexible project plan that could accommodate client's changing criterion. Within a two-month period, had three deliverables in place: 1) Internet access to customer booths and meeting rooms; 2) virtual office/kiosk area; and 3) connectivity/data sharing with disparate systems, as well as establishing the infrastructural foundation needed for electronic commerce.

- **Successfully forecast current and nearly available technologies for adaptation to current business processes** for Palenti Optical. Evaluated and selected appropriate Internet and intranet technologies.
  — Implemented successful pilot intranet for 700-users that incorporated workforce look ups, department information, Internet access, group calendaring, news, secure access to remote sites. Evaluated and implemented secure firewalls.
  — Performed Y2K evaluation on hardware, operating systems and software, enterprisewide and generated action plan that was eventually adopted and currently in place.

- **With Larsen Consulting, was responsible for internal infrastructure for California** with more than 1500 users and served on team responsible for rollout of Netware 4.1, in both North America and South America. Established standards, systemwide, of 2300 file servers for 15 major offices and 35-50 smaller offices. Standards are still functional, 30+ months later.

- **Evaluated and implemented pilot PC-based network for Hamilton AFB. Awarded the Air Force Commendation Medal in recognition of development of network solutions aimed at streamlining unit tasks.** Due to these streamlining efforts, over 25 manned positions were reclassified and the personnel were released back to frontline, mission critical aircraft maintenance.

- continued -

James O'Neil   Page 2

EXPERIENCE

DIRECTOR / OPERATIONS CONSULTANT, ZEON Global Services   **1998 to present**

Promote and provide "best in class" information technology solutions, project management, and management / operations consulting to large clients. Projects have included:

- Network infrastructure design and installation for global automobile manufacturer's international customer assistance call center including Help Desk software evaluation and solution rollout.
- Computer lab/data center design for project-related applications at a RBOC.
- Consolidation and standardization of infrastructure and operations for a multiple media, multiple operating system, and multiple location paper business forms company.
- Replacement of North American SNA network with TCP/IP-based connectivity including physical and application analysis, redesign and implementation to support a SAP and intranet rollout.
- Project managed / established technical requirements for a PeopleSoft design and build team.
- Determined data requirements for a software company's headquarters move. These requirements included data center layout, Internet connectivity (DS3, T1, ISDN), and WAN circuit redesigns.

IT SERVICES MANAGER, Palenti Optical, USA   **1996-98**

Joined this global optical lens manufacturing company during a period of major transition. Established a clear chain of command and provided positive leadership, vision, and direction for both IT personnel and systems organization. Information and voice operations included complex multiplatform telecommunication, AS/400, data network (IP/IPX/SNA) and PC support.

- Designed and implemented network infrastructure improvements and migrations through effective project and resource management. Coordinated technical and human resource aspects of strategic and daily IS operations, achieving buy-in on previously disputed issues.
- Created and implemented Internet security strategy.
- Designed and implemented an enterprisewide multisubnet TCP/IP network.
- Managed 350-workspace build-out to include responsibility for: cabling plant, server room design, move and setup of PCs and servers.
- Additional projects included: Y2K vulnerability evaluation; intranet rollout; Groupware/Email upgrades; and Windows NT Server 4.0 migrations.

NETWORK ANALYST, Larsen Consulting, Inc.   **1995-96**

Lead network administrator for Larsen Consulting's Northern California practice. Provided third-level support, training and mentoring for technical support staff.

- Project team leader for a number of build-outs and upgrades to include coordination of infrastructure planning, procurement, configuration and installation (Netware 4.1, Lotus Notes, and TCP/IP).
- Performed strategic budgeting planning for multimillion dollar technology implementation.

NCOIC - COMPUTER MANAGEMENT, U.S. Air Force   **1984-95**

Identified business requirements, performed cost-benefit analysis and technical research, and presented case to install Novell-based, Ethernet network for Hamilton AFB to streamline operations. Awarded Air Force Commendation Medal for this work. Assumed operational responsibility for the network to include:

- Maintenance of WAN links with 56K, T1 and remote node connectivity; all software/hardware upgrades, troubleshooting and repairs; requirement analysis and procurement; data archive and operational security; user training; and network design and installation for other units.
- Wrote networked relational database solutions to include training requirements, personnel data, rating information, storing / retrieving critical information for aircraft parts ordering, tool checkout, time compliance inspections, personnel injury tracking, and human resource management reports.

EDUCATION

Embry Riddle Aeronautical University, Daytona Beach, Florida
  Bachelor of Science, Professional Aeronautics (3.44/4.0)
Solano Community College, Suisun, California
  Associate of Science, Biology / **Associate of Science,** Chemistry
Associate of Applied Science, Aircraft Maintenance Technologies, Community College of the Air Force

MARC L. DONOVAN

233 Belmont Way, Palm Beach, FL 33408
(561) 555-1212 / email@email.com

SUMMARY

Accomplished, multitalented **IT Management Professional,** offering a unique combination of leadership, technical, and people skills, exercised in small to enterprise-sized environments. Quick study, able to understand, assimilate, and convey new and evolving technologies.

Organization / Leadership—High level of skill in planning, coordinating, and motivating people successfully to complete clearly defined objectives. Skilled in staff selection, supervision, training, budgeting, and interdepartmental liaison. A highly organized, detail-oriented individual, effective with all levels of management and staff.

Technical—Seasoned systems professional, MCSE, experienced in project management, advanced applications, system enhancements, troubleshooting, and OS migrations. Experience includes servers and PCs, LAN/WAN, extensive TCP/IP troubleshooting, Windows NT 3.51/4.0/2000, MS Terminal Server, Citrix Metaframe, Windows 9x, Windows 3x, MS LAN Manager, DOS, Novell 3.12, Unix SVR4, diagnosis of connectivity issues, 3270, and VT emulation. Configuration and administration of Oracle and MS SQL databases. Productivity applications—MS Office, MS Mail/Exchange/Outlook, CC Mail, Lotus Notes. Internet applications—MS Front Page, Dreamweaver, Internet Explorer, Netscape Navigator, and Composer. Graphics applications—Photoshop, Paint Shop Pro, AutoCAD, PageMaker, Visio.

EXPERIENCE

AT&T WIRELESS SERVICES—West Palm Beach, FL
1996 to Present

IT Director—National Development Integration   1998 to Present
Part of a national team charged with planning the implementation and ongoing sustainment of all Windows NT/2000 server-based applications in the AT&T Wireless environment. Included homegrown and third-party apps. Worked with internal business customers to develop business requirements, estimate costs, assess products, and uncover alternatives. Major accomplishments include: Project leader for migration of six critical MS Access/SQL-based financial apps to national Citrix thin client sustainment model. Project leader in planning and executing the upgrade of all Windows NT files, messaging, print, and application servers to Windows 2000. Received extensive training in SDF (Software Development Framework) software development methodology.

LAN and Desktop Manager—South Florida   1996 to 1998
Charged with a team of 8 in support of 10 major sites in the South Florida area. Sustained 30+ servers and over 1500 laptops and desktops from Vero Beach to Miami. Developed many of the overall support policies and procedures for the Southeast region. Designed and built a Citrix Metaframe-based environment for sharing MS Access-based financial applications across the national environment. Developed and deployed LAN and Desktop Web site, including Web page authoring, using MS IIS 4.0 and Front Page 98. Responsible for preparing the entire South Florida environment for Y2K, including upgrading all servers from NT 3.51 to 4.0 with appropriate Service Packs, patches, and Bios upgrades, and upgrading all clients to a Win98 or NT4.0 Y2K-certified image. Member of team that developed standardized national log-on script. Deployed national Connect Direct (NDM) data drop site.

MARC L. DONOVAN

EXPERIENCE *(Continued)*

BUSINESS RECORDS CORPORATION—West Palm Beach, FL
1991 to 1996

Oracle Beta Testing and Support, Installer, LAN Administrator
Acted as LAN Administrator while also providing installation, support, and testing functions for a Windows/Oracle-based voter registration data tracking system. Supported four major municipality accounts, including Broward County, with day-to-day troubleshooting via PC Anywhere, Oracle bug checking, and continued enhancements. Performed two major version upgrades. Member of testing team in charge of prerelease quality assurance. Maintained Novell 3.12 environment. Deployed MS Mail to all users. Deployed Cheyenne ARCserve, and implemented back-up procedures.

THE HARTFORD INSURANCE GROUP—Hartford, CT
1985 to 1991

Home Office Systems Administrator
Provided comprehensive technical support for the commercial division of a Top 10 insurance company. Performed installation, configuration, enhancements, user training, and problem solving of PC workstations and WAN. Part of a team supporting 30+ regional offices and home office (3000+ PCs). Traveled to seven national sites as part of a "SWAT" team, installing the client/server network. Migrated all servers from OS/2 to Unix—Fall 1992. Trained new Systems Administrators on use of hardware and software. In-depth Windows 3.0/3.1 troubleshooting. Created numerous DOS batch programs. Edited/created UNIX shell scripts. Member of team that developed network configuration management system. Project lead in configuration and deployment of Remedy help desk management system. Wrote/produced all documentation and training material. Received award in recognition of the project (11/94). Acquired advanced knowledge of NCR Micro channel desktop and server products.

EDUCATION

UNIVERSITY OF MIAMI, Coral Gables, FL
Bachelors of Science: Technology Management, 1984

Professional Development:
Updated Microsoft Training—MS 1560—Updating Support Skills from Windows NT to Windows 2000 and MS 1572—Implementing and Managing MS Exchange 2000, Administering and Supporting MS SQL 7.0, 2001; AT&T School of Business and Technology, Master's Certificate, Project Management, 2000.

Citrix Metaframe Certification Training, 1999; Microsoft Certified Systems Engineer, 1998—Including TCP/IP 4.0 and IIS 4.0

National Computer Security Association
Desktop and LAN Security, Server System Security, and Internet Security Certificates, 1997; Microsoft Certified Professional, 1997; Lotus Notes Consultant Certification Training—Application Development and Administration, 1995.

Reference upon Request

48—IT PROFESSIONAL

LORENCE TREBEL
1420 Heatherley Drive SW
Farmington Hills, Michigan 48335

248.555.5776
emailadddress@emailaddress.com

PROFESSIONAL OVERVIEW

Information Technology Professional. Hands-on visionary with advanced technical expertise. Strong skillset in developing, analyzing, and implementing complex network environments. Extensive product knowledge in hardware/ software deliverables. Successfully meets the challenge of remaining current with new and developing technology.

Excellent qualifications in general management, human resources, client relations, training, and communication in a cutting-edge environment.

Demonstrated leadership with customers and consistent quality in the technical development of colleagues/subordinates. Confident in abilities and committed to performance excellence, providing stability and growth in computing environments.

KEY STRENGTHS

▸ Exceptionally advanced technical knowledge with an ability to manage complex disciplines and circumstances. Provides competence under pressure in highly complicated situations.

▸ Well-developed organizational skills; identifies work plans, considers priorities, forecasts problems, and envisions solutions. Follows up efficiently.

▸ Generates a positive impression while interacting with and supporting customers, as well as cultivating a secure corporate impact to ensure project success.

▸ Clear and convincing oral communication skills; maintains logic and clarity in pressure/intense situations. Extremely clear, succinct, and thorough writing skills; well-prepared in routine or complex subjects.

▸ Proven training/development abilities in cultivating talents within highly-complex environments; adapts style to recipient.

▸ Industry and environment knowledge includes aerospace, healthcare, automotive, manufacturing, wholesale/retail, and finance.

RECENT EXPERIENCE

COMPUWARE CORPORATION   Farmington Hills, Michigan
Specializing in computer information systems management.
PROFESSIONAL STAFF CONSULTANT, 1994-current
Provide leadership in project management through planning, developing, implementing, and managing system and subsystem strategies for Fortune 100 companies.
▸ Analyze, design, present, and implement effective computer system methods that increase corporate productivity.
▸ Work closely with clients to assess individual needs and support effectively.
▸ Train network teams to work cohesively; maintain contact for ongoing instruction.
Achievements:
▸ Top-ranked consultant in the company nationally.
▸ Redesigned money transfer processing for a major retailer which ensured stability of the system, increased efficiency of the work flow, and improved system operating efficiency by 400%.
▸ Drafted and implemented networking standards that provided reliability and growth to computing environments.
▸ Project managed a national, multisite network upgrade (including proposals, forecasts, and submissions) encompassing more than 2000 end users; on time and within budget.

(Continued)

PREVIOUS EXPERIENCE

INTELLIGENCE NETWORK SYSTEMS , INC.   Bloomfield Hills, Michigan
MANAGER — Technical Services, 1992-94
Responsible for the direction and management of technical services for value-added reseller
activities, including installation, support, maintenance of products, and service contracts.
Supervised a staff of 20 technical specialists.
- ▸ Evaluated new and projected technologies for company growth.
- ▸ Interacted with clients and acted as liaison between executive management for customer
  support, conflict resolution, design specifications, quality, and project/program progress.
- ▸ Provided training and ongoing support to technicians and customers.

SIERRA MAGNETIC SYSTEMS COMPANY   Ypsilanti, Michigan
NETWORK/OPERATING SYSTEM SPECIALIST, 1990-92
Traveled extensively throughout the nation supporting the large computer manufacturing
firm. Led training assignments for the top 140 VARs in the nation.
- ▸ Provided technical support, training, and consultation to corporate clients, internal
  technical staff, marketing, and sales group.
- ▸ Attended trade shows; furnished technical information on company product lines.
- ▸ Successfully resolved 100% of all internal/external assignments.

COMPUTERWORLD — **SERVICE MANAGER/TECHNICIAN**, 1987-89

SELF-EMPLOYED — **CONSULTANT/INFORMATION BROKER**, 1984-current

EDUCATION / PROFESSIONAL DEVELOPMENT

SCHOOLCRAFT COLLEGE   Livonia, Michigan
   Concentration: Computer Science

DALE CARNEGIE — Effective Speaking and Human Relations

IBM Training Certified: PS/2 Hardware Services; OS/2; DOS Networking; LAN Server,
   Quality Service Skills.

Novell Training Certified: NetWare System Manager and Advanced System Manager;
   NetWare Service and Support.

Microsoft: Windows Technical Certification.

Synoptics Certified: Ethernet Connectivity; Token Ring Connectivity; TCP/IP Fundamentals;
   LattisNet Manager.

Netframe: VAR Service Certification; Advanced Application Processor; Advanced
   Benchmark & Network Tuning.

TECHNICAL ADDENDUM

OS Platforms: NetWare; OS/2; Windows 3.x, 95, 98, NT 3.x & 4.x; DOS; Macintosh; SCO
   UNIX; Xenix; Linux; Solaris; A/IX; HP/UX; LAN Manager; LAN Server; Banyan Vines.

Hardware Platforms: AST; Compaq; Dell; Gateway; HP; IBM; Macintosh; NCR; Netframe; Sun.

Topologies: Ethernet; Token Ring; FDDI; ISDN; T1; ATM; Frame Relay.

Protocols: TCP/IP; IPX/SPX; AppleTalk; Netbeui; Netbios.

General: routers, bridges, concentrators, switches; project analysis, deployment and
   management; remote access gateways; specification of hardware/software; development
   of documentation for operations and end users; backup strategies; disaster recovery;
   performance measurement and tuning; network and information security; network
   analysis, administration, architecture, design, migration, and troubleshooting.

LORENCE TREBEL
1420 Heatherley Drive SW — Farmington Hills, Michigan 48335 — 248.555.5776

49—LAN ENGINEER

PATRICK SWINDELL, CNE

123 Reilly Road • Greenville, North Carolina 29720 • (555) 555-5555 • patswindell@yahoo.com

CAREER SUMMARY

- **Highly skilled, senior NETWORK ENGINEER with expertise in Novell NetWare, Windows NT, and Lotus Notes operations, administration, and management**
- **Experienced PROJECT MANAGER with proven record of successful project completion within budget and time deadlines**
- **Widely capable of operating across entire client-server spectrum of applications, methodologies, and connectivity**
- **Strong TEAM LEADER able to motivate and encourage engineers to high levels of productivity and efficiency while maximizing morale and job satisfaction**

TECHNICAL SKILLS

Ethernet
Token Ring
Novell Netware 4.x, 5.x
Windows NT Server
IntraNetware
TCP/IP
IPX/SPX
DNS
Intel LANDesk Management Suite
Novell Application Launcher
Novell ZEN Works

Lotus Notes
Lotus Freelance Graphics
Micrographx Flowcharter
MS Access
PC Anywhere
SQL Server
Citrix Winframe
Citrix Metaframe
Norton Antivirus Corporate Edition
Powerquest Drive Image
Rumba

PROFESSIONAL EXPERIENCE

PJS.com • Research Triangle Park, North Carolina

LAN ENGINEER III / TEAM LEADER   **1998-PRESENT**

Managed complex technology projects throughout full life cycle including costing, budget management, and documentation. Coordinated technology with business units to determine best network solutions for project needs Led enterprisewide software and hardware deployments. Served as group leader to Level III Support team consisting of 5 Level III LAN Engineers managing 150 file servers, both NetWare and NT-based. Applied expertise in NT, Lotus Notes, and NetWare on complex issues and served as escalation point for Level III support. Administered automating application deployments facilitating support actions for Level I and II engineers.

(Continued)

49—LAN ENGINEER (CONT.)

Pat Swindell, CNE • Page 2

LAN Engineer III continued...

- **Directed complex, parallel rollout project of Lotus Notes from RFP stage to deployment/support. Coordinated with vendor and managed subcontractors to successfully redeploy 4500 Lotus Notes clients and configuration/deployment of 15 Lotus Domino servers.**
- **Successfully deployed 40 of company's 150 servers with zero loss of productivity and completely within time/budget constraints.**
- **Achieved deployment of 35 servers and upgraded from NetWare 3.x to 4.x, successfully meeting an aggressive 3-month deadline for Y2K compliance.**

LAN Engineer II   **1995-1998**

Applied technical expertise in hands-on fashion to network projects and software rollouts. Developed and integrated automated application deployment using ZEN Works and original applications. Assured client-server integrity and AS/400 connectivity. Worked as part of a 4-person team on deployment of NetWare for SAA and MS SNA Server projects.

- **Teamed with vendor and internal teams to create and deploy Rumba as enterprisewide host emulation for connectivity to AS/400 and Digital VAX mainframes; trained 1st, 2nd, and 3rd level support teams on operations.**
- **Successfully created and deployed standardized desktops for entire corporation using PowerQuest Drive Image in preparation for Windows 95 deployment.**
- **Managed numerous server conversion and upgrade projects moving from NetWare 3.x to 4.11. Upgraded servers, migrated information/data, and assured functionality for end users.**

Staff Programmer   **1994-1995**

Teamed on implementation of production scheduling application for division. Worked directly with Industrial Engineers on specifications due to educational background and knowledge of process. Served as liaison between Industrial Engineers and vendor on application needs and customization.

EDUCATION AND TRAINING

Bachelor of Science – Industrial Engineering
North Carolina State University
1988 • Class Valedictorian

Certified NetWare Engineer (CNE)
4.x, 5.x • 1997

"Business Management and Leadership Development" – University of South Carolina, 1999

CIVIC INVOLVEMENT

Eagle Scout – Boy Scouts of America
Civitan Club – Member since 1998

50—LANGUAGE SPECIFIC PROGRAMMER

E. Mark Young

5678 Terry Avenue
Bristol, CT 06010

emailaddress@emailaddress.com

Home: **860.555.4321**
Business: 860.555.1234

SOFTWARE DEVELOPMENT / UNIX / LINUX / DATABASE
Web, distributed and object-oriented programming
using a light client / client-server / n-tier model

- Strong object-oriented design and development skills; fluent in C, C++, Java, Perl, Javascript, HTML, DHTML, C and Bourne Shell, SQL, CORBA, RMI, Livelink OScript.
- Skilled in development, maintenance and enhancement of applications.
- E-business application experience encompasses interfacing IS development projects to the Web and Web development.

Operating Systems: Linux, UNIX (Solaris Sparc and x86, AIX, HP-UX), Windows NT/95/98, DEC VAX VMS
Server Applications: UNIX/Linux (BIND, Sendmail, SSH, NFS, Samba), Apache, JServ/JRun/Tomcat, IIS, LiveLink.
Programming Languages: C, C++, Java, Perl, Assembler (ix86,VAX,6502,6800), C and Bourne Shell, CORBA, RMI, OpenGL, UNIX System Programming (RPC, Sockets, etc.), XWindows (Some Motif/Gtk/Qt/Java AWT and Swing), Javascript, HTML/DHTML, XML, Livelink OScript, Java Server Pages (JSP), Active Server Pages (ASP).
Database Systems: Oracle, PostgreSQL, Microsoft SQL Server, Microsoft Access, MiniSQL/MySQL
Graphics: 2D and 3D programming, OpenGL
Networking: HTTP/HTTPS, TCP/IP, PPP
Security Applications: PGP, OpenSSL/SSLeay, SSH, Linux Firewall

PROFESSIONAL EXPERIENCE:

A Software Development Company, Hartford, Connecticut   10/97 - Present
Software Developer
Contracted through **High Technology (HiTech)** to **Major Pharmaceutical Corporation** to develop software applications on UNIX servers to facilitate the research and development of pharmaceuticals. Used Apache, Perl, Java, CORBA, HTML, Oracle 8.

Project: Revised Data Viewer (DV) to facilitate accessibility and manipulation of Oracle relational database on a Perl-based server for evaluation of scientific data. Used Web-based interface to display views of clinical data. Enhanced and extended viewing functionality. Broadened paradigm from single to multiple data sources. Added statistical capabilities to server to enhance views and facilitate research calculations. Substantially increased research productivity.

Pilot Project: Developed prototype for Electronic Monitoring Forms (EMF); created supporting documentation. Prototype incorporates electronic signatures to expedite the process of document correction and to facilitate electronic transmission of documents, both between researchers and into automated filing system. This EMF prototype is now pending FDA Part 11 compliance approval.

(Continued on Page Two)

163

Perform research & development on Linux with Java servlets, RMI, PostgreSQL, SSL, and PGP. Additional projects:

Community-Technical College, Bristol, CT: Created online informational site for college courses, faculty and departments, utilizing Java servlets and JDBC.

Local Public Television (LPTV): Assisted in development of an online auction system which has successfully replaced the previous Achalkboard@ auction method. Created on a Linux server using PostgreSQL and Java servlets.

InformationSpecialists, Bristol, CT   1/96 - 10/97
Software Engineer/Database Engineer
Wrote/ran database inventory software. Aided in CGI and GIS development.

PROFESSIONAL DEVELOPMENT:

Livelink OScript: MorningStar, Baltimore, MD
Continual self-development in Java, CORBA, RMI, and other programming languages/tools.

EDUCATION:

UNIVERSITY OF HARTFORD, Ward College of Technology
B.S. Electronic Engineering Technology: 3.7 GPA

51—MAIL ADMINISTRATOR

Lori Denman

1234 Westpark Boulevard • Euless, Texas 76040 • (555) 555-5555 • cell: (000) 000-

KEY QUALIFICATIONS

Experienced technical professional with strong abilities in network mail operations on a global scale
Established experience in network environments including both NT and Novell
Positive communications skills demonstrated through excellent record of team cooperation and customer relations
Dedicated work ethic — flexible in schedule — goal-oriented — self-guided

TECHNICAL EXPERTISE

Windows NT	MS Outlook	MVS
Novell LAN Network	Micro Focus NetExpress	TSO
MS Exchange	IMS	MS Office Suite
Unix	JCL	ISDN
Lotus Notes	EASYTRIEVE PLUS	TCP/IP
MS Mail	TELON	PPP
CC:Mail	Macintosh	POP3

PROFESSIONAL EXPERIENCE

MailSolutions.com • Ft. Worth, Texas

MAIL ADMINISTRATOR   **1998- PRESENT**

Supported in house and global mail servers and supervised 13 Email Analysts in daily operations of outsourced mail administration operations. Served as third-level escalation point for all complex, technical difficulties. Coordinated with Security Team on infiltration issues and user administration. Documented incidences and provided networkwide security updates. Trained new Email Analysts on procedures and operations. Provided discovery information to new accounts on spectrum of products and solutions.

> Worked with FCC and FBI on successful tracking and acquisition of security threat to major account through message tracking and security monitoring.

EMAIL TECHNICAL ANALYST   **1997-1998**

Worked diligently to provide mail administration across a global WAN in a Novell environment without any loss of productivity or server time. Migrated mailboxes from server to server requiring servers to be brought down remotely and regenerated without loss of service to Local Users, despite differences in time zones. Monitored mail servers and file sizes. Updated employee information in databases to provide accurate information.

> Administered email for large, Fortune 500 companies such as American Airlines and Coca-Cola on a global scale, working across time zones without loss of server operability to end users

EDUCATION AND TRAINING

Bachelor of Science — Information Systems   THE UNIVERSITY OF TEXAS AT ARLINGTON — 1999
Training:
> DB2 • IMS • TSO Environments • Xpediter • File-Aid

52—MANAGEMENT CONSULTANT (E-MAIL RESUME)

Renee Christian
2724 Cameron Street
Washington, DC 20008
W (703) 555-1212, H (202) 555-1212
renee.christian@mail.argi.net

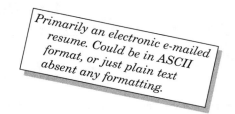
Primarily an electronic e-mailed resume. Could be in ASCII format, or just plain text absent any formatting.

EXPERIENCE

A.T. Kearney - EDS Management Consulting Services
Washington, DC
Principal, 1996 - present
Senior Manager, 1994-1996

Specialized in the development of business plans for emerging wireline and wireless telecommunications companies. Responsible for client relationship management and sales into preexisting client base. Responsible for managing large (up to 30 people) work teams. Provided advice to senior management on a broad variety of strategic and operational subjects, including:
-Business strategy and planning
-Financial modeling
-Competitive assessment
-Market segmentation
-Operations design and optimization
-Mergers and acquisitions
-Implementation assistance
-Churn management

Deloitte & Touche Management Consulting
Washington, DC
Manager, 1993-1994
Senior Consultant, 1991-1993

Primarily focused on developing market-entry strategies for telecommunications clients. Developed very strong financial modeling skills. Responsible for managing smaller projects and developing client deliverables.

EDUCATION

B.S. in Physics, Montana State University, 1989
MBA in Finance, Carnegie Mellon University, 1991

PUBLICATIONS / SPEECHES

"An Ice Age is Coming to the Wireless World: A Perspective on the Future of Mobile Telephony in the United States," 1995
Thought Leadership Series, EDS Management Consulting

"Analysis of the FCC's Order Regarding Ameritech's Application to Provide InterLATA Toll Services Within the State of Michigan," A.T. Kearney White Paper, 1997

Presented at over two dozen industry conferences, workshops, and panels

> *More conventional resume layout,*
> *with good "Career Profile" and*
> *"Areas of Expertise" sections.*
> *Very clean and professional.*

MARK DALGLISH

897 Village Drive
Springfield, VA 22150
Home: (703) 555-4387 - Fax: (703) 555-0843
E-mail: email@emailaddress.com

E-MARKETING / ON-LINE MARKETING DIRECTOR
Award-Winning Pioneer and Expert in Web / Internet / New Media Marketing

---

CAREER PROFILE

Web-savvy marketing professional accomplished in creating and leading high-impact marketing campaigns that consistently meet aggressive e-business goals. Initiated groundbreaking programs and delivered large revenue gains. Excel in both start-up and mature corporate environments. Strong leader known for tenacity and positive "can-do" attitude. Fully fluent in interactive and Internet technologies and tools.

AREAS OF EXPERTISE

- Web, Print, & Broadcast Advertising
- Business Development Initiatives
- Community Building & Customer Loyalty
- E-Business Strategies & Technologies
- Product Launch Strategy & Execution

- Partnership & Alliance Building
- On-line Relationship Marketing
- Market Awareness Building
- User Acquisition & Retention
- Staff Development & Leadership

PROFESSIONAL HISTORY

ComputerTrends.com **1998 - Present**
Dynamic start up e-business offering PC-related sales, service, and support in the business-to-business (B2B) and business-to-consumer (B2C) markets.

E-MARKETING DIRECTOR

- Led development and execution of marketing strategies and new business initiatives that drove rapid growth, from the ground floor to $8.2 million.

- Pioneered a fully functional marketing department infrastructure, including policies and procedures, streamlined business processes, and a talented marketing and communications team.

- Created and deployed unique advertising campaigns proven successful in positioning the company with a competitive distinction. Won national attention for innovative and edgy ads that piqued interest in the target markets.

- Delivered 54% ROI from marketing efforts by employing a shrewd balance of Internet and traditional print and broadcast medias to maximize results.

- Negotiated and structured 8 major business partnerships and alliances; built and led successful win-win programs through cost-effective co-marketing initiatives.

Real Estate Sales, Inc. **1994 - 1998**
Leading national real estate brokerage company with more than 4000 offices and 50,000 sales associates in 50 U.S. states.

SENIOR MARKETING MANAGER

- Guided strategic planning, development, and leadership for all marketing and external communications strategies. Managed a 25-person team and $20 million annual budget.

- Coordinated creation and implementation of all print and broadcast advertising, image building, collateral sales support materials, direct mail, special events, relationship marketing, and electronic marketing.

- Conceived and launched the most extensive real estate Web site on the Internet with over 1.2 million listings, generating 770,000 unique visitors each week and fortifying sales with more than 2500 customer leads each month.

(Continued)

MARK DALGLISH

PROFESSIONAL HISTORY CONTINUED

National ISP, Inc.   **1988 - 1994**
One of the nationwide largest Internet service providers, known for consistent positioning as a leading-edge provider of on-line services to consumers and businesses.

MARKETING & COMMUNICATIONS MANAGER

- Spearheaded strategy development and implementation, growing revenues more than $15 million by launching the company's on-line services within the retail environment.

- Revitalized languishing member acquisitions; conceived and initiated a special "Member get a Member" on-line promotion that was credited with consistently generating 68% of total membership.

- Negotiated and contracted against the competition for the company to be the sole on-line service exhibitor at Disney's Epcot Center, a position that ramped membership by 135,000 users the first year.

- Directed an 8-person staff; resolved challenging performance, ethical, and employee issues through aggressive corrective actions and a leadership style that inspired top performance.

Omni Advertising   **1984 - 1988**
Large advertising agency serving a diverse B2C and B2B clientele, overseeing the creation and execution of multimillion dollar campaigns.

ACCOUNT EXECUTIVE (1985 - 1988)
ASSISTANT ACCOUNT EXECUTIVE (1984 - 1985)

- Planned strategies and repositioned a major cable network from a vertical sports network to a horizontal family channel; guided all consumer and affiliate marketing on both the local and national level.

- Conceptualized, developed, and implemented advertising and marketing programs for a portfolio of 10 major accounts. Personally designed and produced 3 critically-acclaimed, award-winning television spots.

- Played an instrumental role in driving the most successful new cable network launch in history, topping over 60 million subscribers in two years despite a highly competitive market with limited channel space.

EDUCATION & TRAINING

M.B.A., Marketing and Communications
Boston University, MA (1990)

B.S., Business Administration
University of Kentucky, Lexington (1984)

Recent Continuing Education:
- 7 Habits of Highly Successful People, Stephen Covey Leadership
- Delegation & Team Effort, Boston University, Executive Education
- Building Customer Loyalty, The Duncan Group

PROFESSIONAL ACTIVITIES

Building your Digital Business - Featured speaker, BMA conference, 1999
High-Impact Marketing - Keynote speaker, NAFME conference, 1999
Preparing your Business for a Digital World – Keynote speaker, IAPM conference 1998

ASSOCIATIONS

Business Marketing Association – Current Board of Directors, Past President
Power Marketing Association – Current Board of Directors
American Marketing Association – Current Member

> *Large font size for name might be a little aggressive, depending on position and individual. Good summary to open and supporting details in "Experience" section.*

DEENA MARZETTI

Director of Media Integration - Executive Web Producer

e-mail@e-mailaddress.com

503-555-5030

❖ Six years of success in promoting the strategic vision of e-commerce sites through Web design, architecture, and content.

❖ Serve as the nexus among all Web disciplines, interactive/design agencies, external partners, internal designers and developers, hosting providers, and content providers.

❖ Demonstrated skill in managing production work flow from brainstorming phase through award-winning implementation in a variety of media, capitalizing on the core competencies of technical and creative teams.

❖ Expert project management, effectively identifying and managing milestones, dependencies, and bottlenecks by creating production standards, gathering initial user requirements, collecting user feedback, generating and refining specifications for the development cycle.

❖ Innovative design of user interfaces and site navigation features, co-creating and managing the logical flow of content. Exceptional knowledge of copy writing, editing, graphic design, typography, and film/video production.

❖ In depth knowledge of Web usability, cross browser environments, navigation, content management, technical development, hosting, site metrics, and databases.

❖ Proficient in HTML, dHTML, JavaScript, Cold Fusion, ASP, PhotoShop, Dreamweaver, NT, IIS, SQL-Server, Illustrator, Fireworks, ImageReady, GoLive, PageMill, FTP, MS Office, and MS Project.

EXPERIENCE

CyberShoppingMall.com, Seattle, WA   1998-Present
Director of Media Integration

❖ Support the corporate mission of delivering the fastest, most effective merchandising and display technology systems to maximize sales and advertising for clients of this provider of next-generation e-commerce sites and 3D applications.

❖ Direct a team of 12 in the ongoing development and exploitation of core and complementary technologies on company and client Web sites.

❖ Provide project leadership for Web site production, including: budget control, production schedule, status reporting, deliverables definition and accomplishment, client/ project team coordination, and quality assurance.

❖ Team with executive producer and art director to implement HTML and graphics, guiding all facets of content development.

❖ Collaborate with product managers to develop long-term strategic objectives, product specifications, and implementation tactics. Devise and implement new Web solutions in partnership with the JSP/ASP/database development team.

❖ Develop and execute annual plan outlining Web projects and budgets, as well as online marketing campaigns and budgets. Build and maintain relationships with interactive Web service agencies and Internet service providers.

❖ Execute, monitor, and continually improve e-commerce programs. Collaborate with IS, Distribution, and Brand teams to gather and deliver content in line with marketing and e-commerce objectives.

❖ Manage project and production schedules as necessary to meet deadlines and budgets. Generate Web site reports, analyze data, and utilize information for online marketing decisions.

CONTINUED NEXT PAGE

DEENA MARZETTI

DEENA MARZETTI

Page 2 ~ e-mail@e-mailaddress.com ~ 503-555-5030

EXPERIENCE
CONTINUED

NaturoHealth.com, San Francisco, CA   1997-1998
Media Integration Consultant

❖ Redesigned architecture and content for leading natural health e-commerce/portal site. Created structure, organization, and navigation for multiple customer-focused channels.

❖ Implemented interactive features, banner ads, affiliate programs, and links. Supervised HTML and graphic design teams. Interfaced with engineering, database management, merchandising, marketing, and business development departments.

❖ Completed project a month ahead of schedule and $25,000 under budget.

NetsMakeADeal.com, Los Angeles, CA   1996-1997
User Interface Project Manager

❖ Managed front-end development for a high-traffic e-commerce Web site. Coordinated efforts with back-end team for integration of site functionality.

❖ Sourced writers, designers, and technical specialists and supervised production process. Recruited and managed HTML/JavaScript developers. Motivated staffs and fostered positive, productive team environment.

❖ Designed graphical elements, including logos, layout, ads, and icons. Managed/maintained server files using PCAnywhere and FTP protocols, and ad-rotator middle-ware.

❖ Provided guidance on development of shopping cart and transaction interfaces. Balanced long-term projects with bi-weekly releases, fixes, and site updates.

❖ Served as Customer Advocate, identifying and organizing customer focus groups and online feedback. Solved user and site problems by translating important functional issues into technical solutions.

❖ Generated site activity reports, analyzing data from multiple perspectives. Utilized information for online marketing decisions as well as ISP accountability for uptime, latency, and connectivity.

The New Media Group, Inc., Los Angeles, CA   1994-1996
Producer

❖ Produced high-end Web applications for entertainment, e-commerce, B2B, and consumer organizations. Managed high-profile clients including AOL, Discovery Online, PBS Online, Intel, and The World Bank.

EDUCATION & AFFILIATIONS

❖ Certified Web Administration & Development Professional, Certified Intranet/Internet Professional, 1999, Learning Tree International.
❖ Bachelor of Arts, Communications and English, University of Washington, 1990
❖ Member, Association for Internet Professionals
❖ Member, Association for Multimedia Communications

55—METAFRAME/SERVER SPECIALIST

Dorothy Nieto

142 Mill Run Lane
ovi, Michigan 48375
idence: 248.555.9735

emailaddress@emailaddress

> *Excellent concise resume. Good use of "Professional Profile" and overall layout. Notice how the second-page "Technical Addendum" gives the readers all the information they should need to grasp this candidate's qualifications.*

PROFESSIONAL PROFILE

Ambitious Metaframe/Server Specialist with a broad background in complex technical system support. Experienced analyst who accepts personal responsibility for assignments and initiates strong independent effort. Understands and applies technology applications in a high-tech environment. Well-developed technical skills implementing and supporting corporate system initiatives. Background includes:

- Technical Project Management
- Hardware/Software/Network Applications
- WACN/CAN/LAN/MAN/WAN Support

- System Analysis & Troubleshooting
- Training & User Support
- Business & Technical Writing

EXPERIENCE

CITY NATIONAL BANK   West Bloomfield, Michigan
METAFRAME/SERVER SPECIALIST, 1998-current
Deliver information system technical support at the headquarters of national banking operations. Manage projects that support mortgage applications and online banking concerns; assist in troubleshooting operations.

- Manage technical projects; build/rebuild files; transport files to headquarter departments and branches via internal (Bravura) system.
- Troubleshoot a broad range of hardware/software issues; assist customers with specific online loan fulfillment, application, and online banking problems.
- Handle an average of 30 concerns daily with a resolution factor of 94%. *(Typical daily volume averages 10-12 concerns with a resolution closing of 25%.)*

EDS (Electronic Data Systems)   Troy, Michigan
BUSINESS ANALYST, 1997-98
Provided system administration and technical assistance for more than 8,000 DaimlerChrysler dealerships worldwide, DC personnel, and contract employees.

- Trained and supervised new hires and other employees for online dealership project.
- Served as Subject Matter Expert for a team of 15 employees troubleshooting technical hardware issues on LAN/WAN/MAN.
- Member of satellite repoint team for worldwide program.

WRITEON   Novi, Michigan
OWNER/WRITER, 1995-current
Entrepreneurial business utilizing creativity and unique writing skills to create corporate advertising material and newsletters, company forms and letters, and e-commerce business.

- Manage all business operations through Internet, mail order, catalogue, and point-of-sale merchandising.

MEDICAL CLINIC   Ann Arbor, Michigan
OFFICE ADMINISTRATOR, 1992-97
Managed diverse office functions and AP/AR procedures for highly specialized medical clinic. Applied complex computerized documentation techniques for general accounting, advertising, correspondence, and overall office processes.

EDUCATION & TRAINING

OAKLAND UNIVERSITY   Auburn Hills, Michigan
Computer Information Systems & Business Management curriculum toward BA degree

Technical Addendum – attached

(Continued)

55—METAFRAME/SERVER SPECIALIST (CONT.)

OPERATING SYSTEMS
Windows 3.1, 95, 98, NT; Linux

COMPUTERS
Workstations/PCs/Desktops: Compaqs, IBM, Dell, NEC, Gateway, Hitachi SuperScan 752, Macintosh, notebooks/laptops

LAN/WAN/WACN and OTHER APPLICATIONS
Lotus Notes, Quattro Pro, WordPerfect, Rconsole, Pconsole, PowerPoint, Netscape, AOL (America Online), Microsoft Internet Explorer, Adobe Acrobat, DCCNET, TELNET. Microsoft Office, Microsoft Excel, Microsoft Outlook & Express; Quicken, ClarisWorks, DC Security Guardian (in-house application); Adobe Photoshop, Lotus 1-2-3

CALL TRACKING APPLICATIONS
Lotus Notes, Vantive, and R.E.M.

UTILITIES, TOOLS, & DIAL-UP CONNECTIONS (ADAPTERS)
PC Anywhere, MCI WorldCom, FS UserLink, RAS (Remote Access System), NetWare Tools, MS-DOS, Ping Connectivity, HP JetAdmin, and WebTelnet. Ethernet cards/adapters

LANGUAGES
SQL Script Plus 8.0, Basic HTML

PROTOCOLS/DEVICES
TCP/IP, IPX, SPX

SERVERS
IBM, Windows NT 4.0, SQL, Metaframe

HARDWARE
Modems (Internal/External). NIC (network cards). Printers: HP DeskJet, LaserJet, fax, scan & print, tape drives, backup tapes and cleaning cartridges. HUB (Netilligent), UPS (APC SMART, battery backup system), LAN, SCSI, and crossover cables, SCSI drives, hard drives, monitors, CD-ROMS, CPUs, satellites (Earthstation), DIU (Digital Interface Unit)

NETWORKS
WACN/CAN/LAN/MAN/WAN, mapping to a network drive, Galpools, notes, file, and print servers, satellite server network, and Novell Interware

TROUBLESHOOTING & CONFIGURATION
Printer driver downloads - adding/deleting, remapping - installing/configuration, troubleshooting error messages on networks, specific applications, personal computers/ workstations/laptops/notebooks as well as file/notes/print servers, and tape drives, HUB and satellite errors. Network connectivity: Server/Workstation lockups, frozen, server down. Move/add/change requests, password resets, workstation setup, adding icons, mail encryption, attaching, detaching, and viewing documents; user ID requests, delivery failure, I/O reports. LAN connectivity, shared/missing drives, authorization to shared and public folders, hardware breaks/fixes, physical connectivity. General workstation troubleshooting: screen savers, resolution, launching applications, pinging, passwords in boot-up sector, setup (F10 configurations), and launching applications. Cold and warm boots; reboots and booting issues. Hardware dispatch and service

56—MIS DIRECTOR

STEPHEN N. HOLLAND

120 Cambridge * Berkley, Michigan 48072 * 248.555.1212 * email@email.com

DIRECTOR MIS

Manager in BigS Consulting Firm
Successful Manager of People, Process, and Technology
eCommerce Expertise in Growth and Profit Generation

A motivated, innovative, growth-oriented IT Consultant with positive, contagious energy who builds teams, creates relationships, and earns trust. Strategically and tactfully resolves and troubleshoots problems. A high-impact, multidimensional IT professional respected by his peers/superiors with a verifiable record of achievement of exceeding expectations.

CORE STRENGTHS

Information systems issues, risks, development, implementation	Business process analysis and improvement
Vision, strategy, and assessing market opportunities	Product development and enhancement
Teaching, leading, and empowering team members	Business and technical acumen
Relationship development skills; building strategic alliances	Web design and E-commerce technology

PROFESSIONAL EXPERIENCE

ERNST & YOUNG, LLP, Detroit, Michigan   1997 to Current
MIS Director

MIS Director for the Information Systems Assurance and Advisory Services (ISAAS) practice. A history of success delivering measurable value to a myriad of clients in multiple industries, from Fortune 1000 to small, high-growth companies. Extensive experience managing risk as organizations apply technology to complex internal and external business processes. Strategically focused in eProcurement, Internet security, venture acceleration, business process analysis/design, and IT strategy. Helped Ernst & Young develop eProcurement and eCommerce methodologies and build market share. Creates teams, empowers people, and delivers results. Innovative thinker. Pursuit leader on sales efforts. Delivers measurable value on every project.

- Lake Erie region ISAAS eProcurement and eCommerce leader.
- Selected to deliver eCommerce presentation at the annual national Ernst & Young accounting update meeting.
- Selected as ISAAS leader on Ann Arbor territory expansion and pursuit team.
- Increased revenue streams through demonstrating value to clients' IT organization and business processes.
- Successfully managed client expectations on all projects resulting in additional work/favorable client referrals.
- Instrumental in building the ISAAS practice, trained staff/senior consultants in successful client service delivery.
- Industry expertise includes healthcare, insurance, manufacturing, and banking.

Listing of Ernst & Young Major Projects:

Project Name	Description
Venture Acceleration	Accelerated venture business plans to first round of funding. Activities include business modeling, revenue modeling, content sourcing, value chain analysis, competitive analysis, and product definition and design.
Business Plan Assessment	Assessed start-up business plans.
eProcurement	Managed and led strategic eProcurement ROT and diagnostic assessments
Internet Security	Implemented Axent's Technologies NetProwler and Intruder Alert host and network-based intrusion detection software.
Internet Security	Assessed online systems security of B2B transportation provider.
Business Process Analysis	Defined business process improvement opportunities for a myriad of clients in multiple industries.
IT Strategy	Conducted an IT departmental budget assessment.
Due Diligence	Assessed ASP internet start-up as due diligence for potential Venture Capitalist.
Systems Consulting	Defined and assessed technical and functional requirements.

(Continued)

Stephen N. Holland Page two
PROFESSIONAL EXPERIENCE

BLUE CROSS & BLUE SHIELD OF MICHIGAN, Southfield, Michigan   1994 to 1997
Workflow & Imaging Consultant, Contract through Computer Methods Corporation
Assisted Blue Cross Blue Shield in the design of the dental claims imaging system. Was the only consultant on the business side of the imaging project. Led client teams in defining business process and system requirements for various automated work flow queues. Defined detail process flows for work flow and imaging system design. Codeveloped system reporting requirements with client management team.

- Selected by users/management to facilitate business process improvement initiatives with orthodontic work team.
- Defined and established benchmark criteria for the Dental Imaging System to measure overall project success.
- Designed, developed, and implemented dental claim appeals-tracking database that is still in use today.

COMPUTER METHODS CORPORATION (CMC), Livonia, Michigan   1987 to 1994
Project Manager (1992–94)
Employed with CMC for over five years as a Project Manager, Account Executive, and Business Analyst for this $30-million software consulting firm. Reported directly to the President and CEO for three years. Selected in 1997 to lead the Imaging Technologies business unit after much employee turnover, customer dissatisfaction, and lack of organizational structure. Instrumental in achieving stability, increasing revenues, cutting costs, consolidating customer confidence.

- Directed Imaging Technologies business unit operations, responsible for $1.2 million in annual revenues.
- Successfully negotiated new business and renewal contracts with small and Fortune 1000 clients.
- Consistently increased group profitability on a quarterly basis.
- Comanaged implementation of OCR technology integrated with custom-developed claims adjudication software.
- Successfully managed department's staff of 30+ people (programmers, network admin, and administrative staff).
- Responsible for business unit financial planning and budgeting.

Account Executive (1990–92)

- Responsible for high-growth, middle-market clientele sector, successfully increased annual sector revenue.
- Sold client/server solutions, wrote and presented comprehensive proposals for custom application development, established new revenue streams.
- Main liaison between customer and development team, managed customer expectations.
- Selected as sales and marketing contact for Microsoft's Solution Provider program.

Business Analyst (1987–90)
- Defined user, business, and system requirements for scope and design documents.
- Identified & tracked corporate quality measurables, lead contributor to Ford's on-site Q1 quality audit.

EDUCATION / TRAINING

Bachelor of Arts Degree, 1993   **ALBION COLLEGE, Albion, Michigan**

Dual Majors: **Mathematics**, GPA: 3.8 / 4.0; **Economics**, GPA: 3.8 /4.0
Concentration: Carl A. Gerstacker Professional Management Program; Business Study Exchange, Germany, Summer, 1993

Training: Certified Document Imaging Architect (expected 2/2001); Commerce One eProcurement Technical Training; People-Soft Application Controls Training

ACTIVITIES

Junior Achievement High School Economics Teacher and Consultant
Troy High School, Volunteer Football Coach
Albion College Class Agent, Class of '93; Albion College Leadership Campaign Committee Member

57—MIS MANAGER

GARY NOGUERA

15 Marshwood Road, Brightwaters, NY 11706
voice ● 516-555-5555   e-mail ● gn@aol.com

Senior-level Information Systems Group Manager

- Bottom-line oriented executive with over fifteen years of comprehensive experience in profitable oversight of teams *and* technology. Produce consistent achievements in cutting-edge information systems management, team management, contract negotiations, purchasing logistics, and expense reduction. Utilize an anticipatory management style to drive results in a rapidly changing industry.

- Manage information systems group supporting production and business operations for Newsday, the nation's seventh largest newspaper. Supervise 48 direct reports and control $5 million+ operating budget. Research, assess, and approve technology purchases. Implement system improvements to maintain profitable, competitive, and quality-driven production processes.

Key Management and Technology Abilities

- Advanced Technologies
- Resource Management
- Project Planning/Budgets
- Project Management
- Expense Reduction
- Team Building/Motivation
- Presentations
- Capital Expenditure Planning

- Technology Needs Assessment
- Technology Rightsizing/Upgrades
- Win-Win Negotiations
- RFP Development/Review
- Vendor Partnerships
- Network Administration
- Project Lifecycle
- UNIX, SUN, LAN, WAN

- Systems Configuration
- Systems Implementation
- Parallel Systems Operation
- Intranet Development
- Technology Integration
- Disaster Recovery
- Systems Security
- Year 2000 Solutions

Summary of Major Accomplishments

- Reorganized entire Newsday Business Systems operation and hardware for 20% productivity improvement and a $230 thousand savings against operating expenses. Reduced footprint, allowing department's relocation to main building, freeing old location for lucrative commercial rental.

- Recruited and led team of volunteers to independently develop Information Systems Department's Intranet Server. Program was so successful that it was adopted companywide and became part of Information Systems Department's long-range strategic plan.

- Led project team that planned and implemented Newsday $4.8 million pagination project representing cutting-edge production technology. Project delivered ROI in only two and one-half years.

- Increased productivity and reduced expenses by purchase of new Tivoli system, replacing "manual" monitoring/installation method which provided fast-response central network monitoring, asset management, and LAN central software distribution to 1,200 desktops and 35 servers.

- Developed and implemented $680 thousand network project that replaced old copper Ethernets with a fiber-optic backbone and Cat5 10baseT wiring to the desktop utilizing dynamic switching hubs.

(Continued)

GARY NOGUERA   page two

Network, Client Server, and Software Technology

- Fiber-Optic Backbone
- LAN and WAN
- Wide Area Networks Through T-1 lines
- Class B Internet license
- TCP / IP
- Firewall One, Hub Watch
- Wellfleet and Cisco Routers
- Dial and Dedicated Remote Communications
- Frame Relay
- DEC 900 Dynamic Switching Hubs
- Switched and Shared Ethernet Circuits

- Tivoli LAN Management system
- UNIX Operating Systems
- SUN Solaris and Raid Disk Technology
- Sybase Relational Database
- WinFrame Syntrex for Thin Client/Fat Server
- NT Alpha Server with Microsoft Mail
- Windows 3.1, 95, NT (Client and Server)
- Microsoft Office
- Norton Anti-Virus
- Microsoft Project and Support Magic
- Total Intranet Development and HTML Code

Career Development

NEWSDAY, INC., MELVILLE, NY   1982 to present

Director, Information Systems Group 1995 to present
Publishing Systems Manager 1984 to 1995
Editorial Project Manager 1982 to 1984

Manage 48 employees and oversee a $5.6 million budget to research, plan, install,integrate, and maintain hardware, software and networks to support 2,000 internal and external customers at *Newsday's* New York, Long Island, and Washington DC facilities. Areas of responsibility include:

- **Publishing Group**—handles all support for print functions of publication: software, hardware, operating systems, desktop installations, upgrades, repairs 24X7 365 days.

- **Business Systems Group**—the actual operations team. Includes systems programmers and data center staff for *Newsday* and the *Baltimore Sun*. Team also handles testing and implementation of the business systems disaster recovery plan for 24-hour data center catastrophe recovery.

- **Networking Group**—the technical team. Designs, implements, installs, monitors, and repairs LAN and WAN systems in New York City, Long Island, and Washington DC.

Conduct strategic planning including system upgrades, and capital, operating and line item budgets. Develop RFPs, execute ROI analysis, and negotiate/review contracts. Control departmental purchasing and resource management. Track expenses and maintain budget integrity. Produce management and staff reviews, determine salary increases and payroll budget.

Lead project teams, and manage projects using Microsoft Project and Support Magic to direct teams handling internal and client hardware and software installations. Perform system reliability analysis and cost justifications on system replacements.

Education

Certificate in Information Systems Management, Hofstra University, Uniondale, NY 1994

Bachelor of Science in Business (Magna Cum Laude), Hofstra University, Uniondale, NY 1980

58—MULTIMEDIA DEVELOPER

Eye-catching resume, reverse print works well to divide sections.

KAREN SMITH

P.O. BOX 000 • DRIPPING SPRINGS, TEXAS 78788 • (512) 555-5555 • ksmith@rocketmail.com

MULTIMEDIA SOFTWARE DEVELOPMENT • TECHNICAL LEADERSHIP • BUSINESS MANAGEMENT
COMPUTER-BASED TRAINING • E-COMMERCE APPLICATIONS DEVELOPMENT

Accomplished Applications Manager with solid experience in Project Management, Business Leadership, and Software Development. Outstanding technical skills and ability to lead development teams, coordinate resources, and build constructive, positive communications between players to reach goals and high standards of professional excellence. Reputation for achieving project success in hard turnaround situations.

TECHNICAL SKILLS

Authorware	Acrobat
Director	Dimensions
HTML Scripting	Toast
DeBabelizer	Filemaker Pro
Fireworks	FastTrack
Flash	QuarkXPress
Dreamweaver	Norton Utilities
PhotoShop	
Illustrator	

Digital Video Editing Tools
Premier
AfterEffects
QuickTime

Digital Audio Production Tools
SoundEdit
Sound Forge

PROFESSIONAL EXPERIENCE

Bigbrain.com • Austin, Texas

APPLICATIONS DEVELOPMENT MANAGER

1997-1999

Led in-house software development operations and technical development of instructional applications, software-based marketing products, and related development systems and tools. Directed software application development projects for CDROM products requiring Authorware or Lingo coding and dynamic **multimedia technologies using video, audio, and** animation software tools. Managed in-house team in development of Internet content delivery systems involving Java-based NetDynamics core program, HTML, VHTML, and CGI scripting designed for Oracle tie-in. Led development team of 5 programmers and various outsourced project teams on project specifications and progression. Worked directly with editorial groups and project teams on content issues. Wrote project budgets and schedules; established performance benchmarks and technical standards.

- **Led initiation of publisher's first ever Internet deployment of content involving over 5000 pages of e-commerce ready information including online catalog, marketing content, and editorial content**
- **Served as Lead Technical Manager and Project Manager for award-winning development of foreign language CDROM**

(Continued)

177

LEAD APPLICATIONS DEVELOPER   1996-1997

Lead Authorware developer and Technical Project Manager directing team on complex development of World Language CDROM educational series involving audio, video, audio recording, and interactive instruction. Created infrastructure and designed complex code enabling student response tracking, performance evaluation, and language laboratory functionality.

- **Won CITE award for performance and contribution toward making "World Language" company's single most popular, best-selling CDROM product.**

PROJECT PROGRAMMER   1995-1996

Promoted to Lead Programmer within one week of beginning position. Devoted entire 12 months to writing/rescuing corrupted code to achieve major development project turnaround. Spurred creation of in-house technical department within New Media department. Set pace for development schedule, working long hours in a 9-5 industry.

TD Productions • Austin, Texas

PROGRAMMER   1993-1994

Executive management experience outside industry encompassing:
- *Management of multi-unit business expansion and operations of high energy entrepreneurial startups*
- *Personnel development and team building*
- *Financial management and direction from business unit level to corporate levels*

CAREER RECOGNITIONS

BigBrain.com CITE Award for Publishing Excellence – 1997

Featured Digital Artist – "Art Journeys," PBS distributed educational program

Coordinator/Project Development Manager for multimedia products that achieved 9 national awards of excellence from independent sources

PROFESSIONAL AFFILIATIONS

Austin Area Macromedia Users Group
IICS

EDUCATION AND TRAINING

Bachelor of Arts • Trinity University, San Antonio, Texas

Web Development and Design Certification Program
University of Texas Professional Development Center

HTML Scripting I and II - Austin Community College
"Presenting Data and Information" Edward Tufte, Austin, Texas
"Flash Workshop" Ojai Digital Arts Center, Ojai, California
Extensive Multimedia Training and Coursework – See attached Addendum

59—MULTIMEDIA DIRECTOR

GREGORY A. BENUSCAK

15 Tweed Boulevard, Grandview, New York 10983 • (845) 555-5555 • gbenny@isp.com

SENIOR SALES & MARKETING EXECUTIVE

Multimedia, Entertainment • Television & Film Industries Start-Up, Turnaround & Rapid Growth

---

Innovative and dynamic Multimedia professional with 15+ years of expertise driving revenue, market, and profit growth for products, services, and multichannel contracts. Proven skills in opening new markets by building solid partnerships across traditional and Internet channels. Possess the ability to create dynamic business models and establish performance-driven, cost-effective organizations. Outstanding communications, team leadership, and intuitive skills.

AREAS OF EXPERTISE

- Relationship Management & Client Retention
- Product/Service Development & Launch
- Sales & Contract Negotiations
- Market Expansion & New Business Development

- Team Building & Organizational Development
- Process Reengineering & Quality Improvement
- Licensing & Intellectual Property Agreements
- Technology, Website Design, & Internet Strategy

PROFESSIONAL EXPERIENCE

Worldwide Media Communication – New York, New York   1997 to Present
DIRECTOR OF SALES & MARKETING OPERATIONS

Senior Marketing & Operations Executive focusing on expanding this regional service company to its next level of competitiveness by leveraging Internet resources and emerging technologies. Developed a new sales/ marketing strategy and redesigned collaterals to accelerate growth and gain competitive positioning. Lead sales, marketing, and business development initiatives to boost revenues/profits. Manage a staff of eight.

- Defined long-term business objectives, technology structures, and upgraded technologies to optimize digital capabilities projected to drive a 100% increase in revenues/global client base.
- Launched Website to capitalize on global business opportunities. Revamped advertising and targeted campaigns to specific market niches (e.g., telecom, insurance, high-tech).
- Optimized Internet opportunities to identify clients for outsourced interactive business.
- Generated new revenue stream with the introduction of teleconferencing transcription services that generated 50% of total company revenues.
- Developed client relations with Netscape, Yahoo, Sheraton, Exxon, and Avon, and expanded client base from 52 to 100+. Led negotiations for lucrative one-time deals and profitable long-term contracts.
- Built consensus across all functional lines (Communications, PR, Marketing, Customer Service) to facilitate market planning initiatives, strengthen client satisfaction, and enhance revenue performance.

(Continued)

GREGORY A. BENUSCAK • PAGE TWO

15 Tweed Blvd, Grandview, New York 10983 • (845) 398-5555 • gbenny@isp.com

---

Mainstream Arts – Los Angeles, California   1996 to 1997

DIRECTOR OF MULTIMEDIA AFFAIRS

Recruited to this multibillion dollar company specializing in media/interactive entertainment products. Given responsibility for managing business affairs relating to intellectual property licensing, royalty rate structures and celebrity agreements with professional athletes to promote products. Built cooperative working relationships across the legal and sales/marketing functions and with external customers/partners.
- **Facilitated new product development and market launch for video game products endorsed by celebrities.**
- **Structured intellectual property contracts with national sports leagues.**
- **Facilitated licensing agreement with animation house for the development of Wing Commander for television and video markets.**

Affiliated Consulting, Los Angeles/San Francisco, California   1990 to 1996
MEDIA DIRECTOR

Leveraged industry knowledge/qualifications and provided expertise in strategic planning, relationship management, merchandising/licensing agreements, contract negotiations, and sales/business development for international media, film and television corporations. Key clients included Island Pictures, World Films, Inc., Atlantic Entertainment Group and Le Cordon Bleu.
- **Structured/executed agreements and facilitated negotiations involving asset purchase of foreign/U.S. titles feature film library with major studio releases and global distribution.**
- **Revamped marketing/business plan and acquired $1 million in assets which subsequently sold in two years at $50 million.**

Twentieth Century Fox Studio, Los Angeles, CA   1982 to 1990
Vice President - Television Sales (1987 to 1990) • Director of Television Sales (1985 to 1987)
Director of Ancillary Sales (1983 to 1985) • Publicity/Sales Representative (1982 to 1983)

Fast-track promotion with what was then a virtual start-up independent film, television, and production company. Advanced rapidly while the corporation grew to $50 million in sales. Held responsibility for sales, marketing, business development, and new product introductions, staffing, and account management. Oversaw public speaking and trade show representation. Analyzed industry/business trends and developed appropriate models and products to guide market expansion. Recruited/directed staff of 10 and managed a $5+ million product acquisition/marketing budget.
- **Played a key role in building the company from 15 employees and 50+ titles to 100+ employees and over 500 titles. Doubled divisional revenues to over $20 million.**
- **Expanded market penetration in untapped sectors (e.g., military, airlines, education, small market syndication) and generated new revenue streams.**

EDUCATION

BACHELOR OF ARTS – COMMUNCIAITONS
New York University – New York, New York

60—NETWORK ARCHITECT

Mike Goga

234 Mariners Way, Lake Elsinore, California 92530 ● 909 555-6225
mgoga@yahoo.com

PROFILE

Confident, competent, and organized Network Architect with considerable, diverse experience augmented by specialized, industry-related training. Microsoft Certified Systems Engineer (MCSE) with track record of reengineering cost effective, high-performance technology solutions and networks to improve asset performance, operational efficiencies, and reduce expenses. Solid history of delivering outstanding customer service. Proven ability to build and manage creative, highly energized, focused teams. Qualifications include knowledge, skills, and abilities in:

Computer Systems	Network Administration	Project Management
Information Technology	Operational Planning	Strategic Planning

PROFESSIONAL EXPERIENCE

OUTBACK SYSTEMS INTEGRATORS, Lake Elsinore, California – 1996 to present

Network Architect and Systems Administrator for a company specializing in custom designed outsourced procurement solutions. Responsibilities include architecting the network infrastructure to support a team responsible for deploying, running, and maintaining network systems used to provide business solutions. Oversee the teams' research and network design process. Develop the technology enabling production systems to remain up and available to customers. Scope of responsibility also includes maintaining office network and involves installation and configuration of all equipment such as PCs, printers, scanners, hubs, and routers. Oversee and diagnose systems problems. Conduct staff training to ensure proper utilization of new equipment and network usage.

Directed design, implementation, and operation of network project; completed within established budget, in a timely manner with no unplanned interruption of work.
Implemented Windows NT on existing network; maximized productivity and efficiency.

SCHLYBERG ENGINEERING, Long Beach, California – 1994 to 1996

Information Systems Support Technician reporting to the Office Adminstrator for an architectural and design firm. Installed and configured all new PCs, printers, scanners, and plotters. Oversaw daily back-up and recovery of files; installation and implementation of networkwide software upgrades, computers, printers, plotters, and copiers. Directed leasing program of all office equipment.

Installed new server; switched operating system from Novell to Windows NT.
Implemented new design software and new back-up software resulting in faster and more efficient network, increased office productivity, and elimination of network crashes on heavy-load occasions.

COMPUTER TECHNOLOGY

Software Applications: Microsoft Office, QuickBooks, ACT, MicroStation
Computer Hardware: PCs, Monitors, Printers, Scanners, Plotters, Hubs, Routers
Programming Languages: Q-Basic
Operating Systems: Windows 95/98, Windows NT and NT Terminal Server, Novell, Citrix
Network Protocols: TCP/IP, Net Bevi, IPX/SPX
Client/Server Architecture: Two-Tier Arch, Single Server and Distributed Server, Server Farms
LAN/WAN Technologies: Ethernet, Token Ring Networks, Routers, Switches, Network Adapters
Systems Interconnectivity: Analog and Digital Dial-up and dedicated lines T-1 Lines

EDUCATION AND PROFESSIONAL TRAINING

Mt. Jacinto College, Menifee Valley, California
        Associate of Science – Major: Computer Technology
        Certificated Computer Systems Program of Study
          Microsoft Certified Systems Engineer (MCSE)

Alternative Technologies, Inc., San Marcos, California
        Implementing CITRIX Software in an NT Terminal Server Environment

Patricia Capizzi

892 #B Rose Bud Lane, San Diego, California 92131 ● 858 555-1234
pcapizzi@hotmail.com

SENIOR NETWORK ENGINEER ● SENIOR SYSTEMS ENGINEER

PROFILE

Competent, confident, client-oriented information technology professional with considerable experience augmented by a graduate level education in Computer Science and refined by specialized, industry-related training. Flexible and focused, with unique analytical problem-solving ability. Exceptional knowledge of and expertise in hardware, software, and applications for defense and industry. Global perspective based upon life, travels, and work abroad. Significant software engineering analysis expertise including software design and development. Bilingual/Bicultural: Farsi. Expertise includes competence in:

- Cost Estimating/Controls
- Customer Interface/Liaison
- Global Business Development
- ISO 9000 Standards

- Operations & Maintenance
- Performance Improvements
- Performance Monitoring
- Process Improvements

- Proposal Development
- Staff Training & Development
- Systems Enhancements
- Technical Marketing Support

STRENGTHS

- Design, Implementation, and Maintenance of LAN/WAN Network Infrastructures
- Computer Systems Design, Development, and Installation
- Customer Service and Technical, On-site Field Support
- New Business Development, Proposals, and Negotiations

PROFESSIONAL EXPERIENCE

CUBIC CORPORATION, San Diego, CA - 1996 to present

Senior Network/Systems Engineer reporting to the Manager, Systems Engineering Department. Provide technical, marketing, and engineering support for the future Combat Training Center/Instrumentation Systems (CTC/IS) developed by CDS. Analyzed systems requirements, customer interface and presentations, proposal development, cost estimating, and, system and software design for international CTCs including Sweden, Norway, and England.

Oversaw activities of Operations and I.S./UNIX departments. Managed implementation of several key projects, including installation of NetApp, upgrading production of the mail server, and redesign and reimplementation of the companywide Legato Networker installation. Resolved difficult and persistent technical issues arising on-site, specializing in back-end database servers and in high-availability.

Performed trade study analysis and conceptual design for the Small Unit Operations - Situation Awareness System (SUO+SAS), based on the leading edge secure cellular/wireless communications and robust networking technologies. Analyzed requirements; developed system specifications and architecture.

Conducted extensive research and development related to the future generations of Combat Training Systems and their interoperability based on the Distributed Interactive Simulation (DIS) protocols, the High Level Architecture (HLA) standards, and the ATM networking technology. Research included: Object Oriented Analysis and Design based on the UML standards, feasibility study for software development based on Common Object Request Broker Architecture (CORBA) and Java.

Orchestrated activities of 12-person team during transition, operation, and maintenance of a large instrumentation system at the Combat Maneuver Training Center (CMTC) in Germany.
- Led ongoing prototype design and development for the next generation of Analyst Workstations based on distributed object technology using Java Development Kit (JDK) Swing set and CORBA products.

(Continued on next page)

PROFESSIONAL EXPERIENCE (Continued)

INTERNATIONAL COMPUTER SCIENCES CORP., (ICSC), San Diego, California - 1990 to 1996

Computer Scientist. Responsibilities included: System software security and product support, software evaluation and selection, networking and system performance monitoring of a VAX cluster environment.

- Designed and developed software utilities to support software sizing and performance measurements of a large financial system, developed for the Department of the Navy.

I-NET E-BIZ CORPORATION, San Jose, California - 1986 to 1990

Senior Programmer Analyst. Designed, programmed, operated, and maintained multiprocessing Tactical Aircrew Combat Training Systems (TACTS). Developed software packages providing executive control functions for the Ocean View Measurement and Debriefing Systems (OVMDS).

- Developed and provided direct software support for the Automatic Fair Collection Systems.
- Designed, developed, and installed software to provide an executive control function and capability for real-time recording and retrieval of data from a multiple-disk system.

EDUCATION

Pacific West University, Los Angeles, California
     Master of Science - Computer Science and Technology
     Master of Science – International Business Management

Tehran University, Tehran, Iran
     Bachelor of Science in Business and Economics

COMPUTER TECHNOLOGY

- Data Acquisition
- High-Level Architecture
- Networking
- Object-Oriented Analysis
- OnLine System Administration
- Real-Time Applications
- Research & Development
- Software Design
- Systems Administration
- Systems Engineering
- Systems Security
- Systems Software

SOFTWARE

Cicso GSRs, BGP, SNMP, RMON, RMONII, EIGRP CISCO, IOS, HSRP, EtherNet Switches, Network Design, LAN/WAN Analysis, Multiplatform Web and Object-Orientated Systems, X-Window, UNIX, JAVA, CORBA, OOAD, OODB, TCP/IP, DIS, HLA, Informix, Oracle, SQL, DCL, Ada, FORTRAN, C, Assembly, Rational Rose, DOORS, RTM, JFC, JDBC, IDL, JBuilder

HARDWARE

Sun Microsystems:	Solaris, NFS, NOS
Silicon Graphics:	IRIX, System and Network Administration
Digital Equipment:	VRM, DECNET, NCP, SPM
Concurrent (MPS3200):	OS/32, System Programming
Personal Computers:	Windows-95, Windows-NT, MS-Office

LICENSURE, CREDENTIALS, AND CLEARANCE

- MCSD:Windows Internal Architecture 1 & 2
- Professional Certificate in Systems Engineering, UCSD Extension, 1998
- U.S. Government Final Top Secret Security Clearance based upon December 1989 BI

62—NETWORK OPERATIONS MANAGER

KEITH JOHNSON

15869 Calle Mazatan • Morgan Hill, California 95037 • (408) 778-5555 • kjohnson@isp.com

CAREER OVERVIEW

A results-oriented **Network Operations Manager / Professional** with progressive career in information systems for both domestic and international environments. Decisive and goal oriented, able to set realistic priorities to coordinate and complete multiple complex projects simultaneously. Demonstrated ability to adapt readily to new situations while maintaining consistently superior levels of productivity. A proactive leadership style which instills confidence in peers and staff. Broad based exposure to all aspects of information technology strategies with proven strengths in devising and implementing improved approaches to internal technology auditing.

AREAS OF STRENGTH

- *Information Systems*
- *Worldwide Audit*
- *Coordination Information*
- *Application Development*
- *Communications*
- *Network Information Technology*
- *Asset Security*
- *Internal Controls*
- *Team Building*

PROFESSIONAL EXPERIENCE

I.B.M. Inc. • 1969/Present
Chief Information Officer, Network Systems Storage Division - United States
San Jose, CA • 1996/Present
- Manage day-to day operations and overall $142 million budget of SSD Network Information Technology investments.
- Develop team and management system and implement effective controls to achieve communications to division thru extended team and sitewide employee presentation.
- Negotiate agreements and service contracts for data center services, applications development, and maintenance of $75 million contract.
Selected Accomplishments:
- *Reduced IT division spending by $23.5 million; improving productivity by 18%.*
- *Designed division Lotus Notes development strategies for the deployment to 3000 end users worldwide within 3 months including upgrades for employee workstations.*
- *Developed and implemented division approval for containment of applications development expenditures to fund Year 2000 project and strategic systems development.*

(Continued)

184

KEITH JOHNSON
(Page 2)

Manager, Information Processing Audit Competency Group Corporate Internal Audit
Armonk, NY • 1990/1996
- Directed information system audits worldwide including information asset security, system service and application development.
- Managed operational audits of ISSC and Advantis.

Selected Accomplishments:
- Coordinated and managed multiple audits conducted concurrently worldwide.
- Reduced duration of on-site field work and improved customer satisfaction by 18% year-to-year.
- Completed course work and received Bachelor's degree while on 100% worldwide travel assignments.

Senior Internal Auditor, Corporate Internal Auditor
Stamford, CT • 1988/1990
- Led and performed various types of information processing audits worldwide.

Technical Assistant to Site Director of Business Support Systems
Bethesda, MD • 1987/1988
- Supervised administrative and personnel support, site issue management.
- Directed the preparation of reports and coordination of executive visits and staff meetings.

Senior Project Manager, Purchase Billing Business Administrative Systems
Bethesda, MD • 1986/1987
- Acted as second-line manager responsible for application ownership, requirements, definition, application development/maintenance and function testing of customer purchase billing systems.

CICS Function Test Manager
Bethesda, MD •1985/1986
- Managed stability and reliability of application change top CICS production environments.
- Established function test environments and formal testing procedures.
- Maintained code library management systems.

Inventory and Billing Development Manager
Bethesda, MD • 1983/1984
- Oversaw the development and maintenance of billing and inventory systems for OP heritage systems.
- Developed consolidation projects and coordinated management and system support personnel.

EDUCATION

- **Syracuse University** - Syracuse, New York
  Bachelor of Science • Business Administration/Finance • 1996
  Magna Cum Laude • GPA 3.6

WALT JOHNSON

30 Dale Road #22	Plainville, CT 06062	emailaddress@emailaddress.com	(860) 555-2230

NETWORK OPERATIONS SPECIALIST
Application Development / System Administration

Extensive computer proficiency in a variety of programming languages, hardware platforms, and software applications. Enterprise-level Lotus Notes / Domino application developer, using Lotus, IBM, Microsoft, Sun Microsystems, and third party development tools. Diverse computer and engineering technical knowledge, including work flow analysis, systems integration, systems testing, interface bus design, instrumentation, avionics, communications, metrology, component level repair / calibration. Excellent written and verbal communication skills; familiar with OOP design, project team management, and UML tools. Project management includes:

Design   **Development**   **Documentation**   **Prototyping**   **Testing**   **Resource Management**

PROFESSIONAL EXPERIENCE

PRICELINE.COM, Webhouse Club, Stamford, CT   11/99 – Present
Network Specialist, Priceline Webhouse Club Network Operations Center
    Contracted through IT Contract Service to monitor all aspects of Internet traffic at the Network Operations Center. Monitor usage of several hundred Web and database servers daily, maintaining load balancing of front- and back-end servers. Troubleshoot and solve technical problems using remote reporting and administration tools.

REGIONAL TELECOMMUNICATION COMPANY, Hartford, CT   1/95 – 9/99
Programmer / Systems Analyst (2/96 – 9/99)
    Contracted through IT Contract Services. Developed enterprisewide work flow Lotus Notes applications; provided ongoing support in a Domino 4.6x server environment. Application was designed to automate communications among dealers, customer service, account executives, and marketing, including use of Lotus Fax Server. Customized client-server applications to exchange data between NSF, SQL, DB2 and Oracle databases and custom in-house applications; utilized OBDC, Zmerge, Lotus Script, and Java Script programming knowledge.

Lotus Notes Support Consultant (1/95 – 2/96)
    Contracted through IT Contract Services as Lotus Notes Desktop Support and Server Administrator for 400+ licensed Lotus Notes users, interfaced to Corporate Domain of 7000+ users. Performed e-mail account administration, technical consultation, user installation, user training, and system troubleshooting. Administrator of LAN-based Domino production / development servers connected to Corporate WAN.

INDEPENDENT COMPUTER CONSULTANT, Plainville, CT   1990 – Present
    Services: Web site development, software application design, systems administration, training, network installations, value-added reselling, desktop support, system maintenance / repair / upgrades, and custom-designed interface hardware. Client base has grown by referral to 100+.

MAJOR AIRCRAFT COMPANY, Stratton, CT   1993 - 1994
Contract Metrology Engineer
- Participated on select 5-member team assembled to achieve compliance with stringent military metrology standards. Updated antiquated equipment calibration procedures/documentation; developed new procedures for MIL-45662-A compliance. Disciplines included electronic, hydraulic, pneumatic, temperature, humidity, optics RF, and specialized manufacturing process equipment. Researched ISO 9000 compliance requirements needed for certification.

(Continued)

WALT JOHNSON

ALLGEN CORPORATION, a division of BCD TECHNOLOGIES, Newbury, MA   1989 - 1990
Contract Project Manager, Navigational Data Unit Program
Took over leadership of an 18-month project already 9 months behind schedule. Directed the efforts of mechanical engineering, electrical engineering, CAD, and technical publication departments. Turned project around within 90 days; successfully completed final design and testing within the original 18-month parameters.

- Company was awarded contract bonus of $250K by meeting original project milestones.

MAJOR AIRCRAFT COMPANY, Stratton, CT   1974 - 1989
Senior Project Manager/Working Supervisor, Avionics Test (1987 - 1989)
Successfully designed Integrated Bench Test Facility (static helicopter simulator) to test prototype and existing equipment. Supervised over 15 engineers, engineering assistants, and other support personnel.

- Originally designed for in-house use only, the project was so successful that it resulted in a multimillion dollar purchase of additional units by the federal government.

Early MAJOR AIRCRAFT positions included:
Senior Project Engineer, Instrumentation (1984 - 1987)
Repair/Calibration Technician, Metrology Laboratory (1979 - 1984)
Flight and Ground Test Engineering Aide, Instrumentation (1974 - 1979)

EDUCATION / CONTINUING EDUCATION

ENGINEERING INSTITUTE, Fairfield, CT
    B.S. Electrical Engineering, 1984
    A.S. Electrical Engineering, 1982

Regional Telecommunication Company: Web Development Techniques, Domino Application Development, including Domino Designer v.4.6.
Continuing Microsoft, IBM, and Novell sponsored hardware / software development technical workshops.
Major Aircraft: Total Quality Management (TQM); Engineering CAD workshop.
U.S. Armed Forces: Instructor Training Certificate; Electronics Repair Technician; LORAN Technician.

COMPUTER SKILLS (Working skills with all; current proficiency level varies.)

Programming: Visual Basic; COM; DCOM; ASP; ADO; XML; LotusScript; Lotus Notes API, VB Script; ActiveX; Java; JavaScript; Visual J++; HTML; DHTML; Visual InterDev; CGI; Perl Script; Fortran 77; Pascal; Visual C++.
Web Design: Domino Designer; FrontPage 2000; NetObjects Fusion, Coldfusion; PhotoShop 5.x; PaintShop Pro; Debablizer.
Database: MSSQL 6.5; IBM DB2; Oracle 7; MS Access; MS Visual Foxpro; dBASE; DataEase; Paradox.
Operating Systems: Windows 2000; Windows NT 4.0; Windows 95; WFW 3.11; DOS. OS/2; IBM AIX; IBM AS/400; Linux.
Network Operating Systems: Windows 2000 Server; Windows NT 4.0; Windows 95; Novell; Banyan.
Organizational Programs: Lotus Organizer; MS Schedule+.
GroupWare/E-mail: Lotus Notes / Domino 3.x, 4.x, 5.x; MS Exchange / Outlook.
Word Processing: MS Word; Lotus WordPro; Corel WordPerfect.
Spreadsheets: MS Excel; Lotus 1-2-3.

Hardware: PC, R6000, AS/400, IBM 360, DEC PDP 11, DEC VAX, Cisco, Apple, S100, CNC machines.

Online Careerfolio...

John Wang

Click on Link to Review ...

Summary

Education

Experience

Technology

Affiliations

References

Contact

Silicon Valley Region
(555) 555.5555
E-mail ~ johnwang@mediaone.net
E-folio ~ http://www.careerfolios.com/johnwang

Very creative and appealing layout. Web enabled for navigation; could be compelling for electronic reviewing.

SUMMARY

E-Commerce Executive with substantial record as a leader and manager of new-economy initiatives. Envisioned tactics that capitalized on Internet opportunities, launched core e-initiatives, and achieved first-to-market status in Web and traditional markets. Enterprise planning, P&L, and management skills reflect strengths in Web marketing, business development, strategic alliance development and negotiations, global sales, and technology product development and management. Career highlights:

➤ **General Management:** Authored marketing, fiscal, and operating strategies that drove e-sales from start-up level to $23 million in less than one year, with conservative predictions of $77 million in recurring revenue by next year end.

➤ **Business Development, Alliance Initiatives:** Structured and negotiated watershed deal with **America Online**, gaining valuable cobranding leverage for company.

➤ **Product / Brand Management:** Conceptualized innovative Internet device—marketed and managed product that shipped 200,000 units in less than 1 year.

➤ **Fiscal Management:** Owned division balance sheet and P&L responsibilities (up to US$80 million). Undertook reengineering initiatives that captured hard-dollar savings of $18 million.

➤ **High-Profile:** Invited speaker at national and international technology summits. Interviewed by **CBSmarketwatch.com**, **CNBC**, **CNN**; quoted in ***Fast Company*** and tech publications regarding emerging technology. (Click links for reprints.)

EDUCATION

MBA ~ Entrepreneurial Management: Duke University Fuqua School of Business, Durham, North Carolina.

BS degree ~ Finance: University of California, Santa Barbara.

65—ONLINE COMMUNITY MANAGER

DEBRA PETERSON
15505 Margra Lane • Austin, Texas 78748
512-555-5555
generalhospital.guide@about.com

Good layout and summary up front.

WEBMASTER • ONLINE COMMUNITY MANAGER

An award winning Online Community Manager with extensive expertise in developing and implementing compelling and innovate features to increase membership and build traffic. Demonstrated ability to establish strong rapport with both community members and celebrities to drive and sustain membership levels. Computer expertise encompasses Windows 95 & 98, Unix, HTML, CGI, Scripting, JAVA, and an extensive knowledge of the Internet. Core competencies include:

- **Graphic Design**
- **Traffic Increases**
- **Networking**
- **Programming**

- **Web Site Development**
- **Community Relations**
- **Internet Research**
- **Celebrity Chat Management**

PROFESSIONAL EXPERIENCE

About.com - New York, New York • 1998 – Present
ON-LINE COMMUNITY MANAGER - PRIVATE CONTRACTOR
- Maintain all facets of this entertainment Website focusing on the serial television drama General Hospital.
- Regularly search the Internet for all relevant links pertaining to General Hospital and affiliated shows ensuring accurate posting of information to assist members with searches.
- Select a fan site for "Best of the Net" based upon material, layout, and presentation on a monthly basis.
- Coordinate "Scoops" with private inside sources and develop newsletters for e-mail publication.
- Develop weekly features and polls regarding current plot lines designed to increase site traffic.
- Collect and post cast member photos for community use and downloads.
- Arrange star chats with General Hospital's most popular cast members.
- Meet with cast members for interviews and to promote individual actor events.

ADDITIONAL EXPERIENCE

NATIONAL SEMICONDUCTOR – Tucson, Arizona • 1982 – 1991
QUALITY CONTROL INSPECTOR

Managed Quality Control inspections for MIL Aero Division performing temperature, stress, and product testing.

Clean layout and easy-to-read format.

Steve Miller

12436 Tarrytown Road   -   New York, NY 10023
H: 212-555-3124   -   **W: 212-555-6342**
Emailaddress@emailaddress.com

E-business Editorial Professional with over ten years of award-winning journalistic experience. Expertise in spearheading the development of compelling online content to drive sales and circulation.

PROFESSIONAL EXPERIENCE:

LARGE PUBLISHING COMPANY, INC., Corporate Communications, New York, NY
Editor, *State-of-the-Art Magazine*   4/97-Present
Edit and publish monthly e-magazine with a circulation of 85,000 employees worldwide. Manage a staff of four; assign free-lance writers and photographers. Plan, develop and organize high-quality content; collaborate with visual designers to select graphics and enhance layout. Cooperate with Web development, marketing and business development departments to deliver attractive and informative finished product.

- Led relaunch of Internet magazine, refurbished in January 1999.
- Both circulation and content have doubled since inception of new e-magazine format.

Senior Writer, *State-of-the-Art Magazine*   5/95-4/97
Reported and wrote feature articles on business, entertainment, and technology. Art directed photo shoots. Wrote headlines and news briefs. Assigned and edited free-lance stories.

- Helped develop *State-of-the-Art Magazine*'s first online version.

THE CONNECTICUT DAILY, Bridgeport, CT
Staff Writer/Columnist   1993-1995
General assignment reporter covering crime, education, health, and social services for large circulation regional daily. Coordinated coverage for one of the state's largest cities. Wrote bi-weekly column.

- Contributed weekend pieces on regional and national issues including a Sunday A-1 series on a major local employer and investigative stories on computer crime and police ethics.

THE SHORELINE ADVOCATE, Shoreline, CT
Staff Writer   1989-1993
Covered city government, housing, environment, and politics, including 1990 and 1992 Congressional races for this 50,000 circulation daily. Conceived and led award-winning series.

FREE-LANCE WORK:

Personality Magazine; Teen Personality; Personality en Español, New York, NY
Stringer   1/98-Present
Reported stories for the New York bureau on celebrities, events, and human interest including cover stories on Pop Divas and celebrity singers, *Teen Personality* "Weighty Issues" and *Personality En Español* cover story.

(Continued)

Steve Miller -   Page 2

WWWW-AM, Nashville, TN
Correspondent   1998
 Contributed reports on entertainment events to "Nashville Now," a drive-time show on this 50,000 watt station.

HEALTH TODAY, New York, NY
Contributor   1995-1996
 Reported and wrote front-of-book environmental health stories.

EDUCATION:

 M.S. Journalism, MAJOR UNIVERSITY, New York, NY
 B.A. English, STATE COLLEGE, Burlington, VT
 • Graduated Magna cum laude
 • Phi Beta Kappa / State College chapter

RELATED SKILLS:

 Languages: French, Spanish
 Computer: MS Word, Excel, Quark, HTML, Photoshop, LEXIS-NEXIS; Web-savvy

AWARDS:

SOCIETY OF PROFESSIONAL JOURNALISTS
 • First place, General Reporting, 1994
 • Honorable Mention, In-depth Reporting, 1994
 • First place, In-depth Reporting, 1993
 • First place, Spot News, 1993
 • First place, Spot News, 1990

Portfolio available upon request

Clean "Profile" section and shading adds a little style. Overall good layout.

Mary Beth Rouse

mbrouse@aol.com □ 8800 West 18th Street, Denver, CO 80201 □ 303-555-1819

Profile

- Capable and creative **Senior Online Editor** with eight years of progressive experience in journalism seeking promotion to Director of Publications.

- Outstanding ability to develop innovative "look and feel" of online information while establishing and maintaining high editorial standards. Dedicated to driving the development of new strategies for a new medium, continually pushing the envelope of print and broadcast forms.

- Key strength in networking and collaborating cross-functionally to build the business of a national media company, setting strategy with other local managers.

- Highly productive and organized, balancing multiple projects under extremely demanding deadlines. Well-versed in developing editorial calendars, organizing production schedules, managing budgets, and coaching staffs of up to 20.

- Articulate, persuasive communicator, with excellent public relations and writing skills. Frequent presenter at national journalism conventions on the topic of Web publishing.

Experience

CitySearch.com, Denver, CO   1996-Present
Publisher of Comprehensive Local City Guides on the World Wide Web
Editor-in-Chief, Denver.CitySearch.com

- Guarantee accurate and up-to-date coverage of all CitySearch topics, including news, sports, weather, arts and entertainment events, community activities, recreation, shopping, and professional services in the Denver metropolitan area.

- Collaborate extensively with business groups and marketing staff to site enhancements, continually reviewing content to ensure meeting the mission and business requirements of the company.

- Incorporate a standard approach and consistency in AP style, grammar, and voice. Establish and improve content update processes across all departments.

- Motivate and train an online publishing team of 20. Provide coaching to enhance reporting, writing, fact-checking, and editing skills, as well as building editorial judgment.

- Develop and maintain a broad network of industry contacts. Review and publish wire-service news stories to online news site throughout each business day.

- Frequently represent CitySearch.com as an invited speaker at national and regional journalism conventions on the topic of the evolution and future of New Media.

CompuServe, Inc., Columbus, OH   1993-1996
Online Editor

- Developed and reorganized content for interactive communities and online editions of PC Week, Inter@ctive Week, and Computer Shopper magazines.

- Functioned as liaison between the newspaper's online and print staffs, facilitating multiple daily updates of the Internet edition.

- Coordinated efforts of marketing, technical, and editorial content providers. Directed a graphic design team to improve menu graphics, logos, and icons. Identified internal and external resources for ongoing community management. Drove development of multimedia elements, opinion polls, and forums.

▪ **Continued Page 2**

Mary Beth Rouse
Page 2 □ mbrouse@aol.com

Experience, continued

The Ohio State University, Columbus, OH   1989-1993
Editor-in-Chief, The Bulletin - OSU's student newspaper, 1991-1993
Assistant Editor, Student Reporter, 1989-1991

- Wrote and edited copy for each weekly edition. Assisted with layout and paginating of 5-10 pages per issue. Determined and assigned story ideas to staff writers and stringers.

- Instrumental in the paper's achievement of a #3 ranking among American college newspapers (1992) by the Journalism Education Association.

Technical Proficiencies

- In-depth knowledge of the World Wide Web, including all aspects of site design, creation, and server management.

- Working knowledge of Perl, JAVA, Flash, and VBScript/ASP.

- Highly skilled in graphic design and layout to give locally produced online news stories effective and innovative multimedia elements, using PhotoShop, Illustrator, RealAudio and RealVideo media delivery systems, Premiere, SoundEdit, PhotoVista and Apple QuickTime VR.

- More than five years of experience with QuarkXpress.

- Proficient with DOS, Windows, Windows95/98, NT, MacOS, and UNIX operating systems.

- Extensive experience using HyperText Markup Language (HTML) and Web-page design techniques.

Education

Bachelor of Arts, Journalism with minor in English, 1992
The Ohio State University, Columbus, OH

Charter member of The Ohio State University's student chapter of Society of Professional Journalists.

Professional Organizations

Society of American Business Editors and Writers

Association of American Publishers

International Webmasters Association

Martin B. Parish

3041 Patriot Road * Baltimore, MD 21045
410.555.5244 * MBP@aol.con

PRODUCT MANAGER
- Staying ahead of a warp-speed, forward-moving, high-tech industry -

PRODUCT
DEVELOPMENT

RESEARCH &
DEVELOPMENT

DEVELOPMENT &
SOURCING

NEGOTIATIONS &
PROCUREMENT

COST-EFFECTIVE
MANAGEMENT

PRODUCT GROWTH &
PROCESSES

NURTURE
LONG-TERM
CLIENT
RELATIONSHIPS

MANUFACTURING
OPERATIONS

SHIPPING &
DISTRIBUTION

BUSINESS PLAN
DEVELOPMENT

PROJECT
MANAGEMENT

SYSTEMS AND
WORK FLOWS

CREATE COMPLEX
POWERPOINT
PRESENTATIONS

WORD, NT,
INTERNET,
QUICKBOOKS,
EXCEL, ACCESS

PROFESSIONAL VALUE OFFERED

Highly creative, profit-driven Product Manager with a proven record of accomplishments, and a keen ability to develop new business opportunities, successfully launching new products into the marketplace. Develop products, introduce product line maintenance, documentation, and integration.

PROFESSIONAL EMPLOYMENT

Technical Product Specialist
e-Entertainment, Inc., Reston, Virginia   **1995 to Present**
e-Entertainment, Inc., specializes in the complete production of electronic entertainment products including technical design, engineering, component sourcing, manufacturing, assembly, package design and distribution. The company has grown from start-up operations to $7.5M volume with national distribution in an extremely competitive high-tech market.

SCOPE OF OPERATIONS

• Achieved strong and sustainable revenue for the company through demonstrated knowledge of financial and product management practices. Expertly determine long-range objectives and manage projects within or below established budgets.

• Competent expertise of highly specialized electronic entertainment products. Envision products, work with business development, and marketing to create and execute product strategies. Research industry trends. Review the competitive landscape of the industry and expertly translate market analyses into ongoing product development.

• Gather technical requirements, prepare proposals, and manage the implementation of product features with corporate operations, marketing, and sales efforts. Create and monitor business metrics. Analyze revenue streams, establish and manage costs, draft schedules and product delivery. Keen insight for reviewing processes and advising production and operations.

Selected Achievements

♦ Instrumental in building a start-up dot.com company from the ground floor to three sites with 65,000 square feet of manufacturing space, millions of dollars of capital equipment, a warehouse with distribution capability, and an annual volume of $7.5M.

♦ Successfully positioned and marketed a CD game product, clinching the market and doubling annual revenue for the company.

♦ Improved quality product ratings by 16% implementing a continuous improvement process. Execute operational aspects of market trials and key customer sampling.

♦ Planned and drafted a formal, master production schedule for annual and five-year product manufacturing plans based on current and projected trends.

♦ Expanded vendor sourcing and captured over $500K in material and cost reductions.

(Continued)

Martin B. Parish, Page 2

Product Manager/Market Segment Manager
Molecular Sciences Company, Baltimore, Maryland   **1990 to 1995**
* Molecular Sciences Company is the world's largest manufacturer and distributor of state-of-the-art research products and electrophoresis apparatus used in gene research—moving toward the Millennium.

SCOPE OF OPERATIONS

- Prepared business and marketing plans to include pricing, market strategy, and forecasting. Designed and implemented numerous marketing plans for several markets—with each market fully exceeding the quota. Monitored competitors—gathered and analyzed competitive market intelligence and determined competitive trends within the market.

- Project Management: Coordinated engineering, marketing, and outside vendor tasks for each new product. Established inspection, diagnostic, and installation procedures as required. Assessed processes and designed customer-friendly products. Researched, developed, and implemented policies and procedures.

Selected Achievements

- Assembled a cross-functional team to address productivity, efficiency, product quality, and distribution issues—resulting in improved relations between marketing and business operations in the launch and promotion of a new product line, with a significant increase of 26% in annual sales.

- Controlled over $2.6M in capital plant and equipment assets engaging the company in new and even more profitable business opportunities. Evaluated molding processes to best suit specific products.

- Envisioned and designed a presentation binder instrumental in closing million-dollar plus sale projects, with several essential customers.

- Published a District Brochure, the standard for promoting equipment. Composed operation and maintenance manuals for company equipment.

- Participated in various promotional programs. Created and delivered complex PowerPoint presentations. Displayed and promoted products at trade shows. Conducted customer visits.

- Working with engineers, developed and marketed approximately 40 different genetic research products, creating the benchmark of electrophoresis apparatus used in gene research, with an annual contract of $2.5M. Oversaw design processes, contracting, operations/production, and distribution for plastic medical technology products. Researched and determined best raw materials suppliers to purchase from.

EDUCATION

MBA, Radford University, Virginia, 1990
BS in Economics, University of Maryland, 1988

TRADE ORGANIZATIONS

Society of Product Managers, National Program Chairman, 1999 to 2001

Daniel S. Schmitz
784 Callaway Drive ● Kansas City, Kansas 66011 ● 913-555-4416

Professional Experience

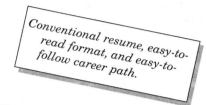

Conventional resume, easy-to-read format, and easy-to-follow career path.

SPRINT CORPORATION
April 1992 to Present

Senior Product Manager, Long Distance Division, 1997 to Present

- Developed and implemented a new network platform called Sprint ION.
- Made sales presentations to 40 of the Fortune 100 list of companies explaining converged network services and how Sprint ION represented this new approach to voice and data networking.
- Developed product implementation process for new platform including, training, support of the sales staff, and resolution of issues related to implementation.

Manager of Finance Markets, Local Telecom Division, 1992 to September 1997

- Responsible for the development of applications sold to the financial markets in the 19 states in which the Local Telecom division of Sprint operates.
- Developed market strategy to address the finance markets, including the generation of an overall market plan and application marketing plans.
- Made multiple sales and marketing presentations in support of the sales process to customers of the seven regional operating companies.
- Taught training classes for sales and marketing personnel to acquaint them with the consultative sales process within the banking markets.
- Wrote a business case for a new related business for Sprint.

FARM & HOME SAVINGS INFORMATION SYSTEMS
FARM & HOME FINANCIAL CORPORATION
1987 to 1992

Vice President of New Product Development Farm & Home Financial Corporation,
1989 to 1992

- Directed a staff of 34 in the areas of Telecommunications, Operations, and Computer Systems.
- Managed all aspects of software purchase from design, to security, to negotiation of contract and price as well as the implementation process.
- Handled the coordination of all acquisitions and mergers from the data processing perspective.

Vice President, Manager of Information Support, 1987 to 1989

- Managed a staff of 8 people responsible for the sales and marketing of outsource services.
- Responsible for the evolution and implementation of application systems.
- Held primary responsibility for budget tracking and reporting for the company.
- Maintained a business plan and set priorities for enhancement to the system.

(Continued)

Daniel S. Schmitz   *Page 2*

FINANCIAL INFORMATION TRUST
December 1974 to November 1987

Regional Director of Member Services, 1983 to 1987

- Managed a staff of eleven people, five dedicated to telephone support and six dedicated to sales and on-site support of financial institutions in a six state area.
- Had expanded duties that included sales and support responsibilities and met or exceeded overall objectives for territory during every year in which I managed region.
- Participated in the analysis of multiple software packages for utilization at the Trust.
- Held responsibility for the direction of field support staff in the areas of sales to existing and potential customers.
- Maintained an action plan and budget with reporting on a monthly basis to senior management.

Account Manager, 1976 to 1983

- Was responsible for the sale, service, and subsequent support of financial institution in a three-state territory.
- Met or exceeded sales objectives during all 8 years in which I had responsibility for the territory.
- Held responsibility as the correspondent banking representative for member institution of the Federal Home Loan Bank of Des Moines.

Account Representative, 1974 to 1976

- Learned financial processing and financial institution management.

ARDAN WHOLESALE
1973 to 1974

Branch Accounting Manager

- Responsible for store accounting staff at corporate headquarters.
- Directed the accounting and auditing function in 8 stores in 5 states.

Education

Simpson College, Indianola, Iowa
Bachelor of Arts in Business Administration, May 1973

REFERENCES
References will be furnished upon request.

Good resume that illustrates technical strengths and key-words throughout.

SETH MILLER

575654 Lane Boulevard, La Mirada, California 91943 ● (858) 555-1946
smiller@aol.com

PROGRAMMER

Competent, intelligent, and personable computer professional with considerable experience developing and programming database and computer support programs. Computer literate in a wide variety of technology and software applications. Proven record of success in training end-user staffs in technical aspects of computer program products. Developed excellent reputation for creating, designing, presenting, implementing, and evaluating accurate and effective processes. Formal academic studies are reinforced by technological expertise enhanced by specialized professional training. Skills include:

☑ Communications	☑ Program Analysis	☑ Strategic Planning
☑ Computer Languages	☑ Program Development	☑ Support Services
☑ Management Skills	☑ Program Evaluation	☑ Systems Requirements
☑ Organizational Skills	☑ Repair and Maintenance	☑ Telecommunications
☑ Policies and Procedures	☑ Quality Assurance	☑ Troubleshooting

COMPUTER LANGUAGES AND ENVIRONMENTS

C(DOS, Windows, and UNIX), C++ (DOS, Windows, OS/2), DELPHI, Java, Pascal and Turbo Vision (OOPS), Basic (DOS), Visual Basic (Windows), HTML, Perl, JavaScript, CGI, SQL, Prolog, VB for Application, FORTRAN, ASSEMBLY (x86, 8031, VAX, PDP-11), HPL (Hardware Programming Language), Ladder Logic, Continuous Control Chart (CCC)

COMPUTER AND OTHER SYSTEMS

VAX 11/780, Micro VAX, UNISYS, and AS/400. IBM PC SeriesX86, Cicso Routers series 4500, AS5100 Access Server, Process Control and Real-time machines like Honeywell UDC Series 9000, LAN, WAN, PLC Network, and Zworld PLC

OPERATING SYSTEMS, ENVIRONMENTS, DATABASES AND PACKAGES

DOS, Windows 95/98/NT, NT-RAS, UNIX, LINUX, VMS, ALTRIX, OS/2, PCDM, SCADA, NETWARE, INTERNET, SQL Server, Oracle, Access, FoxPro, MS Project, MS Office, AutoCad, Orcad, Erwin, Casewise

PROFESSIONAL EXPERIENCE

NAVAL FACILITIES ENGINEERING COMMAND, La Mesa, California – 1997 to present

Programmer, Project Management, Analysis, and Development Department. Oversee development and implementation of documentation, security, and formal management systems for command customers. Act as Management Analyst in the Operations and Systems Division providing technical support of existing program applications aimed at developing and implementing new applications in support of the Public Works community.

- Managed and developed Visual C (Win32), JavaScript and Oracle based billing, inventory, accounts management, and MIS systems.
- Incorporated change in the billing and account management systems by implementing Roaming services by GRIC.

(Continued on next page)

PROFESSIONAL EXPERIENCE *(Continued)*

NAVAL FACILITIES ENGINEERING COMMAND, Coronado, California – 1993 to 1997

Programmer and Computer Specialist in the Information Management Support Section involved in supporting existing applications in the Family Housing Activity Management Information System (FAMIS) program and technical representation to projects aimed at new applications development and implementation.

- Spearheaded creation and development of the FAMIS program, 1995.

HOUSING DEPARTMENT, Marine Corps Base, Camp Pendleton, California – 1990 to 1993

Programmer and Computer Specialist in the Facilities Division involved in coordinating and integrating technical computer aspects with administrative matters such as standards management, acquisition and configuration management, ADP security, and risk management.

- Oversaw development of commandwide management analysis techniques.

ISMO, 1stForce Service Support Group (FSSG), Camp Pendleton, California – 1988 to 1990

Computer Programmer and Analyst providing Site Coordinator and Database Administrator assistance and production requirements coordination to ensure sufficient scheduling flexibility and equipment capacity to meet peak production needs, maintain accurate automated workload schedules, and processing times. Prepared, designed, and wrote complex computer application programs, procedures, and systems for the military information systems management program.

- Coordinated and simultaneously administered programs for 38 cross-functional, multitiered military organizations in multiple locations.
- Nominated for Navy Achievement Medal for significant accomplishments as a Programmer, Team Leader, and Analyst.

EDUCATION

Southern Illinois University, Carbondale, Illinois
     Master of Science - Computer Information Systems

National University, San Diego, California – GPA: 3.9 Cum Laude
     Bachelor of Science - Major: Information Technology

PROFESSIONAL DEVELOPMENT AND TRAINING

Irvine Training Center, Irvine, California
     Administering ENS for NetWare

David Maibor Associates, Inc. Seminars, Long Beach, California
     Software Development and Documentation: EIA/IEEE J-STD-016 and ISO/IEC 12207

Appropriate personal and professional references are available.

Jennifer Southworth

104 N. Meyers Drive • Hazel Park, Michigan 48030 • emailaddress@emailaddress.com • 248.555.0955

PROFESSIONAL PROFILE

Skilled project manager and savvy Internet steward. Track record of successful product introduction and implementation. Dynamic self-starter with a strong sense of responsibility and positive, aggressive attitude.

Creative problem solver who applies technical skills and business knowledge to achieve improved results. Able to manage complex programs and multiple projects simultaneously. Productive as both individual contributor and team member. Excellent communication and relationship-building skills.

"Jennifer continues to deliver a strong, consistent performance. Her positive attitude and attacking style help keep those around her focused on solving complex problems."

"She always takes the initiative, works extremely well on her own, and rarely needs follow-up on action items."

"Her professional conduct and technical wisdom have earned her the respect of her peers and management."

.. C. Laurencelle, Manager

ACHIEVEMENTS

- ❂ Recognized for success in the delivery of user training and support programs that *outpaced the competition and provided 24-hour support to internal/external customers worldwide*.
- ❂ Conducted an analysis to reduce online search complexity. *Implementation of the design reduced timing issues without affecting the overall design.*
- ❂ Integral member of team that convinced management to allow the team to develop a tool that addressed a major Website integrity issue. *Resulted in an improved design and greatly improved customer satisfaction.*

EXPERIENCE

MITSUBISHI TECHNICAL CENTER, U.S.A., INC.　　　　　　　　　　　　　　　Plymouth, Michigan
INTERNET ANALYST, 1998-current
Interface with IS/IT and outside agencies to develop and implement systems which advance development of comprehensive international Web presence to grow/increase business efforts.
- ❂ Pilot new software and technologies which support the Internet site.
- ❂ Develop Internet strategy to provide a competitive advantage.
- ❂ Define metrics for success, analyze and interpret data, breed Web strategies and tactics and present reasoning to upper management.

MARKETING SPECIALIST, 1996-98

THE DAVIS:MARTIN GROUP　　　　　　　　　　　　　　　　　　　　　　Detroit, Michigan
COPYWRITER/ADMINISTRATIVE ASSISTANT – 1995-96
- ❂ Provided design and writing skills for client campaigns in boutique design firm specializing in creating printed materials and Website development.

EDUCATION & PROFESSIONAL DEVELOPMENT

EASTERN MICHIGAN UNIVERSITY　　　　　　　　　　　　　　　　　　　Ypsilanti, Michigan
Master of Arts in Composition and Rhetoric course work

OLIVET NAZARENE UNIVERSITY　　　　　　　　　　　　　　　　　　　　Kankakee, Illinois
BACHELOR'S DEGREE IN ENGLISH, 1993 – Minor: Business Marketing

Jeff Kilpatrick

7 Camelot Court, Stratford by Del Mar, California 92014 ● (858) 555-6328
jkilpatrick@savis.com

PUBLIC RELATIONS SPECIALIST ● MARKETING STRATEGIST

Confident, competent, and results-oriented professional with considerable, cross-functional experience in public relations, marketing, strategic planning, and competitive positioning reinforced by strong campaign management skills and an innate, creative talent. Diverse expertise is augmented by a formal education in Business Administration. Keen troubleshooting skills; able to identify, carefully assess, and quickly resolve problems. Positive attitude; personable and professional demeanor. Computer literate in a variety of software applications and Internet technologies. Qualifications include:

- Accounts Management
- Business Development
- Communications
- Competitive Analysis

- E-Mail Marketing
- Internet Marketing
- Investor Relations
- Market Analysis

- Market Research
- Media Relations
- Special Events
- Strategic Planning

EDUCATION AND PROFESSIONAL DEVELOPMENT

University of Southern California, Los Angeles, California
Master of Science in **Marketing and Public Relations**
Bachelor of Science in **Business Administration**

University of Southern California, Los Angeles, California
Leadership for the 21st Century Seminar—Live Remote with Peter F. Drucker

PROFESSIONAL EXPERIENCE

E-MPe3.com, San Jose, California – 1998 to present

Public Relations Director responsible for overseeing strategic IPO planning, implementing crises management, coordinating global marketing activities with public relations campaigns, managing the public relations agency, and conducting an effective marketing and public relations program. Planned, directed, developed and communicated information designed to market the company.

Key participant in largest private Internet IPO in history of stock market and key strategist in original marketing team of a multibillion Internet music service provider.
Successfully launched media relations campaign for E-MPe3.com Initial Public Offering (IPO). Coordinated all publicity efforts with more than 300 media outlets including *New York Times*, *Wall Street Journal*, *US News and World Report*, *Time*, *USA Today*, *Los Angeles Time*, *Wired*, *CNET*, *The Industry Standard*, Business 2.0, thestreet.com, CNN, CNBC, Fox News, etc.
Coordinated post IPO media tour interviews with Good Morning America, CNN, CNBC, Bloomberg News, British Broadcasting Company, *Business Week*, *Wall Street Journal*,

Partner Marketing Director responsible for implementing business development programs and contracts. Scope of responsibility included managing client relations, matrix teams, internal communications, and identifying new avenues to generate new revenues. Primary member of focus group developing, identifying, implementing, and communicating strategic plans and

(Continued on next page)

Jeff Kilpatrick

7 Camelot Court, Stratford by Del Mar, California 92014 ● (858) 555-6328

Resume   *Page Two*

PROFESSIONAL EXPERIENCE *(Continued)*

quarterly revenues, enhancing clients' marketplace presence, increasing corporate awareness and profitability.

Managed major corporate accounts generating 95% + of quarterly revenues. Communicated unique and innovative management techniques to increase site traffic and enhance brand awareness through diversified market strategies.

Callaway Golf Company / Odyssey Golf, Inc., Carlsbad, California - 1995 to 1998

Public Relations Specialist and Marketing Manager reporting to the Vice President of Marketing. Recruited by President/CEO. Planned and conducted public relations program designed to create and maintain a favorable public image for the company. Planned, directed, developed, and communicated information designed to increase public awareness of programs, accomplishments, and products. Developed and released feature articles, editorial interviews, press releases, and publications. Cultivated event press support, promotional items, and corporate imaging by contacting editors, writers, and media representatives in the United States and Europe. Directed efforts in building media outlets to ensure a strong publicity presence. Fostered strong relationships with the media and public. Communicated company image to international distributors, corporate accounts, suppliers, and manufacturers.

- Challenged to develop a publicity campaign to sell the company story; implemented successful international radio, television, and newsprint publicity campaigns.
- Key participant 1998 NFL Super Bowl Media Day at San Diego Convention Center.
- Coordinated Stronomic System launch on Odyssey Golf Media Day at Callaway Golf Center, Las Vegas, Nevada, 1998 International PGA Show.
- Represented Odyssey Golf at the 1998 Callaway Golf Shareholders meeting.
- Key team participant in discussion meetings to implement a strategic marketing plan.

    Public Relations and Special Markets Executive. Challenged to introduce new products, develop new business, and expand corporate accounts in the special markets arena.

    Key participant in sales and marketing team effort that increased sales from $4.5 million to $17 million, to $38 million, and finally to $67 + million in annual sales over a four year period.

CALIFORNIA DISTRIBUTING, La Costa, California - 1993 to 1995

Sales Manager reporting to the President. Oversaw all activities of the sales team and administrative support personnel engaged in selling commercial and industrial construction equipment. Supervised the daily sales effort. Trained and oriented all sales representatives.

- Started National Equipment Warehouse Catalog Sales Division de novo.
- Increased sales significantly by implementing the national sales catalog.

REFERENCES

Appropriate personal and professional references are available.

73—QUALITY ASSURANCE MANAGER

PAUL AYERS

1201 Slipper Court * Columbia,
(410) 555-8073 * Email: PA@yahoo.com

CAREER PROFILE

HIGH TECH QUALITY ASSURANCE MANAGEMENT

TQM / QA / Internal Controls •Evaluate Process & Design Improvements • Inspector Analysis • Project Manager • Establish Procedures • R&D •EIT (Engineer in Training) Windows NT • Lotus 1-2-3 •Access • Excel • Word • TCP/IP • PowerPoint • Unix
Write & Publish Training Materials and Policy

Five years' direct experience in testing and systems implementation in an e-commerce environment. Ten years' experience in QA and risk management. Expertly map business processes, analyze test conditions and results. Utilize testing tools and automated e-commerce tools including Mercury. Strong technical and analytical skills.

Progressive record of accomplishments for analyzing in-place operations and determining solutions: consistently develop systems and processes highly increasing work productivity and efficiency.

PROFESSIONAL EXPERIENCE

QUALITY EFFECTIVENESS MANAGER   **1996 TO PRESENT**
CC SOLUTIONS, BALTIMORE, MD

☑ Recruited by this cutting-edge Internet solutions provider, specializing in high-tech computer chip development, sale, and delivery, to review and strengthen process improvement initiatives and define requirements for operational need. Direct and monitor QA in three separate facilities. Manage and account for a budget of $2.2M. Review and revise policy. Manage multiple projects and meet deadlines.

☑ *Enthusiastic management style—lead by example. Assemble talented working teams to diagnose and resolve operational problems. Genuinely listen to employees and encourage vision meetings, whereby ideas are suggested for implementation (these meetings are held without management present, to mobilize resources and enhance staff creativity).*

☑ Designed and incorporated a TQ control structured management system program with strict guidelines, bringing the company in alignment with industry standards, receiving high marks from users and clients. Developed ISO-9000 process schematics ensuring adherence to regulatory standards. Constantly gather data, oversee equipment operations, assess operational procedures and develop and implement fully reactive and proactive measures to expedite operations.

☑ Assessed root causes for a six month backlog in data entry and records management resulting in the design of new schedules, contracting an administrative employee for four months, and streamlining records procedures, which decreased the backlog in two and one half months to a manageable level.

☑ Within six months of coming on board, effectively reduced warehouse stockpiling, moving products into the market and increasing distribution capacity by 17%.

☑ Devised and implemented a customer satisfaction survey tool with returns of better than 70%, used to correct problem areas and enhance successes in services and products.

☑ Research and introduce the best practices in key QA areas, i.e., test and performance automation, quality metrics, layers testing techniques, user-centered design, and reliability engineering. Write concise reports providing in-depth analyses regarding product and service quality, defending conclusions, and offering practical solutions. Prepare and conduct presentations and training sessions in the fundamentals of TQL.

(Continued)

203

QUALITY ASSURANCE SPECIALIST

1990 to 1996
Bowman Technologies, Reston, VA

☑ Reviewed processes, set policies and protocols, and met with Configuration Management, Change Management, Risk Management and Testing areas.

☑ Created a change/risk management committee resulting in automation for change management and implementation of risk management tools.

☑ Instrumental in division achieving industry ratings.

☑ Successfully evaluated a software development project noting six deficiencies. Provided immediate corrective remarks, monitored the implementation of corrective actions, and conducted follow-up testing.

☑ Prepared and executed test scripts, documented results, and evaluated the quality of the system. Managed a team of testers.

☑ Defined and implemented software development processes including Requirements, Design, Construction, Test, and Delivery.

☑ Evaluated and documented operations, created organizational procedures, data conversion, and other implementation tasks.

MILITARY SERVICE

SIGNAL COMMUNICATIONS SPECIALIST (SECRET CLEARANCE)

1986 TO 1990
UNITED STATES ARMY

☑ Supervised, installed, operated, and maintained multichannel communications equipment including communications security equipment. Interpreted Signal Operating Instructions extracts, circuit routing lists, and system traffic designs. Applied internal QA measures.

EDUCATION

BS, Civil Engineering, University of Maryland, 1990
President of the Student Chapter of the American Society of Civil Engineers

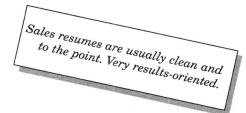
Sales resumes are usually clean and to the point. Very results-oriented.

Suzanne Bolar

1212 Easy St. - Orange, CA 92867 - (714) 555-1212 - sbolar@worklink.org

SUMMARY

- Top sales performer in software, video, and broadcasting-related industries.
- Web literate and eager to learn more.

SIGNIFICANT EXPERIENCE

Sales Related:
- Coordinated product sales in relation to client Websites
- Increased new accounts by 33% in 1999
- Successfully prospected and managed client base in twelve states
- Achieved top sales results ($300K+ in 1998/1999) for pre/postproduction, duplication, printing, packaging, and fulfillment
- Developed software sales, training, and installation technical assistance strategies

Production Related:
- Expertly coordinated video, CD, etc., pre/postproduction, duplication and international formats
- Conceived, wrote, produced, and hosted one company's first video catalogue
- Produced, wrote, and hosted special interest reports for news segments and award-winning magazine program
- Produced/hosted in-flight audio interview, news, and special segment programs for major U.S. airlines

Senior Account Executive - NewWord Media INTL., Los Angeles, CA 1998-present
    (video, audio, and CD services)
Senior Account Executive - PSI KAPPA Video, Inc., Anaheim, CA 1993-1997
    (video and audio services)
News Anchor and Program Producer, SOMEtvCable, Inc., Somewhere, CA 1990-1996
    (TV magazine program)
Account Executive - WHYNOT, INC., Boston, MA 1989-1990
    (securities database software company)
Narrator/Spokesperson - VaVoom Voice Productions, Los Angeles, CA 1990-present
    (Voice-over for commercial/industrial ads worldwide on video, CD, etc.)

EDUCATION

B.S. Communications, University of California at Los Angeles (UCLA)
Computer Programming and Business Writing, Harvard University
Fundamentals of Public Relations and Writing for P.R., UCLA

RELATED DATA:
Member of WWW Professionals, well traveled, energetic, & creative.

DAVID HEINTZELMAN

78 Lafayette Street
Erie, PA 16508
Email: emailaddress@email.com

Home: (814) 555-6543
Office: (814) 555-2109
Cell: (814) 555-0327

SALES / SALES MANAGEMENT EXECUTIVE
CUTTING-EDGE COMPUTER & INTERNET TECHNOLOGIES

*Key Account Management ♦ New Business Development ♦ Direct Sales & Reseller Partnerships
Consultative & Solution Sales ♦ Networking & Relationship Building ♦ Contract Negotiations*

PROFILE

Dynamic 14-year sales career reflecting pioneering experience and record-breaking performance in the computer and Internet industries. Remain on the cutting edge, driving new business through key accounts and establishing strategic partnerships and dealer relationships to increase channel revenue.

♦ Expert in sophisticated e-commerce sales models and vast knowledge of both the e-business marketplace and the capabilities and complexities of products.

♦ Outstanding success in building and maintaining relationships with key corporate decision makers, establishing large-volume, high-profit accounts with excellent levels of retention, and loyalty.

♦ Exceptionally well organized with a track record that demonstrates self-motivation, creativity, and initiative to achieve both personal and corporate goals

"David is a dynamic leader and arguably one of the best salespeople that has ever worked on any of the sales teams I have managed. I highly recommend David for a position within any organization."

— *VP of Sales, Millennium Software*

PROFESSIONAL EXPERIENCE

1998 - Present

Web Communications, Philadelphia, PA

DISTRICT SALES MANAGER

Execute direct and channel partner sales models for advanced e-commerce software applications. Target a broad market, meeting sophisticated e-business needs for customers that include Fortune 500s and emerging dot.coms. Interface directly with top-level executives, negotiate high-dollar contracts, and coordinate implementation. Manage accounts and orchestrate post-sale professional services and resources.

Key Achievements:

♦ Achieved 186% of quota and qualified for "President's Club." Grew sales to $4 million within 6 months and positioned as the top #2 rep in the company.

♦ Established alliances with 10 major integration partners and attained ranking as the top #1 sales producer within just one year, generating $7.6 million annually.

♦ Delivered $2.8 million revenue, selling 2 of the first 5 units in North America of a newly released, cutting-edge e-commerce business solution.

♦ Opened a completely unworked territory, surpassing all sales goals in spite of challenges associated with the sale of a v.1 release product with no reference sites.

♦ Generated the highest volume of new accounts companywide, and was recognized with a "President's Achievement Award," the company's most prestigious honor.

(Continued)

DAVID HEINTZELMAN Page 2

1994 - 1998 **Millennium Software, Boston, MA**

AREA SALES MANAGER (1995 - 1998)
SENIOR ACCOUNT EXECUTIVE (1994 - 1995)

Built a territory spanning Maine to Pennsylvania for this $5 billion provider of Web development tools, Web-based applications, and consulting services. Rapidly achieved goals and refocused to resolve challenging sales and personnel issues. Led a 10-person team generating $15 million annually through sales of middleware and application-server solutions in enterprise software space.

Key Achievements:

♦ Transformed an underproducing sales team, immediately resolving long-standing problems, and instituting incentives that elevated performance while building morale and motivation. Ramped area sales 550%+ in under 3 years.

♦ Surpassed personal quota, generating more than 200% of license sales goals and 175% of service sales goals. Overachieved area sales objectives every eligible year.

♦ Identified, pursued, and closed the largest license deal in company history, contributing millions of dollars through annually recurring revenue.

♦ Penetrated dozens of profitable B2B accounts, individually valued at up to $2.5 million, with major Fortune 500 customers.

♦ Championed creative marketing initiatives, including seminar series with partners, sponsorship of national Java user groups, and speaking engagements in Internet and e-commerce space.

1991 - 1994 **Multimedia, Inc., Saddlebrook, NJ**

EAST COAST TERRITORY MANAGER

Sold and marketed multimedia, computer-based training, graphics and 3-D design, photo-imaging, sound editing, and Web-page development tools to key Fortune 500 and 1000 accounts. Supervised the sales force in all East Coast trade shows and industry events. Drove sales of more than $8 million annually through consumer distribution channels; delivered an average 145% of channel quota.

1986 - 1991 Early career includes inside/outside sales experience with two large computer resellers targeting both consumer and business markets.

EDUCATION & TRAINING

B.S., Business Administration (1986)
University of California, Los Angeles

Extensive professional training in the areas of sales, relationship building, and leadership. Certified for IBM, Apple, and Compaq sales. Completed Novell Network sales training.

TECHNICAL SKILLS

Skilled with MAC OS, Windows 3.11, 95, 98, NT, and NT Server, MS Office (Word, PowerPoint, Excel, Access, Project, and Outlook), Director, FreeHand, Authorware, Soundedit 16, Extreme 3D, Backstage Desktop Studio, CC:Mail, Lotus Notes, Novell GroupWise, ACT, MS FrontPage, and Vivo Active Producer. Advanced Internet skills.

76—SALES ENGINEER (E-MAIL RESUME)

William H. Garrou
123 Any Ave * Mytown, USA 00000
H 123 456 7890   W 123 456 7890

Summary of Qualifications

* Public Speaking/ Presentation Skills
* Technical Writing
* In-Depth Technical Knowledge of Data Networking including: Frame Relay, Managed Network Services, TCP/IP (Dial and Dedicated), Security, ATM, Network Design and Implementation, Router Configuration and Emerging Technologies

Professional History

Sprint Corporation, Greensboro, NC
September 1999 to Present
Sprint ION Business Development Manager
National Accounts overlay sales manager for Southeast Region. Responsible for leading Sprint sales in the southeast national accounts region.

Sprint Corporation, Greensboro, NC
March 1998 to Present
Area Consulting Engineer
Area Support for Eastern United States. Reported directly to Director of Application Engineering. Drove product development issues and disseminated information to field presales support groups. Delivered presentations to internal and external customers at all levels. Worked on Sprint ION product and process development. Responsible for leading Regional ION Support Teams in the sales cycle for Sprint ION opportunities including account planning, network design, customer presentation, and contract negotiation. Contributed in the development of marketing and pricing strategy for Sprint ION.

Sprint Corporation, Greensboro, NC
1995 to 1998
Regional Consulting Engineer
Senior engineering position provided expert level consulting, design and sales support for data networking and emerging technology opportunities. Responsible for ensuring success of all strategic sales opportunities involving data. Heavily involved in qualification, positioning, contract negotiation, and closing throughout the sales cycle. Worked directly with sales management team during account planning and strategic opportunity review. RCE team leader: worked closely with management on key initiatives including product development and rollout. Supervised Network Engineers in North Carolina. Responsibilities also included mentoring the sales support field engineers; developed technical training curriculum and instructed specific courses such as IP Services, Security Services, and Frame Relay.

Sprint Corporation, Greensboro, NC
1990 to 1995
Network Engineer
Responsibilities included presales engineering of data opportunities. Completed verbal and written responses to Request for Proposals on all levels including executive briefings, technical overviews, solution presentation, and

(Continued)

208

detailed engineering briefings. Performed cost analysis on different network designs in order to provide complete and detailed responses to proposals. Prepared order packages and tracked orders through provisioning process to implementation. Worked with customer to ensure satisfaction of products and services "post-sell." Ongoing life-cycle support of data accounts for growth, redesign, and change management.

Sprint Corporation, Washington, DC
1989 to 1990
Test and Acceptance Engineer
Responsibilities included the supervision of all activity on Sprint's northeast U.S. fiber network related to the actual splicing and testing of the backbone cable. Coordinated work activity with Sprint internal groups, construction contractors, and Sprint field technicians on an as needed basis to complete backbone cable maintenance and repair. Developed career pathing and assisted with merit reviews for Sprint field technicians. Developed annual budgets for backbone cable maintenance and repair.

American Spliceco Inc., Columbia, MD
1985 to 1989
Operations Manager
Responsibilities included: personnel acquisition, development and motivation, profit/loss for splicing/testing division, including generation of bid responses and quotes for additional work, capital expenses and operating budget, coordination of work schedule to meet deadlines.

Education
East Carolina University, Greenville, NC, 1984
BS Industrial Technology/ Manufacturing and Management

Sally Nelson

Layout very clean and professional. Good title and profile section at top.

398 Menominee Village Way
Lake Orion, Michigan 48360

residence: 248.555.3738
cell: 248.555.4114 / *fax:* 248.555.3739
email: emailaddress@emailaddress.com

SALES $ MARKETING $ SALES MANAGEMENT
Internet Banking & Financial Service Industries

Senior Sales and Business Development Executive with proven ability to drive business growth through aggressive sales initiatives that deliver revenue growth, market share, and market penetration. Conceptual thinker and strategic planner who balances sales production and sales leadership. Experienced in technology/product launch and market expansion. Well-versed in dealing with diverse operational units (Legal, IS/IT, Finance, HR, Investor Relations).

Cross-Functional Team Building & Leadership	Consultative Sales
Internet Business Development & Implementation	Contract Terms & Negotiation
Competitive Analysis & Product Positioning	Relationship Marketing

Strong background in identifying, establishing, and managing strategic relationships to leverage and generate significant business opportunities. Talented motivator with keen business acumen.

EXPERIENCE

INTERCHANGE MARKET SYSTEMS CORPORATION

INTERNET SALES DIRECTOR OF U.S. OPERATIONS, 2000-current

Lead sales management for Canadian software developer of middleware bridge products that link broker/dealer's core processing system with retail customers directly through Internet channel to enable online customer trade options with their existing broker instead of e-trade brokerage firms.

- Recruited as member of expansion team to launch market presence in the United States and establish a beachhead; select and position a veteran sales team and set Internet strategies in place.
- Forecast European, Latin American, and Australian markets; exploit market feasibility.

PCPS SOFTWARE/ZEENET, INC.

DIRECTOR OF SALES, 1999-2000

Headed the sales and marketing efforts of Internet banking software solutions to community banks and bank holding companies in the Michigan market.

- Originated an e-commerce portal for each of the Internet banking clients, including an electronic bill-payment feature.
- Successfully secured endorsement of Independent Bankers Bank for additional channel marketing.

MUTUAL TRUST GROUP

VICE PRESIDENT OF Midwest Marketing Division, 1998-99

Established newly-created position to launch turnkey counselor selling program throughout sales and nonsales units of the company. Managed nine account VPs throughout the Midwest.

- Expanded revenue 12% in first eight months. Achieved #1 ranking among peer group by end of third quarter.
- Redesigned pricing structure for corporate P&C product line to block competition and preserve market share.

Continued

Experience (continued)

GREYHAM INSURANCE GROUP

VICE PRESIDENT OF Business Development, 1991-98

Championed entry into bank-operated investment centers with community banks. Contracted 25% of the target market in first 12 months; secured endorsement of Michigan Bankers Association.

- Established pivotal relationships with Michigan's largest bank holding companies: NBD (Detroit), First of America (Kalamazoo), Old Kent (Grand Rapids), Michigan National (Farmington Hills).

- Developed professional links with Michigan's largest mortgage companies (Source One and GMAC); gained connections with major thrift corporations (Great Lakes Bancorp and Standard Federal Bank).

- Chaired executive committee that expanded corporate product lines and systems support resulting in 600% revenue growth over five years.

MUTUAL LIFE INSURANCE COMPANY [1973-91]

REGIONAL VICE PRESIDENT (Detroit, Michigan), 1988-91

Managed staff of 45 sales managers, sales representatives, and service personnel domiciled in 12 Midwestern states. Implemented captive insurance/reinsurance marketed throughout banking and mortgage institutions.

- Directed successful ventures with GMAC and Michigan League of Savings Institutions.

- Coordinated production goals and attainment, sales strategies, and budget projections.

GROUP VICE PRESIDENT (Chicago, Illinois), 1984-88

Implemented entry into universal life insurance market for customer groups of financial institutions and employer groups.

- Negotiated reinsurance and ceding agreements with major industry leaders, including Fortune 500 firms.

- Selected, trained, and supervised sales and service team that won top national honors in 1986, 1987, and 1988.

REGIONAL MANAGER (Tampa, Florida), 1977-84

Recruited to direct expansion into Puerto Rico and Virgin Islands.

- Increased corporate market share in Florida from 8% to 45% over six years.

SALES REPRESENTATIVE (Columbus, Ohio) 1973-77

Sold more than 150 new client relationships in three years.

- Sales Rep of the Year 1974 and 1976.

EDUCATION

HANOVER COLLEGE, Hanover, Indiana

BA DEGREE IN ECONOMICS & POLITICAL SCIENCE, 1973

Sally Nelson *(page 2)*

398 Menominee Village Way
Lake Orion, Michigan 48360

residence: 248.555.3738
cell: 248.555.4114 / *fax:* 248.555.3739
email: emailaddress@emailaddress.com

Novell.

> *Good use of titles at top of resume, and of "Technical Skills" inventory on page 2. "Training and Education" leverages relevant seminars, important in this industry.*

Steven A. Bartlett, CNE

1807 Slaughter Lane • Austin, Texas 78749
(512) 555-5555 • STEVE@YAHOO.COM

Presales Engineering • Product Management • Network Engineering • Tech Support

EMPLOYMENT HISTORY

TManage, Inc.

PRESALES SUPPORT ENGINEER
Austin, Texas 2000-present

Provided technology expertise in the sales process for new accounts. Worked in tandem with Sales Representatives on professional consulting and program sales for telecommuting services and packages. Conducted technology discoveries for new customers, documented findings, and made recommendations for technology solutions as part of telecommuting package. Served as main point of contact on LAN/WAN and connectivity issues with established accounts and ensured speedy resolutions to difficulties. Gave multiple presentations to executive management of established and prospective accounts concerning technology scope.

DIRECTOR OF TECHNICAL SUPPORT/PRODUCT MANAGER
Austin, Texas 1999

Provided technical leadership and assistance in creating technical backbone capabilities, consistently dedicating 100+ hour-weeks in early stages of company operation. Managed Tech Support teams working multiple telecommuting contracts across the country and served as Interim Technical Support Representative in the Atlanta office supporting largest account. Managed team building actions, recruitment, and training for tech professionals, establishing core group of "best in class" Tech Support Organization. Evaluated, tested, and recommended all technical products for support of contracts. Gave technical presentations to accounts and prospective customers on technical scope of telecommuting programs. Traveled extensively for strategic business development.

- **Teamed on design and implementation of complete network and telecommunications infrastructure for corporate relocation. Worked with subcontractors, negotiated with service providers, and coordinated all technical needs for employees and senior management. Supervised technical operations equipment installations and operability.**
- **Played key role in initial launch of technical program with all clients including BellSouth, HP, and Compaq.**
- **Led team action to rectify crucial equipment malfunction for key account with minimum downtime, achieving executive commendation and complete customer satisfaction.**
- **Received executive commendation for performance during corporate relocation.**

Nortel Networks

SENIOR TELECOMMUNICATIONS ENGINEER
Nashville, Tennessee   1997-1999

Provided third-tier technical support in HOMEbase Operations giving expert assistance to over 3400 telecommuters as part of world's largest telecommuting program. Served as Team Leader for Tech Support Team for HOMEbase customers. Installed, troubleshot, and maintained systems using Ascend Pipeline routers, Ascend Max 4000 Switches, MCK Switch Extenders, Nortel Meridian Home Office II, and Ethernet TCP/IP connectivity in a Windows 95 environment.

- **Designed and implemented procedures plan for conversion of users from bridging to routing increasing network efficiency and customer satisfaction.**
- **Received award for high performance in clearing backload of 800 calls in a newly acquired Tech Support queue.**

TECHNICAL SKILLS

Novell Netware 4.1 and 3.1x	Advanced Telephone Systems
Windows NT Workstation and Server	Nortel Meridian Home Office II
Ethernet	MCK Digital Switch Extenders
Ascend Pipelines, Max 4000	TCP/IP, IPX/SPX, Appletalk
Jetstream Front Desk	Microsoft Office 97, 2000
MS Windows 98/2000	MS Outlook 98, 2000
MS Exchange Server	ISDN
Virtual Private Networks – PPTP/IPSec	DSL
Voice over IP – Calista, Nortel	Nortel Connectivity Extranet Server
Multiplexers	Cisco ISDN Routers
LAN/WAN design/installation	Meridian Mail

TRAINING and EDUCATION

Certified Netware Engineer, New Horizons Computer Learning Center • 1997

Technology Certifications:
Ascend – Pipeline, NavisAccess
Gandalf/Mitel   **Windows 9x**
Windows NT   **Teltone**

Navis Access Network Management, Ascend Technologies, San Jose, California. 1998
Watchguard Firewall Training – Austin, 1999
Cisco VPN Training – Austin, 2000

United States Air Force – 1989-1995 • Honorable Discharge • Top Secret SBI Clearance
Communications Computer Systems Control Specialist Training, Keesler, AFB, Mississippi

GRACE BAILEY
777 Picard Lane
Foster City, California 94404

650-555-2828
gracebailey88@msn.com

Conventional layout and approach for concise resume.

EXECUTIVE SUMMARY

Highly effective, knowledgeable, and dedicated **SAP Consultant / Systems Security and Integration executive.** Provide decisive leadership and consensus in technology selection and development. Drive creation of integrated, robust systems.

- **Significant contributor to numerous ERP / SAP projects,** from project manager and team leader to consulting within Fortune 500 companies.
- **Introduce stable business solutions and address future expansion projections** through Business Object Modeling and reusable apps.
- **Deploy systems featuring high availability, secure processing,** failure handling, component framework integrity, asynchronous messaging, and incorporate the latest in modular system design.
- **Key strengths in:**
  — Functional SAP consulting
  — Project start-up / closeout
  — Business process redesign
  — Methodology application
  — Enterprise applications integration
  — SAP solutions and transaction processing
  — Fault-tolerant and high availability systems
  — International experience (U.S., Europe, South Africa) / U.S. Green Card.

EXPERIENCE

1997 to present

Shere Khan Financial

VICE PRESIDENT, SAP Consulting and Training
Global and national responsibility for all aspects of consulting and training for three product lines within this publicly traded company. Applications include business modeling in SAP R/3 (Live Model), applications integration in SAP R/3 (LiveInterface) and business process modeling (LiveAnalyst).

- Built department from the ground up, hand-picking 16-member team, selecting technology and building reciprocal vendor relationships. Led a cross-organizational team of over 25 developers in building the next generation trading application for Shere Khan Financial.
- Recent Enterprise SAP/XML/Java system developed is currently in Beta phase; tasked with automating functions previously performed by staff and incorporating modular systems/apps to meeting increasing demands as well as ensuring system stability and security. Results to date include a projected recurring savings for new market ventures / product introductions as well as a multimillion dollar reduction in risk exposure.
- In recognition of expertise in emerging technologies, SAP integration, security and business applications, was tapped to serve on companywide Technology Review Board. Instrumental in actions to implement a stronger governance and harmonize technical decisions company-wide.

1996-97

PROJECT MANAGER, Magnavox, System Integration Center
Subcontracted through IBM with overall responsibility for the integrated system design in an "engineer to order" environment. Successfully implemented SAP R/3 Project System, Financial, Controlling, Materials Management, Sales and Distribution, Production Planning, and Human Resources modules. Jointly responsible for the development and management of project timeline, methodology (WISDDM), and other project management functions.

- continued -

Grace Bailey
Page 2

EXPERIENCE *(Continued)*

1995-96   **MANAGER, CLIENT SERVICES, East-West Consulting Group**
Involved in multiple SAP R/3 projects covering a spectrum of industries. Work included presales activities, methodology (FastTrack 4SAP), project management, business process redesign, software configuration, scoping and planning, training and thorough knowledge transfer to clients. Provided SAP functional focus on Controlling and Financial modules with an emphasis on integration to Logistics modules. Actively participated in West Coast recruiting and marketing efforts and internal company initiatives. Projects included:
- **Harris Digitech, Capital Team Project Lead** — Responsible for project management of Capital team for business reengineering and SAP functional consultants. Capital team scope included Project Systems, Sales and Distribution, and Assets Management.
- **Mergatroyd, Systems Integration Center, Project Manager** — Responsible for all project management activities and management of team of SAP consultants. Produced client with detailed Scoping and Planning and methodology approach within an "engineer to order" business environment.
- **Fyr Networks, Quality Assurance** — Provided project quality assurance and mentoring for the SAP Financial and Controlling consultants.
- **Hewlett Packard, Test & Measurement Organization** — Responsible for the Financial and Controlling configuration of SAP R/3 within a Sales and Distribution environment for steering committee presentation. Additionally, served as Financial Cost Accounting and Integration Team Lead and liaison between other global Hewlett Packard financial projects. Responsibilities included SAP Financial, Cost Accounting, Product Costing, and SAP Hierarchy processes including providing SAP functional training and process definitions.

1992-95   **SENIOR CONSULTANT, Global Consulting Solutions**
Involved in development of SAP implementation methodology (FastTrack) and development of the ICS Accelerator SAP training program. Provided functional SAP presentations, overviews, training and consulting. Involved in definitions of company current and future business processes.   Served as Lead Consultant and Team Lead on projects for PG&E, Microsoft, Exxon, USA, Exxon Chemicals, USA, General Mills, and ICI.

1989-92   **APPLICATIONS CONSULTANT, Cognitive Systems**
Implemented SAP Financials within large national and international companies. Supported SAP presales within the financial modules. Provided SAP training. Designed and developed ABAP programs to fulfill client requirements. Clients included: South African Airlines, Robert Bosch, SA, Hoechst, SA, and Mobil Oil.

EDUCATION, TRAINING, and CERTIFICATIONS
Executive M.B.A., Wits Graduate School of Business Administration, 1991
- Distinctions in: Marketing Management, Productivity Management, Organizational Behavior, Accounting, and Finance.

SAP International One-Year Training Program, SAP, Switzerland, 1988-89
Bachelor of Commerce, Accounting, University of Cape Town, South Africa, 1983-86

SAP certified Financial and Controlling consultant *(detailed list of modules available upon request)*

80—SECURITY ARCHITECT

GARY AARON

48 Garlic Field Way, Watsonville, California 95076
(408) 555-9183/ gaaaron@netscape.com

SECURITY ARCHITECT

QUALIFICATIONS
- Successful background in designing, deploying, and supporting distributed computing environments combined with a strong knowledge of router deployment and configuration.
- Develop and deploy robust security schemas that incorporate redundant solutions, electronic auditing, intrusion detection, 24x7 system/network monitoring, research services, and identification of "attack signatures."
- Solid experience with Cisco Routers, UNIX, Netware, and Windows NT. Well versed in director services (DNS, NIS, NDS, and NT Domain) including NDS and NT Domain structures.
- Diplomatic and responsive in communicating with end users and explaining security protocols. Successfully win cooperation and instill the importance of adherence to procedures through clear explanations and a positive approach that emphasizes the benefits of a secure system to end users as well as nontechnical decision makers.
- Effectively use both commercial products and public domain software to probe systems and network access points to learn how "hackers" might infiltrate and compromise systems.

EDUCATION

Bachelor of Science, Computer Science (BSCS), 1996
California Polytechnic University, San Luis Obispo, California

EXPERIENCE

1995 to present

Harrold Digitech, Scotts Valley, California
Started with this digital wireless telecommunications firm as an Intern through Cal Poly and was requested by MIS management to become a full-time employee after graduation.
System includes a PDC, an HTTP server and two FTP servers as well as an AIX box and workstations connected to an ISDN link (128K) with legal addresses.

SYSTEMS SECURITY ARCHITECT /NETWORK ADMINISTRATOR
- Promoted to System Security Architect in 1998 after successfully winning buy-in from nontechnical management to implement firewalls and eliminate public IP addresses in spite of perceived inconveniences by end users (inability to access RealAudio streams, etc.). Educated management on legal ramifications of being involved in the distribution of illicit online material and that their lack of awareness would not reduce their liability.
- Detected major compromise in network security after Sysadmin complained of unprecedented need to add disks to the server. Installed firewall, changed all internal addresses to private and had all passwords changed on the inside. Firewall log showed 300-500 attempts a day. End users immediately could access substantially more server space as well as see a marked increase in connection speeds.

Excellent resume. Very thorou nical skill set overview at end, along with well-written "Professional Experience" section.

LIN HOGUE

800 Capital of Texas • Austin, Texas 78739 • (512) 555-5555 • cell: (512) 111-1111 •

INFORMATION TECHNOLOGY CONSULTANT

Key Qualifications

Established successful track record in Web-based ventures and environments

Over 8 years' experience in PROJECT IMPLEMENTATION, PRODUCT ROLLOUT, and E-commerce venture launch

Knowledgeable in both technology and business issues with abilities to integrate the two to achieve overall strategic goals for client

Expertise in Windows NT, System Migrations, Online Security, and E-commerce

Professional Experience

TECHNICAL DIRECTOR
BlackCorp, Inc.
Austin, Texas
1997-present

Served as security consultant providing expertise in strategy, branding, customer retention, and operations security of online commerce ventures. Evaluated and "shopped" online storefronts to determine areas of revenue loss and problems in order programming. Recommended solutions to close "leaks" through better programming and marketing strategies.

Envisioned, designed, and launched online auction site, growing site annual revenues to over $350,000. Wrote business plan and secured seed funding to actively market site to special collectors market. Evolved venture into ecommerce consulting firm providing network design and administration to small and medium businesses including the Hard Rock Café and General Electric. Managed 4 employees.

Led the pack in launch of auction site, predating Ebay.com and other major auction sites with concept and being first to implement phone/fax auction entry capabilities.
Designed entire e-commerce auction application in Peri.

O/S TEST ENGINEER
Compaq Computer Corporation
Commercial Desktop Division
Houston, Texas
1996-1997

Retained to test and monitor new implementation of Windows NT on all hardware related to Compaq DeskPro systems. Acted as Senior Windows NT Subject Matter Expert for entire desktop line. Coordinated directly with Microsoft on NT compliance testing, bug reports, and resolutions. Provided testing and technical writing for NT CD-ROM and bundled software. Developed innovative test diskettes, test plans, and trained others in use. Worked directly with consumer division on system operability and future deployment strategies.

Led all compliance testing and interface compatibility for Windows NT.
Teamed on testing and development of LS 120 Imation Superdisk and Panasonic Powerdrive PDCD rewritable drives for the DeskPro system.
Managed testing, Quality Assurance, compliance, and deployment for Windows NT on DeskPro line.
Fluent in Spanish – Tested foreign language versions of Windows NT.

(Continued)

217

81—SECURITY SPECIALIST (CONT.)

INDEPENDENT CONSULTANT
Pasadena, Texas
1992-1996

PROVIDED EXPERTISE ON SEVERAL PROJECTS INCLUDING SPECIAL CONTRACT FOR VICEROY/GENERAL ELECTRIC DIVISION ON OPERATING SYSTEM CONVERSION MIGRATING FROM WINDOWS 3.1/UNIX TO WINDOWS 95/NT ENVIRONMENTS AND MANAGED UPGRADE OF EDI SYSTEM. INSTALLED ALL NETWORKING TOOLS, PERFORMED SYSTEMWIDE AUDIT AND NEEDS ANALYSIS ON FRAME RELAY NETWORK. INSTALLED AND SUPPORTED TWO TCP/IP SUBNETS AND INSTRUCTED END USERS IN TCP/IP USE. ASSURED COMPATIBILITY OF SYSTEMS FOR CONVERSION. MANAGED CONVERSION OF ALL SOFTWARE AND CONFIGURATION FOR EACH SYSTEM WITHIN A DECENTRALIZED ENVIRONMENT. TRAINED INDIVIDUAL END USERS ON WINDOWS 95 OPERATIONS.

SUCCESSFULLY MANAGED CONVERSION AND TRAINING OF END USERS WITHOUT LOSS OF WORK TIME IN A 24/7 ENVIRONMENT.

SYSTEMS ADMINISTRATOR
Automated Business Development
Boston, Massachusetts
1995

Configured Novell client systems, managed Lotus Notes and administered TCP/IP subnet. Performed domain registration, troubleshooting, and diagnostics on networks, systems applications, and PCs. Provided cutting edge configuration and programming of digital telephone system and modem pool. Contributed to first ever information sharing via the Internet for mutual fund registration firm. Teamed on presentation of system to investors for successful launch.

Technical Knowledge

Novell NetWare	C++	Ethernet
Windows NT Server	Java	Token Ring
Windows 95/98	HTML	VINES
IBM OS/2	JavaScript	PC/TCP OnNet
Mac OS	Perl	DNS
Linux	VBScript	FTP
Caldera	XML	IMAP
OSF/1	JSP	IPX/SPX
Solaris	ASP	POP3
SunOS	NetBeui	PPP
Visual Basic	Oracle	SMTP
C	MS Access	TCP/IP
Pascal	PC Anywhere	Telnet
SQL	Lotus Notes	
SQL Server	AppleTalk	

Education and Training

Bachelor of Arts – University of Texas
Major: Government • Minor: Computer Science
1997

82—SOFTWARE SYSTEMS OPERATOR

Cindy Rouse

4217 Mayfield Court * Laurel, MD 21045
410.555.0675 * CR@aol.com

**Software Systems Operator
Software Coach**

**Microsoft Windows Environment / LAN, NT
Accounting Software Development
Microsoft Office Suite**

Software Systems Operator **Highland Technology Services
2000 to Present**

❑ Cornerstone support for a multifunctional team of 45 software developers, analysts and database administrators in the process of designing a new finance software package. Familiar with all phases of the software development cycle.

❑ Monitor access to software and control privileges to modules. Distribute passwords. Explain access procedures to team members. Examine and schedule lockouts and review work in progress.

❑ Implement software plans, process data through the system, and run daily backups. Support the software test team: Run software through a test plan and ensure that systems tests thoroughly validate software requirements.

❑ Draft training documentation to assist operators in protocols and applications. Provide technical recommendations and diagnose software problems.

Help Desk Specialist **COMP-USA
1999 to 2000**

❑ Technically proficient with software installation. Fielded an average of 4 software related troubleshooting calls per hour and resolved over 75% without supervisor assistance. Talked each caller through software installation or troubleshooting. Proficient with Microsoft Office Suite and Windows 95/98/NT.

❑ Successfully assisted in-store clients with troubleshooting questions/problems regarding their software installation or use. Installed software for PC users. Professional and courteous while working with all customers.

Student **1999 to 05/2001**

❑ Howard Community College, Anticipated AA Degree in Computer Studies, 2001

Student resumes generally are best leading with educational background and distinguishing accomplishments.

MARK LUDWIG

517-555-2491

RESUME OF QUALIFICATIONS
328 WESTERN MILL
OKEMOS, MICHIGAN 48821

SUMMARY OF QUALIFICATIONS

EDUCATION

Master of Business Administration (expected 1999)
Central Michigan University, Midland, Michigan
GPA 3.0/4.0

Bachelor of Arts in Communications, 1996
Central Michigan University, Midland, Michigan
GPA 3.4/4.0

HONORS/AWARDS
- High School Valedictorian.
- Won citywide Essay Competition senior year in high school.
- Won "Best Essay" Contest out of 800 students at Armstrong State College.
- Invited to statewide Academic Recognition Ceremony at State Capitol.
- Awarded distinguished *Silver A* award from Armstrong State College.

SKILLS/ STRENGTHS
- Strong understanding of financial markets and market development.
- Proficient with all Microsoft Windows-based programs.
- Extensive background with performing strategic analysis of corporations.
- Developed multiple presentations outlining strategic recommendations.
- Proven tact and diplomacy in handling interpersonal relationships.

VOLUNTEER ACTIVITIES AND PREVIOUS WORK EXPERIENCE

Merrill Lynch, Lansing, Michigan
Intern (Summer 1997, 1998)
Performed financial analysis of prospective investment opportunities and worked directly with clients to support account manager.

SIGMA ALPHA MU FRATERNITY, Central Michigan University, MI
Kitchen Steward (Academic Season 1996, 1997, 1998)
Established kitchen procedures, many still in use, for newly chartered chapter of this fraternity. Responsible for food budget, purchasing food and supplies, interviewing and hiring kitchen personnel, supervising kitchen and dining room operations, and preparing food. Also held positions of Scholarship Chairman and Fundraising Chairman.

SPECIAL INTERESTS

Arts and crafts, badminton, beginning golf, and Michigan State University Athletics

Chuck Palmer

1135 Michigan Avenue ∎ East Lansing, MI 48823 ∎ (517) 555-0588

QUALIFICATIONS

- Marketing Degree from Michigan State University
- Tom Hopkins Seminar Attendee
- 2 years' experience selling telephone service and publishing materials
- High level of ambition to begin career

EDUCATION

Michigan State University
East Lansing, Michigan   March 1999
Earned a bachelor of arts in Marketing in under the prescribed four-year course schedule, while financing my own education. My final two years I was totally self-supportive, working an average of thirty hours per week.

Tom Hopkins Seminar
Detroit, Michigan   February 10, 1999
The seminar "How to Master the Art of Selling" shall improve my inherent sales abilities. Learning various personnel skills for applicable situations will be an invaluable asset to my career.

WORK EXPERIENCE

United Parcel Service, Lansing, Michigan   November 1997 to present
Working at UPS enabled me to earn enough to support myself in school. I earned over $12,000 per year, an impressive accomplishment for a college student. As well, I maintained the highest production average at our Center.

Sprint Telephone Division, Lansing, Michigan   1996
Sold local telephone feature services to the consumer market in Lansing. This experience paved the way for my future career path in sales. After three months at Sprint, I was the sales leader among the part-time college students and enjoyed the interaction with the customer. The only reason I left was to move on to UPS, where the part-time earning potential was greater.

OTHER SKILLS

- C/C++ and JAVA NT
- UNIX and LINUX

- Installshield, Microsoft Developer Studio, CVS
- GUI Design, Object-Oriented Design and Design Patterns

- POSIX thread API, Sentinel License Manager, and IRIS Performer.
- WIN32(with Internals), Motif, OpenGL, FOX(Open Source),

85—SYSTEMS ANALYST

Marty Zajic, MCSE

87 Andover Street, San Marcos, California 92038 ● (760) 555-1234

mzajic@spcs.com

Microsoft™	Certified
Professional	
	Systems Engineer

PROFILE

Competent, organized, and analytical professional seeking transition into the field of Computer Science and Information Technology as an Information Systems Analyst, Network Administrator, or Network Manager. IT expertise is supplemented by considerable, diverse experience, formal studies in Information Systems Technology, and refined by specialized, industry-related training. Microsoft Certified Professional (MCP) ID: 1779673. Expertise includes skills and knowledge in:

Problem Analysis	Interpersonal Skills	Project Management
Communication Skills	Multiple-Tasking	Staff Coordination
Computer Applications	Presentation Skills	Strategic Planning
Cross-Functional	Productivity Increases	Troubleshooting

EDUCATION

City College of Albany (CCA), Albany, New York
   Bachelor of Science – Major: Business Administration – GPA: 3.74

Palomar College, San Marcos, California
   Certificated Computer Science and Information Systems Program
      Networking Specialist (Microsoft Certified Systems Engineer) (MCSE)

RELEVANT EXPERIENCE

MANAGEMENT SOLUTIONS, Palo Alto, California – 1999 to present

Senior Systems Analyst reporting to the Director, Information Technology. Scope of responsibility includes supporting all non-ERP related data systems utilizing data reporting tools with a special emphasis on data integration and systems analysis. Coordinate with various departments to identify their needs and solutions for ideal data management procedures and develop customized reports for the sales and management teams. Using SQL and MS Access-based database skills, provide the foundation database structures for PeopleSoft, ADP Payroll, and RetailStar applications including accounts management and reconciliation, maintenance of bank records, troubleshooting accounts activities, spreadsheets, and related database management activities. Collateral duties include assisting the Information Systems Manager with internal diagnostics and installation of computer equipment and systems.

Developed and managed customized finance, sales, and payroll reports within 6 months. Manage a $2.8+ million flexible spending account fund.

CALIFORNIA AIR NATIONAL GUARD, San Diego, California – 1994 to present

Captain in the Infantry Division whose military responsibilities included classified and unclassified assignments throughout California. Primary duties included Systems Analysis assignments involving problem solving, decision making, leadership, training, and staff coordination. Direct liaison with external software vendors (WPDS) in the proper configuration

(Continued on next page)

Marty Zajic, MCSE

87 Andover Street, San Marcos, California 92038 • (760) 555-1234

mzajic@spcs.com

Microsoft™ | Certified
Professional
Systems Engineer

Resume   *Page Two*

RELEVANT EXPERIENCE *(Continued)*

and modification of software to meet user requirements. Led team managing software life cycles from testing to deployment. Oversaw teams performing unit and integrated systems testing.

Orchestrated and oversaw gathering and documenting user requirements for the U.S. Air Force's Government On-Line Data System (GOLD) computer system.

Special assignment included direct participation in fielding a team for a DOS/ADA based maintenance management program for the U.S. Air Force/California Air National Guard. Set up computer equipment and installed software packages. Conducted initial training of computer operators. Completed initial data entries to debug and initialize program. Provided on-site, advanced technical program support in military installations throughout Southern California.

Received Army Commendation Medals for meritorious performance, 1996 and 1997.
Awarded U.S. Government Final Secret Security Clearance based upon NAC.

CALIFORNIA AIR NATIONAL GUARD, San Jose, California – 1990 to 1994

Training Technician, GS-1702-09 reporting to the Operations Officer, 143rd Air Squadron, San Diego, California. Prepared training plans for mobilization, operations, and training of personnel using a variety of sophisticated computer applications.

Completed program to obtain credential as Certified Instructor – Train the Trainer Instruction.

COMPUTER TECHNOLOGY

Database Management: SQL, MS Access, PeopleSoft, ADP Payroll, RetailStar POS Systems, Crystal Report, Excel, and MS Change.
Software Applications: Microsoft Office 2000 & 97; Corel WordPerfect Office Suite; Lotus SmartSuite; QuickBooks Pro; CorelDraw 8; Adobe Illustrator; Internet Explorer; Netscape
Computer hardware: IBM compatible PC (Desktops & Laptops); Monitors; Scanners; Ink Jet & Laser Printers; Modems; Tape Drives; CD-ROM Drives; Routers; Hubs
Programming language: Basic, C, C++
Operating systems: MS-DOS; Windows 95, 98, 2K; Windows NT 4 (Workstation & Server).
Network protocols: TCP/IP; NetBeui; IPX/SPX
Client/Server Architecture: Two-Tier (Server/Workstation) & Three-Tier (Database/Application/Workstation) using Microsoft domain systems
LAN/WAN technologies: 10BaseT; 10Base2; 10Base5.
Interconnectivity: Client/Server & Peer-to-Peer Networking; Networked & Shared Printers.
Online Internet Technologies: Internet Explorer; Netscape.
Office Automation technologies: MS Word 2000; WordPerfect 8; GroupWise; MS Outlook.

Clean layout, particularly page 2. In technical disciplines, it is important to list all technical skills for easy reader identification and keyword searches.

K. "Lucy" Morris

1212 Reston Street - San Mateo, CA 90000 - (714) 555-1212 -   klmorris@earthlink.com

---

SUMMARY OF QUALIFICATIONS

- As a SYSTEMS ARCHITECT, have been involved in complex design, testing, on-line diagnostics, and analysis for storage system installation, maintenance, and upgrade projects, plus high-speed digital signaling bus and related architectures.

- Experienced in full line of software languages and hardware systems utilized in commercial, aerospace, and military program designs.

- Problem solving and service-oriented abilities are complemented by transferable skills including customer liaison, project organization, and department teamwork.

CAREER OVERVIEW

6/1997 - Present

Engineering Staff Member - Big Time Business Communications, Anaheim, CA - Company manufactures communication switches for major and multisite clients such as universities, district hospitals, and nationwide distributors of consumer products. Design and function test systems. Prepare upgrades and revisions for maintenance and updates. Write/edit documentation. Test designs of other software engineers.

1991-1996

Senior Software Engineer - GBU-15 Project Engineering Department, Honeywell, Inc., West Covina, CA - Designed, analyzed, developed, and integrated visually-guided weapons system instructor-station operational software which involved real-time programming and interfacing several processors. Prior responsibility with F-15 Aircraft Maintenance Trainer sections. Chaired Software Review Board.

1986-1991

Member, Technical Staff - Software Engineering Division, Project 311, Hughes, Fullerton, CA - Designed and maintained for simulated environments for a real-time radar system. Prior similar design and analysis assignments with Firelenter. Design and implementation activities ranged from antenna control and operator interface to on-line diagnostics and communications network controls.

(continued)

K. "Lucy" Morris

EDUCATION

1985	**M.S., Computer Science,** California State University, Fullerton
1980	**B.S., Communications,** California State University, Fullerton (emphasis Photo Communications) Honors, Dean's List
1975-1980	Mathematics Studies - UCLA

SOFTWARE LANGUAGES

Microsoft NT, Infomaker, Sybase, C++, Fortran, RPG-II, LISP, APL, assembly language for CDC, Univac, Interdata, Perkin Elmer, and IBM systems

SYSTEMS

HP, PDP 11/70, PDP 11/45, Perkin Elmer 4000, HMP 2000 (AN/UYK-50 or Interdata 716), CDC 4500, Honeywell Level 20, Hewlett Packard 6000+, ASIC I/O topologies and implementation, Windows PC, and UNIX workstations

OTHER SKILLS

- Special experience in resource planning and IT trends, technical proposal writing including ROMS, and estimates and departmental leadership.

- Able to assess new projects and develop time lines and budgets.

PERSONAL

- Fluent in English, Spanish, and Japanese.
- Able to travel/relocate.
- References and salary history available.

87—SYSTEMS ENGINEER

Phone—(714) 555-1212
Home 1212 Easy Street, Orange, CA 92867
EMAIL—email@email.com

TONY B. GOOD

MICROSOFT NETWORK SYSTEMS ENGINEER

BACKGROUND: EDUCATION/PROJECT EXPERIENCE:
Microsoft Systems Engineer Related Education - 3/2/96 - 12/30/96
Industry Technical School   (*1280 hours of class time and hands on*).
Microsoft®Windows™ 3.1 and MS-DOS® 6.2 for Support Professionals
Networking With Microsoft® Windows™ for Workgroups 3.11
Implementing and Supporting Microsoft® Windows® 95-2000, Microsoft® Windows NT™ 3.51,
Microsoft® NT™ Server 3.51 Version 1.0, Microsoft® TCP/IP for Microsoft Windows NT™ 3.51,
2000 ME, Systems Administration for Microsoft® SQL™ Server 6

12/98-Present - POS Automation Manager
Major Wireless Communications Corp.
Hired in as technician. Promoted to current position within six months. Currently manage
automation technicians in West Coast territory. Supervise new equipment installations, support
upgrade and maintenance programs. Confer with managers in U.S. installations at corporate
meetings and online conferences. Utilize complex integration processes during corporate mergers and
reconfigurations.

10/97-11/98 – Office Automation Technician
Online Connecting Point. Working in the I.T. Dept. at Sprint PCS/Cox Communications
support desktop and laptop configurations of a 2500 node Novell/NT network including remote sites
in Las Vegas and San Diego via PC Anywhere. Standard configuration is Win95 with Novell
client32 IPX/SPX and TCP/IP for intranet and Internet. Installations and support include PeopleSoft,
Oracle, Visio, and Support Magic. Hardware configurations are Compaq Prolinea, Deskpro 2000,
4000 and 6000. Laptops are NEC 4050, 4080, 6030, 6050, Toshiba, and Gateway. Utilities
used: Ghost, PQ Magic.

5/1/97 - 8/6/97 – Network and PC Technician
Special Laboratories, Inc.
Provided Server and Network Administration, client configuration, and end-user support in a 500
node network. Administered high-speed Document Scanners, Database Servers, and a 100-slot CD
jukebox.

2/1/97 - 4/21/97 – Network and PC Specialist
The Professional Resources, Inc.   Worked in the M.I.S. Dept. at SpecialtyEyeglass, Inc.
Set up and configured computers, changed drives, cards, main boards, and power supplies.
Moved a 250-node NT network. Installed and maintained operating systems and third-party software.

Page 1 of 2

Phone—(714) 555-1212
Home 1212 Easy Street, Orange, CA 92867
EMAIL—email@email.com

TONY B. GOOD

4/1/98 - Present — Self Employed
MICROSOFT NETWORK SYSTEMS ENGINEER CONSULTANT
Clients included:

A1. Construction Co., Inc.   Anyone Construction Co.
The Ragin'Cajun Companies   Career Sorcery, Etc.

- Installed and configured Microsoft® NT™ Server 4.0, Microsoft® TCP/IP, Microsoft® Windows® 95, and Microsoft® Windows™ for Workgroups 3.11.
- Server and Network Administration, client configuration, and end-user support.
- Set up and configured computers, change drives, cards, main boards, and power supplies.
- Installed and maintained third-party software, such as Netscape Navigator, Office 95, AutoCad 13, Solidworks 97, Norton and Macafee AntiVirus software.
- Purchased new computer systems and components.

1978-1997 - Quality Assurance
Quality Engineering / Ultrasonic Nondestructive Testing Level II
Northrop Grumman Aircraft   Trent Tube a Division of Colt Ind.

- Assisted LAN Administrator with 30-node network of HP150s and PCs with dot matrix and HP LaserJet Printers and flatbed scanners.

Commendations and Accomplishments
"Has good independent thought processes with regard to workplace problems and
solutions, and has the ability to function with minimal oversight and only initial guidance."

Selected to represent department management at facilities meetings.

Designed new universal tool that resulted in a major cut in inspection times.

Performed quality destructive and nondestructive testing on composites, metals, and adhesives to
ensure specifications and procedure requirements were met.

Industry-Sponsored Courses
Unigraphics 101, Geometric Dimensioning and Tolerancing Interpretation, Blueprint Reading,
Ultrasonic level 1 and 2, Dye Penetrant Inspection Level 1, and Radiation Safety.

Military Service
Squad Leader - US Army Airborne

88—SYSTEMS PROGRAMMER

DAVID A. DOSS
136 Marsh Lane
Addison, Texas 7500
(214) 555-2000

QUALIFICATIONS SUMMARY

SYSTEMS PROGRAMMER established in technical support and systems support with strong emphasis on troubleshooting and installation and maintenance of third-party software. Over 8 years' MVS Systems Programmer experience, including SNA networking with VTAM, NCP, and SSP. Over 10 years' VM Systems Programmer experience. First-hand knowledge of computer operations, operations management, and applications programming.

HARDWARE: IBM 3OXX and 37XX, VM/XA SPA, MVS/XA, JES2, VTAM, NCP.
SOFTWARE: SSP, TSO/E, ISPF/PDF, SMP/E, ACF2, RSCSv2, TCP/IP.

EXPERIENCE

9/87–Present | Kelly Air Force Base
CONSULTANT | San Antonio, Texas

Provide all installation, maintenance, and upgrade support for VM/XA 2.1.0 and MVS/XA 2.2.0 operating systems on IBM 4381 designated as a Mission Critical Computer Resource (CBIPO, CBPDO, SMP/E). Control all system and resource access as System Manager (includes ACF2 Administrator). Manage all direct-access storage backups and recovery. Authored operations manuals and procedures. Proficient in ACF/VTAM (3.2.0), ACF/NCP (4.1.0), and ACF/SSP (3.2.0).

- Compiler support for Automated Test Equipment, including rehost implementation, verification, and documentation. Technical support, user support, and training.
- Recovered BETA compiler system used to program ATE equipment in support of F-111 aircraft avionics.
- Developed and implemented fiber optics link in support of Operational Readiness Inspection alternate site requirements.

3/85–9/87 | Santa Rosa Medical Center
SYSTEMS ANALYST/PROGRAMMER | San Antonio, Texas

Maintained and upgraded hospital accounting applications. Authored batch applications to provide input data for Shared Medical Systems RJE host.

SYSTEMS PROGRAMMER

Installed and maintained MVS/XA operating system and all subsystems.

Headed DOS/VSE to MVS/XA conversion team. Developed unique procedures for sharing databases between DOS-based DLI and IMS on the MVS/XA system during the conversion. Authored an application to recover "lost" CICS transient data transactions resulting in the recovery of over $80,000 in hospital revenues.

PERSONAL DATA

Top Secret Cryptographic Clearance, United States Air Force

Author's favorite. Utilizing a left-hand column for a profile of skills is excellent in any discipline. One of the best layouts in this collection.

TECHNICAL PROFICIENCIES

Network/Operating Environments:

- Solaris, AIX, Linux, Novell Netware, VMS/CMS Mainframe, DOS, Windows 95/98/NT, Xwindows, Banyan Vines, SunNet Manager

Network Equipment:

- Cisco (1000, 2500, 4000, 7000 series Routers)

- Bay Networks (Contivity 4000 Extranet Switch, BCN and BLN series Routers, 28000, 58000, and 350T series Ethernet Switching Hubs)

- Synoptics (2813, 3000, 3030, and 5000 series hubs/concentrators)

- 3com (3100 series Terminal Servers, Netbuilder II Routers, Lanplex 2500 series, Linkswitch 3000 series)

- Cyberguard (Firewall), Sniffer, OneTouch.

Programming / Scripting Languages:

- C, C++, Assembly (370,8086,8031,8051), HTML, FORTRAN, BASIC, Visual Basic, Java, Perl, CGI, SQL, Shell Scripting

Protocols / Services:

- IPsec, PPTP, SNMP, TCP/IP, RADIUS, PAP, MSCHAP, DHCP, DNS, FTP, Telnet, RMON, x.509, DES, Triple-DES, FTTH

Applications:

- Microsoft Outlook, Word, Powerpoint, Excel, Project, Access, Bay Networks Optivity, Harris Network Management, Exceed, Lotus ccMail, Ecoscope, Netscape, Internet Explorer, Visio, Informix, Oracle

Tom Sorensen

123 Arlington Court, Denver, CO 80239
e-mail@e-mailaddress.com
303-555-5451

Summary

- **Voice & Data Communications Engineer** with 10+ years of experience seeking continued project leadership role, integrating emergent technologies into comprehensive communications solutions.

- In-depth knowledge of communications network operations. Proven ability to build proficiency in new technologies and collaborate with multidisciplinary project teams to ensure successful project integration.

- Strong skills in coordinating all facets of multiple complex projects, ensuring on-time, on-budget, on-target results.

- Articulate, flexible, and personable communicator, with excellent skills in client and vendor relations. Frequently selected to serve as a project consultant and task force contributor on critical corporate initiatives.

Experience

Internet Fiber, Inc., Denver, CO   1998-Present
FTTH Project Manager

- Design and build Neighborhood Networks™ (customer-owned Internet Fiber networks) using a high-speed fiber to the home (FTTH) architecture for Internet, telephony, and video.

- Perform feasibility studies, determine network requirements and specifications.

- Maintain strong partnerships with top-rated residential homebuilders. Coordinate construction schedules from rough electrical to interior finishing phases.

- Hire and manage telecommunications and network technicians and subcontractors to meet all implementation deadlines.

AT&T / Lucent Technologies, Westminster, CO   1990-1998
Telecommunications Engineer, IP-based Network Services

- Supported implementation of multiple projects, including Interspan Network, IP network services (the AT&T Worldnet backbone), frame relay, ATM, AT&T Broadband services, APS (a PC-based, Unix O/S Voice Recognition Call Processing System), and 900 MHz Spectralink phone systems.

- Determined location of hardware and schedule installations to minimize impact to customers.

- Coordinated all unit and system testing, ensuring 100% turn-up of equipment prior to cut-over.

Education

BS, Telecommunications Engineering, Cum Laude
University of Colorado at Boulder

90—TELECOMMUNICATIONS SALES SUPPORT

> *Conventional yet effective layout. Good summary at top, followed by good detail in the "Experience" section.*

LESLIE A. GAILLARD
3600 Fillmore Street #204, San Francisco, CA 94123, 415-555-7597, lgird@link.net

PROFESSIONAL PROFILE

- 4 years in telecommunications industry
- Specialty in voice and data product management, engineering, and sales engineering support
- Developed technical sales training for Sprint sales
- Performed wide area network [WAN] designs for hundreds of Sprint customers and sales prospects

EXPERIENCE

5/99-Present

SPRINT CORPORATION   San Francisco, CA
Advanced Sales Support Manager/Field Product Manager

- Provided technical and product related support for all West Area Sales Support divisions on leading edge technologies. Acted as a technology consultant for approximately 200 engineering and sales management employees.
- Created and delivered strategic presentations on Converged Network solutions to premiere high technology companies and top-tier funded E-Commerce clients.
- Developed analyses of competitors' product offerings and evaluated customer demand for new product feature offerings through market surveys. Provided recommendations to Marketing and Business Development on needed enhancements to product portfolio.
- Contributed to $1.5 million 1999 revenue for products through speaking engagements at high-profile industry conferences and executive briefings for CTOs and CIOs.
- Conducted monthly product updates and technical training sessions for Engineers and Sales Managers throughout the West area.

1996-1999

SPRINT CORPORATION   Herndon, VA
Systems Design Engineer II, Government Systems Division

- Designed and implemented wide area networks for NASA and Energy Sciences Network (ESNET) using Asynchronous Transfer Mode (ATM) technology.
- Conducted analysis of network design to determine optimal configuration for customer's data traffic profile. Made recommendations and presented design strategy to client.
- Designated as region's Subject Matter Expert on ATM, SONET/DWDM, and Integrated On-Demand Network (ION) Architecture.
- Created product guidelines and coordinated service delivery for Sprint's first OC-12 ATM product.

July-Dec. 1996

SPRINT CORPORATION, ASSOCIATE ENGINEERING PROGRAM   Reston, VA
Associate Engineer

- Completed 6-month rigorous training program on Wide Area Network (WAN) design and telecommunications protocols.
- Promoted to Systems Design Engineer I within 6 months of employment with company.

EDUCATION

COLLEGE OF WILLIAM AND MARY   Williamsburg, VA
Bachelor of Science, May 1996

ADDITIONAL

Extensive knowledge of ISDN, Frame Relay, ATM, TCP/IP, and SONET protocols
Practical experience with configuration of *Fore Systems* ATM switches.
Enjoy Yoga and running.

91—TRANSLATOR

ROBERT C. KNOWLES

2672 Cherry Way * Anaheim, CA 92807
714.555.0213 * RCN@hotmail.com

.........Profile

< Seeking employment as a Linguistics Processing Engineer >
>> Offering Translations and Conversions for a multilingual Web Community <<

< Text Formats >	**XML, RTF, HTML, PDF**
< Scripting Languages>	**JavaScript, VB Script, CGI**
< Operating Systems>	**Unix, MS NT**
< Languages>	**C, Java, Perl**
< Database Systems >	**Sybase Adaptive Server Anywhere 6.0, Sybase Adaptive Server Enterprise 11.9 & 12.0, Sybase Central, ASE TRANSACT- SQL**

> Format data for use by other applications (Import, Export, and Comma-delimited)
> Skilled text processor and memory translator
> Accomplished in navigating the Internet and World Wide Web sites
> Strong background in database management

Experience

Translator   E-Business Solutions, Orange, CA   1997 to Present

 ➢ Develop customized strategies and solutions to manage clients' ongoing and dynamic Web site requirements.
 ➢ Process text and work on translation memory.
 ➢ Identified Unix system specific code and converted and modified it to run on the NT system, saving the company's initial investment in legacy software of over $100K, updating operations and products to current day culture.

Database Administrator   New IT Solutions, Inc., Irvine, CA   1994 to 1997

 ➢ Performed Legacy Data Conversions: Skillfully converted MS Access databases to Adaptive Server Anywhere 6.0 through mapping techniques, temporary tables, and SQL statements. Also, converted ASA 6.0 databases to ASE 11.5 databases using unload commands and the BCP DOS utility (developed a new technique to convert ASA to ASE, using a very intricate process). Created cursors to assist in legacy data conversions.
 ➢ Converted large batch TRANSACT-SQL to stored procedures.

Freelance Web Designer   1994 to Present

 ➢ Design cutting edge sites and Web-based strategies to create high impact response.
 ➢ Skilled with Web interface, navigation, graphic design, and interactive pages.
 ➢ Created over 20 Web sites for high profile clients including Fortune 2000 companies and government agencies.

Education

BS in Computer Science, California Polytechnic University, San Luis Obispo, 1994
>> Graduated with Honors, Dean's List, President—Computer Club, 1 year

92—UNIX ADMINISTRATOR

Comprehensive section on "Professional Expertise" summary is very effective. Layout is very appealing and easy to read as well. Notice spacing between sections and use of section breaks created by the double horizontal lines.

David Hines

5 Madison Way
Bristol, CT 06010
860-555-5234

dhines@compu.net

PROFESSIONAL EXPERTISE

Systems Design / Troubleshooting / Network Administration / Internet Service Provider / System Integration

- Excellent communication and interpersonal skills; proven ability to serve as liaison among business and technical staffs and end users. Highly focused on integrity and exceptional quality of customer service.

- Experienced **UNIX and network administrator** with expertise in performance analysis, troubleshooting, and tuning to enhance the functionality and security of distributed hardware and software components including networks, servers, and operating systems.

- Strong background in both technical and business aspects of Internet service provision, and a healthy understanding of bottom-line profitability.

- MCSE + I certification

Technical Skills:
- **Operating Systems**: Windows 95/98/NT/2000, UNIX (Flavors: FreeBSD, Linux, Solaris, SunOS, Irix, SCO)
- **Telco/Networks**: T-1/T-3/OC-3, ATM/Frame Relay, DSL, ISDN
- **Hardware**: Cisco routers, switches, IOS; Extreme Networks switches; 10/100/gigabit Ethernet
- **Routing Protocols**: BGP, OSPF, RIP
- **Network Protocols and Applications**: TCP/IP, UDP, HTTPS/SSL, DNS, NFS, DHCP, SSH, RADIUS Authentication, NIS, Sendmail, Apache, MS IIS, PGP
- **Programming**: PERL, PHP, HTML, CGI, Shell scripting; self-study in C++/Java.

PROFESSIONAL HISTORY

Management / Business Development / Integration

@jenkinss.com, Bristol, CT   6/94 - Present
Vice President and Chief Technology Officer (6/94 - 4/00); **Integration Coordinator** (4/00 - Present)
Co-founder and Chief Geek Officer of the **first full-service ISP** in the Northeast. Managed all technical aspects of creation and operation, including design/implementation of network from the ground up. Designed WAN & LAN, utilizing BGP and OSPF. Maintained all aspects of DNS, Sendmail, and security. Installed and upgraded software; performed troubleshooting and repair of software, systems and networks. Collaborated with small businesses to provide Internet connections and establish Web service to facilitate e-commerce. Designed, implemented, maintained, and updated Apache/Stronghold Web server, using CGI, HTML, and PHP. Managed technical staff of seven (three first-level technical support, two engineers, one upper-level technical support, and a Webmaster) from recruitment to professional development.

(continued)

David Hines   **Page 2**

Managed the integration of @jenkinss.com and other ISPs purchased simultaneously.

♦ Started company from scratch, building to 100 users in first year of operation and to current subscriber base of 4200, comprised of 50% business and 50% residential. Company has been profitable since its inception.
♦ 1999 revenues: $1.2 million, showing a 30%+ growth in the past year alone.
♦ Provide free Website hosting for a variety of local and national nonprofit organizations.

EARLY CAREER EXPERIENCE

MAJOR-MICRO CORPORATION, Hartford, CT   1/94 - 5/94
Assistant Marketing Manager (contracted)
Assisted in the prepress design and production of marketing and collateral materials for Developer Network. Also helped to redesign the departmental newspaper, advancing its technology from one- to four-color printing.

ABC Printing, Plantsville, CT   1/90-1/94
All-Print, Southington, CT
Manager
Managed all aspects of electronic prepress. Implemented/upgraded software and hardware for heterogeous computer networks.

AFFILIATION

TI-Com (ti-com.com): Member, Board of Directors, 1999 - Present
Served as **Technical Director** for **ISP Forums** in Spring 1999 and Fall 1999. Coordinated/managed computer equipment and network for 2000+ participants; supervised six volunteer technicians. Included wireless show floor (2.4GHz).

References Furnished on Request

93—UNIX ADMINISTRATOR CONSULTANT

> *Excellent resume. Very thorough technical skill set overview followed by detailed "Employment" section.*

SUZANNE COUTEE-CHANG

445 East Avenue
Chicago, IL 60611

Home (407) 555-4688

PROFESSIONAL SUMMARY:

Professional UNIX Systems Administrator with seven years of experience. Experienced in analyzing, supporting and troubleshooting client/server configurations across large scale heterogeneous networks. Also accomplished at providing a high level of customer service and training to end users. Experienced in dealing with vendors from both a hardware and software perspective. Solid knowledge of the following hardware/software:

Hardware/Operating Systems	Software	Applications Used
Sun Sparc (5,10,20,Xterm,Ultra, 1,000,2000) **(Solaris** 1.X & 2.X)	Abaqus	FrameMaker
	Patran	Word Perfect
	C/Fortran Compilers	MS Office
HP 9000 (700,800,C100 Series)	Comsearch/SSAM	Wingz
(HP-UX 9.X & 10.X)	Mapinfo	MAE
	Informix/Oracle	Soft-Windows
Tektronix Xterminals	ER Mapper	PC-Xware
HP & Sun Printers/Plotters	FrameMaker	Action Request System (ARS)
	Paradigm Help Desk	
Sun/Dec Storage Arrays	WinDD	**Others**
DiskSuite, Auspex	Spectrum Help Desk	NFS/NIS/NIS+
	Word Perfect	TCP/IP, Automount
Backup Software	HP Jetadmin	
Legato Networker	Secureid (Security)	
Veritas Netbackup	Sun XtMgr	
Delta Microsystems Budtool	Lotus Notes	
	Tektronix Xpressware	

EMPLOYMENT

8/97 to Present   **MOBIL OIL**   13777 Midway Rd, Farmers Branch, TX
Position: UNIX Systems Administrator (Consultant with Decision Consultants)
Providing client/server, system hardware/software support on SUN/HP/SGI platforms to Engineers, Geophysicists and all other technical staff in the Research Development division which consists of 10 departments. Working with each department on a project basis to implement standardization of all desktop environment including network and operating system configurations. Co-ordinate user migration; provide training to help-desk support personnel on how to respond/log UNIX related calls and providing ongoing procedure documentation. Provide training to new users on general use of workstations.

5/96 to 8/97   **MOTOROLA**   8000 W. Sunrise Blvd, Plantation, FL
Position: UNIX Systems Administrator (Consultant with TechniSource, Inc.)
Provided client system/application support to 800+ client workstations which consisted of developers, engineers, database, and network administrators; provided backup support to server administrators; configure and maintain SUN/HP client workstations for NIS client/server environment; administer/monitor/troubleshoot help desk support calls through use of Action Request HelpDesk software (ARS). Install and configure HP network based printers/plotters. Maintain and update inventory of all HP/SUN equipment on ARS.

(continued)

SUZANNE COUTEE-CHANG   (continued)

6/95 to 5/96	**Verizon Wireless (PrimeCo)**	Six Campus Circle, Westlake, TX

Position: UNIX Systems Administrator

Provided systems support to developers, engineers, database, and network administrators; this included the RF Engineering department and the implementation of a production work environment. Also provided backup technical support to the system administrators in 11 markets on the Sun platform. Installed, configured, maintained, and upgraded Sun/Solaris servers and workstations. Evaluated, tested, installed, and upgraded software packages. Troubleshot help desk calls. Installed and configured HP network printers and plotters. Maintained an NIS+/NIS client/server environment with 15 different domains established. Maintained system backups on Legato Networker. Procured evaluation units, acquired price quotes, generated purchase orders, and tracked maintenance agreements for all UNIX hardware/software within the company and 11 national markets.

8/94 to 5/95	**Southwestern Bell Mobil Systems**	13900 Midway Road, Farmers Branch, TX

Position: UNIX Systems Administrator

Provided system support to developers, database, and network administrators. Also provided backup technical support to system administrators in other markets on both SUN/HP platforms. Installed, configured, maintained and upgraded Sun/Solaris servers and Xterminals, including SUN/HP and Tektronix. Evaluated, tested, installed, and upgraded software packages. Troubleshot help desk calls. Installed and configured HP printers on network.

1/94 to 7/94	**The Future Now**	3410 Midcourt Drive, Ste. 115, Carrollton, TX

Position: UNIX Systems Engineer

Provided presales support to Marketing department. Provided postsales support for implemented solutions at customer site. Installed and configured servers and workstations. Maintained in-house Solutions Center and assisted with internal UNIX Network support and planning. Evaluated and tested new products, and demonstrated new solutions to clients. Assisted with the development and implementation of programs. Provided on-site user-end training.

5/91 to 1/94	**SuperConducting Super Collider Laboratory**	Waxahachie, TX

Position: UNIX Systems Administrator

Provided system, software, client/server support for 600+ users on SUN/HP platforms, which included over 20 servers across 30 routed subnets. Worked closely with engineers, physicists, and technicians to determine and understand user needs, problems, and requests. Installed, configured, upgraded, and maintained SUN workstations, operating systems, tools applications, and hardware. Coordinated major events such as user migration, system relocation, and system installations. Coordinated, managed help desk requests. Setup/maintained user accounts. Configured and maintained Sun and Tektronix printers on printservers. Administered network backups for all systems. Maintained constant contact with vendors to coordinate hardware/software purchase, repairs, warranties, and upgrades.

EDUCATION

1/92 to Present	**Northwood University**	Cedar Hill, TX

Major: Business Management
(Bachelor of Arts Degree Expected Completion Date of 12/98)

PROFESSIONAL COURSES

Sun Microsystems – Solaris Systems Administration, Network Administration, SunOS Systems Administration, Server Administration, NIS+ Administration.

Hewlett Packard - HP-UX Systems Administration (700 & 800 Series)

Nice conventional resume layout, with notable exception of utilizing the Microsoft certification. Depending on your position and ability, using such an endorsement might be a unique differentiator.

12245 Elm Way ◆ Ft. Lauderdale, Florida 33414
(555) 555-5555 ◆ cell: (555) 000-0000
abc@yahoo.com

Hank Garcia

■I **Web Designer...** Experienced in Web site planning, design/coding, launch and marketing... Strong graphic art skills backed by sound technical abilities... Bilingual in Spanish and English... High energy individual with positive outlook, excellent team skills, and recognized talent/ability to meld form and function in an online environment.

■I **Design Experience**
■I **Professional Experience**
■I **Education and Training**
■I **Contact Information**

http://www.risco.com
Corporate Web site for Risco Industries

Designed, coded, and launched 133-page commercial site for multimillion dollar privately held distribution company with a national market base. Developed and wrote content and provided Web marketing strategies for site distribution/registration. Applied skills in HTML, JavaScript, and Cold Fusion to create online catalog of products. Sole Web master tasked to continual maintenance, marketing, and updating of site; keep all product specifications and descriptions up to date and available for both customers and corporate users.

Achieved first time profitability and revenues from online marketed sales of $100,000 for 1998 alone

Web site grew from informal concept to major part of national corporate marketing plan

http://www.mamajuana.net
Public relations/promotions site for popular music group

Planned, designed, and implemented bilingual Web site for promotion of Latin pop music group. Worked with marketing and public relations representatives to develop overall style of site and to accurately achieve client desires for site purpose. Coded entire site in ASP. Maintained content and functionality.

(continued)

Hank Garcia

http://www.new-community.org
Informational site for nonprofit organization

Worked within a team to develop site for community church using FrontPage. Assisted organization in technical issues in addition to site designs – set up NT server and configured PCs.

Experience

Systems Analyst/Programmer
1996-present
Risco Industries ♦ West Palm Beach, Florida
Nationwide distributor of aluminum products on wholesale and business-to-business bases.

Sole designer and Web master for corporate Web site. See above for detailed description.

Maintained prewritten applications in COBOL, C, Perl, and shellscripting. Supported Unix operating systems and software for Risco employees across the nation. Trained new employees on procedures and operations. Worked in team environment to provide outstanding customer service and technical expertise.

Operations Manager
1994-1996
Cactus Bar and Grill♦ Dominican Republic
Popular gathering place and nightspot serving fine food and providing live entertainment to a select market.

Education

Bachelor of Science – Computer Science
Minor: Technical Services
Pontifica Universidad Catolica Madre y Maestra
Dominican Republic ♦ 1994

Legal resident of the United States able to accept and pursue long-term employment in the United States. Documentation will be cheerfully provided.

95—WEB DEVELOPER

Jack Morris
9871 Pinecrest Place #24C
Brandon, Florida 32510
813-555-9779
emailaddress@emailaddress.com

Title and summary at top work well. Good job description with-in the "Experience" section.

WEB DEVELOPMENT / WEB PROGRAMMING / WEB DESIGN / WEBMASTER

Web Developer with experience in multimedia and Web design. Skilled in assessment of client needs and requirements. Capable creator of viable e-business solutions from concept to implementation. Proficiency in JavaScript and Perl scripting languages and Active Server Pages; broad knowledge of database structures. Team builder with strong customer service focus and highly effective communication skills.

Programming: HTML 4.0; ASP 2.0/3.0; VBScript; JavaScript; Perl
Operating Systems: Windows 98/NT/2000; UNIX
Applications: PhotoShop 5.5 / ImageReady 2.0; HomeSite 4.5; MS SQL 7; Dreamweaver 2.0; Microsoft Office 2000; Flash 4; CakeWalk Pro Audio 8.0; Xing AudioCatalyst

EDUCATION / CREDENTIALS
B.A. Education, State University   Graduated with honors, May 1995
Passed Microsoft's Network Essentials examination   March 1999

EXPERIENCE
INTERNETTRAVEL.COM
Web Developer   March 2000 – Present
Work with other programmers, database developer, graphic artists, video encoders, and content staff to create, maintain, and upgrade, travel information Web site. Integrate new products into existing Web pages. Design, develop, and code Web pages using Active Server Pages (ASP), VBScript, JavaScript, MS SQL 7, and HTML 4.0. Oversee development of intranet and Administration Web sites for company.

- Embedded QuickTime video player into Web pages to ensure convenient and seamless viewing of video travel clips on Web site.
- Challenged to integrate proprietary chat and message board applications into Web site. Researched/analyzed products, acquired necessary development tools and successfully completed project, adding functionality and consumer interest to the Web site. Applications used Apache Web server on NT server.
- Co-supervise intern programmer; assign projects and evaluate skills and performance.

MUNICIPAL GOVERNMENT CONSORTIUM
Web Services Administrator   April 1999 – March 2000
Maintained consortium's intranet and Internet sites, accessible by 300 + member organizations. Consulted with member groups to develop their Web sites. Created and/or modified graphics and animations for consortium Web sites. Installed software and hardware; provided technical support for users.

- Implemented online intranet auction utilizing ASP. Site has attracted interest and consultation requests from several municipalities across the country.
- Implemented online message board (Perl).
- Designed, developed, and coded legislative bill tracking system for intranet site, using ASP. System facilitated research and enabled member groups to act quickly on time-sensitive legislative issues.
- Acquired secure server certificate to acceptance of online credit card purchases.
- Compiled 400 + e-mail addresses of associates; developed database and created/distributed weekly e-mail news bulletin with links to consortium Web site. Increased Web site traffic substantially.

(Continued)

Jack Morris   Page 2

INDEPENDENT WEB DEVELOPER   February 2000 - Present
Created and maintain eCommerce site for small commercial enterprise. Assessed customer needs; collaborated with business owner to create visually attractive Web pages and to develop effective online marketing strategies. Researched site's Internet visibility potential. Currently evaluating the possibility of creating database back end for client to display inventory more quickly on Web site.

- Web site consistently ranks in top 9 views in product searches on major search engines.

MUNICIPAL LIBRARY
Computer Support/Trainer   April 1999 – October 1999
Hired to modify existing computer training curriculum for library staff. Instructed classes in Windows NT, MS Office 97 programs and Internet skills. Additionally created, modified, and taught curriculum for public computer training classes (up to ten students per class).

- Provided computer support to patrons using MS Office 97 programs and Internet Explorer 4.

ATTORNEYS-AT-LAW INC.
Legal Assistant   Spring 1994; June 1995 - July 1998
Initially a temporary placement, then hired full-time to provide administrative and clerical support for attorney. Established, organized, and maintained legal records and files. Researched, drafted, and prepared reports, forms, contracts, legal documents, Board minutes, correspondence, and IRS applications. Served as liaison to State University.

- Used MS Access to track payments to client accounts, created a variety of reports quickly and accessed information easily. Maximized productivity while minimizing mistakes.

MUNICIPAL BOARD OF EDUCATION
Math Tutor   August 1994 - June 1995
Tutored students (1st - 5th grades) in math problem-solving strategies. Maintained anecdotal records, individual folders, and periodic progress reports.

- Member of Focus Group that made recommendations for program improvement.

STATE LAW LIBRARY
Librarian Assistant   October 1987 - January 1994
Provided limited supervision of Clerks and Pages. Assisted patrons with use of IBM and Macintosh personal computers.

MUSICIAN
Guitarist/Songwriter
Co-manager: Booked performances; negotiated fees; contacted media, record stores, and radio stations; promotion and marketing; conferred with legal representative and handled other business matters.

References and samples of work available upon request

96—WEB MANAGER

MARK ROULETTE

38538 Zyerne Court • Fremont, California 94536 • (510) 555-2813 • roulette@home.com

WEB MANAGER and DIRECTOR OF ONLINE COMMUNITIES

- Proven experience with an innate ability to learn, create, and integrate new procedures and systems.
- Strong communication skills. Work well with individuals at all levels; serve as an effective liaison between engineering teams and clients/users.
- Provide calm and productive leadership in challenging situations and high-demand environments.

AREAS OF TECHNICAL EXPERTISE

OS:
MacOS, MacOSX, Windows NT 4.0, Windows 95/98, Windows 2000 (beta), HP-UX 9.x & 10.x, Linux

Server Architectures:
IIS 4.0, Apache, Microsoft Site Server, WebStar, and basic WebObjects

Database Systems:
SQL, Access, Filemaker Pro

Languages:
JavaScript, VBScript, Visual Basic, VBA, ASP to SQL DB Scripting (ADO/ODBC), SQL (standard queries and stored procedures), C++, Java, with basic skills in PERL

Web Languages:
HTML, DHTML, CSS1, ASP, Active Channels/Desktop (CDF), ActiveX controls, SSI, with basic skills in XML

Applications:

Web Development:	BBEdit and NotePad (for hand coding), DreamWeaver, NetObjects, FrontPage/Visual InterDev, Composer
Graphics:	Photoshop, Illustrator
Programming:	CodeWarrior, VisualBasic 5/6, Visual C++, VisualJ++, Visual Cafe, Visual InterDev
Web Log Analysis:	WebTrends, FunnelWeb
Help Desk Systems:	Clientele

Certifications:
Level 1 - Microsoft Site Builder Network and Apple Certified Server Engineer

EXPERIENCE

IXIX Product Development, Palo Alto HQ, California, 1995 to present
This product design and development company was recently identified as "the secret weapon of Silicon Valley" by Wired Magazine. IXIX has 300+ employees in ten locations worldwide with six offices throughout the United States and overseas office in London, Milan, Essex, and Tokyo.

WEB MANAGER and DIRECTOR OF ONLINE COMMUNITIES
Solely responsible for all Web management, development and oversight of forums for IXIX.

- Consult to the Engineering community for Web design and programming for client project Extranet sites. Develop Web sites that can be used as a meeting place to share documents, create and modify project schedules, and to discuss various aspects of the project. Use and modify third-party CGI scripts as well as develop custom coding to meet the needs of the project and client.
- Manage all customization and maintenance of the User Support Group's help desk system (Clientele). Heavily modified existing system to improve the functionality and work flow of the User Support Group. This application is a VisualBasic application with an Access database linked to an SQL database. Modifications included interface layout changes, addition of work flow steps, removal of unused features, additions of required features, SQL table addition, modification of existing tables, stored procedure creation/modification, and Access query creation/modification.

- continued -

240

96—WEB MANAGER (CONT.)

IDEO —WEB DEVELOPER / INTRANET MANAGER *(continued)*

- Implement new features and requested functionality from the 300+ members of the user community. Assess the feasibility of requests. Research, define the scope of, and manage these projects under own initiative. Responsible for the graphic design and implementation of the entire look and feel of the corporate intranet. Collaborate and work closely with the User Support and Database Groups.
- Lead in ongoing intensive research for content and forum updates to make site continuously relevant to industry professionals and community participants.
- Involved in the overall schema designing and modification to the Enterprise database and perform schema design for when the needs of an application are not fulfilled by the current database design.
- Develop Web-based applications to extract data from an extensive enterprise database as a resource for project managers, business developers and engineers. Web applications created include:
    - —a Web front end to an SQL-based Clientele Help Desk application
    - —a Vendor DB application
    - —a Patent DB application
    - —an online queriable employee list
    - —an online conference room scheduler
    - —an online recruiting/resume tracking DB
- In previous position as **Macintosh Network Manager,** was responsible for the support, purchasing, maintenance, and troubleshooting of 200+ Macintosh computers. Supervised technician and trained as replacement when promoted to Web Developer.

PREVIOUS EXPERIENCE
MIS Manager, The Volt Group, 1993-95
Fab Technician, Oarboat Technologies, 1992-93
E-5, United States Army (Ft. Benning, Georgia/Ayers Kaserne, Germany), 1989-92
Honorable Discharge - Security Clearance: Top Secret

EDUCATION

A.A., Graphic Design (Print), Master's Institute

Professional/Continuing Education

Diablo College:	C++ Programming
	Applied VisualBasic Programming
Network Frontiers:	Managing AppleTalk Networks
	Designing AppleTalk Networks
	Managing AppleShare Servers & Backup Management
J.D. Edwards:	Basic Administration of JD Edwards Accounting System on AS/400
	Advanced Administration of JD Edwards Accounting System on AS/400
	JD Edwards Accounting System Technical Foundations
IBM:	AS/400 Basic System Management
	AS/400 Advanced System Management
Conferences:	World Wide Developer Conference, Apple Computer , 95, 96, 97, 98, 99
	1999 Conference sessions included topics on WebObjects, WebObjects Apps, SQL/Relational Databases, Advanced HTML/DHTML/ JavaScript, Java Client, Java on MacOSX, and QuickTime.

Mark Ludwig
mludwig @compulink.net

> *Notice that skills are listed according to vertical industry, a very unique approach. Would only recommend this if these vertical industries were important to the prospective employer.*

2036 South Street
Santa Ana, California 92867
714. 555-1212

EXPERTISE:

- Web Site Design/Management
- Configuration & Systems Analysis
- Automated Inspection Equipment
- Multitasking Systems
- Information Architecture
- Artist/Designer Interface
- Net Content and Performance
- In-House Test Equipment
- Software development test/debug with assembly (6809, 68K, 80x86, 8039, 8085, 8900, 80188, TMS-7000, Z-80)
- Visual BASIC , C, Fox Pro, HTML, DHTML, ASP, PICK, PSOS, RTKernal, MTOS, NT & Solaris, JavaScript, CGI-PERL.

ACHIEVEMENT AREAS:

Manufacturing Industry

- Created Windows HP-printer driver for custom font cartridge.
- Maintained high-speed production line real-tie automated inspection equipment.
- Designed/developed application to convert PL-5 macros and stored them with bit-mapped fonts into an HP-compatible font cartridge.
- Created production software to automatically program unique calibration values in EPROM and store information into database.
- Security systems including "time bomb" location & removal.

Health Care Industry:

- Through MS Access & Visual Basic, created user interface for Visual Nurse Monitoring System for Friendly Health Programs.
- Created medical industry firmware

Entertainment Industry:

- Supported in-flight entertainment equipment development
- Customized Tetris style game.
- Wrote modem driver for set-top box for Major Pay for View (MPPV).
- Optimized operating system performance.

RELATED EMPLOYMENT:

1/98-Present	Embedded Systems Consulting - CITY
96-98	Senior Firmware Engineer – Scantreon - CITY
94-96	Senior Programmer, Industrial Dynamics - CITY
91-94	Senior Programmer, United Media, Inc. - CITY
89-91	General Security Co. - CITY

PERSONAL DATA: Michigan State University Booster Club President.

Tom Jensen

8600 Aspen Ridge • Apartment 15
Ann Arbor, Michigan 48103
734.555.1492   tjensen@airmail.com

Very clean one-page resume for a young professional recently out of school. For a recent graduate, education should be moved up front, and having an "Objective" might even be OK since he knows where he wants to go.

Objective

Web-head techie looking for long and short-term Web, Internet, and eCommerce projects and assignments utilizing heavy JAVA, HTML, Web browsers, and MS applications. Highly skilled in troubleshooting and problem-solving complicated situations.

Background in building and updating Web sites, researching projects, and consulting for general business, education, music, movies, games, sports, and independent retail companies.

Education

UNIVERSITY OF MICHIGAN; Ann Arbor, Michigan
COMPUTER TECHNOLOGY curriculum *(undeclared major)*

PIONEER HIGH SCHOOL; Ann Arbor, Michigan
GRADUATE, 1998
- Assisted school in hardware/software integration with all the middle-level schools in the district.
- Presented computer workshops to middle and elementary-level students.

Experience

IKANDOIT; Ann Arbor, Michigan
INDEPENDENT CONTRACTOR — Web Surfing Geek, 1995-current
Undertake challenging projects to assist companies and individuals with software and hardware concerns. Examples include:

Joe's Sport Shop — Built and maintain a Website promoting University of Michigan sport merchandise and sport memorabilia. State-of-the-art site encouraged worldwide business and quadrupled sales in the first year.

ConeZone Coneys — Developed successful marketing and promotional application tools that partnered with Sony to create a movie featurette. Fast-tracked the production and delivered final product in only five weeks.

Ann Arbor Brokerage — Assisted with online trading and brokerage Website to broaden customer base and cross-sell banking services.

TechnoLogic — Mined the Internet to locate and identify potential avenues of growth for startup business.

CosmicWare — Developed cool entertainment, sports, and game Websites (i.e., ZoneGame.com, ZoneKid.com).

Ensemble Group, Inc.

Orchestrating Communication Solutions

BEN CHANG

WIRELESS MANAGEMENT CONSULTANT

DEPLOYMENT STRATEGIES, ORGANIZATIONAL DESIGN, CHANGE MANAGEMENT, SITE DEVELOPMENT, CONSTRUCTION MANAGEMENT, PCS/RF ENGINEERING, AND NETWORK DEPLOYMENT MANAGEMENT.

PROJECT MANAGEMENT

- Multiple Engineering Department operation, staff, and resources management.
- Proposal preparation and contract negotiation.
- Strategy development and formation of strategic alliance(s).
- Establishment of customer relationship.
- Account attainment and management.

RF ENGINEERING TECHNOLOGIES

- Digital: CDMA, TDMA.
- Analog: AMPs – Americas, TACs – International.
- Paging: FLEX (1 way), REFLEX 2.5 (2 way).

ENGINEERING

Design
- Create Initial RF design(s) for bidding of wireless carrier licenses and RFP(s) using propagation, and statistical software.
- Create demographic and morphology calculations for bidding of wireless carrier licenses and RFP models.
- Evaluate and analyze link budgets.
- Direct and create coverage, frequency, and capacity plans.

Implementation
- Implement Q&A procedures to monitor effective installation of RF communication system.
- Direct and implement processes for site noise and interference measurements.
- Monitor Microwave Link relocation process to reduce link and designed network interference.
- Present and submit technology reports to regulatory and local agencies.

(continued)

Ensemble Group, Inc.
Orchestrating Communication Solutions

Optimization

- Implement drive-test procedures resulting in effective measurements in determining RF network performance.
- Train RF Engineering personnel about the effective processes and techniques.
- Create processes and procedures to manage network expansion and RF databases.
- Create procedures to monitor and record all pertinent RF OMC parameter changes.
- Implement and optimize existing and additional CBSC's to alleviate current capacity and system expansion.
- Implement Operational key indicators to persistently improve capacity and cell site dimensioning.

EQUIPMENT/TOOLS

- Safeco-MDM, OPAS; Qualcomm-DM, LPAR; Grayson-CW test equipment; Lucent-AutoPace, HP-E4900, HP-E7450 to E7480 (optimization tools), HP-E7480; MapInfo; ISG-CellDesigner; MSI-PlaNET, LCC-ANET, CelluMate, RSAT, Comarco; Safeco; AEthos-Odyssey, SUN OS UNIX.

PROFESSIONAL EXPERIENCE

PageNet Inc., Dallas, TX	Principal Consultant	6/98 – present
WaveLink Systems Inc., Dallas, TX	Principal Consultant	1/97 – 4/98
Aethos Communications, Dallas, TX	Senior Consultant	3/95 – 3/96
Mobile Systems International, Chicago, IL	Senior Engineer	3/93 – 3/95
Ameritech Cellular, Schaumburg, IL	RF Performance Engineer	5/92 – 3/93
LCC Inc., Arlington, VA	Associate RF Engineer	10/90 – 5/92

WIRELESS NETWORK CONSULTING ENGAGEMENTS

PageNet	Dallas, TX	2-way messaging
	Chicago, IL	REFLEX 25/FLEX
Sprint PCS	Salt Lake City, UT	CDMA
PrimeCo Personal Communications	Dallas MTA, TX	CDMA
PrimeCo Personal Communications	Miami MTA, FL	CDMA
Bell Atlantic Personal Communications	Arlington, VA	CDMA/GSM
Bell South Personal Communications	Atlanta, GA	CDMA/GSM
Ameritech Personal Communications	Hoffman Estates, IL	AMPS
CellNet	London UK	TACS
AirTouch Cellular	Los Angeles, CA	AMPS
Bay Area Cellular	San Francisco, CA	AMPS

EDUCATION

Bachelor of Science in Electrical Engineering, Capitol College, May 1990

100—WIRELESS PROJECT MANAGER

JOSEPH SMITH

123 Elm Street • Seattle, Washington 98072 • (206) 555-5555 • jsmith@sprintmail.com

KEY QUALIFICATIONS

TELECOMMUNICATIONS PROJECT MANAGEMENT NETWORK DESIGN WIRELESS APPLICATIONS

In-depth experience in managing complex, large-scale telecommunications implementation projects involving network design, design implementation, and support

Skilled manager of multiple technical teams tasked to projects across wide geographic regions

Knowledgeable of high speed network design, wireless telecommunications applications, and infrastructure buildout

Excellent record of success in projects completed on time and within budget

TECHNICAL SKILLS

Visio	Windows 98
MapInfo	MS Excel
Schedule+	MS Access
Onyx	MS Word

PROFESSIONAL EXPERIENCE

AWBC.NET • Everett, Washington

CONSULTANT   2000 - present

Retained to provide consultative services on establishment of Spread Spectrum wireless technologies and delivery of High Speed Wireless Internet Access to markets in the Pacific Northwest. Technologies dealt with include DSL, ISDN, Frame Relay, Dedicated Copper Circuits, Wireless Access, VoIP, VLAN, Fractionalized Voice/Data Wireless, IP and Dedicated Voice. Prioritized prospective areas according to spectrum availability in a Point to Multipoint topology and fiber backhaul capabilities to existing IWBC switching facilities. Determined vendor product pricing for wireless network configurations. Wrote procedures for wireless view shed and wireless POP surveys, equipment configurations, and regulatory compliance practices.

ADVANCED WIRELESS TELECOM (AWT) • Bellevue, Washington

SENIOR MANAGER – MARKET DEVELOPMENT   1998-1999

Spearheaded network establishment project in Phoenix market area for AWT involving delivery of services to business customers. Performed advanced planning on network development and coordinated interdepartmental actions to meet project needs. Verified building location and information to create concentric applications and network mapping. Manipulated information on customer prospects to design efficient network infrastructure to best serve market. Member of Network Development/Advanced Planning Team. Plotted and mapped sites using MapInfo.

(continued)

Joe Smith • (206) 555-5555

**Led buildout of most accessible network in nation from start to finish, including establishing physical infrastructure, planning concentric service areas for 60 buildings and 80 broadband customers; led prospect generation for sales team.
Managed team project for developing and implementing market research database in MS Access that stored, manipulated, and synthesized customer demographics; database reports were intrinsic portion of network planning and rollout.
Spearheaded Market Planning data conversion and implementation of Onyx database for utilization in Sales Automation and Market Development.**

SITE DATA SERVICES MANAGER   1997-1998

Administered all licensing and implementation actions for microwave radio site installations across the United States. Coordinated teams for site verification and acquisition, spectrum analysis, and application engineering. Supervised Geographic Information Systems Team for mapping of network design. Analyzed preexisting sites for standards compliance.

**Managed national program involving 270 special project site installations within 8 months; overcame numerous changes in specifications and standards to achieve on time completion.
Managed major project involving development of 2 databases for lease administration and tracking of FCC 38 GHz authorization compliance issues for 290 licensed telecommunications service areas and 1600 locations.
Merged legacy database systems from customer care, field services, site acquisition, application engineering, technical implementation teams, and the network operating center into a single intranet accessible MS Access/SQL database.**

SITE SERVICES MANAGER   1996-1997

Developed policy and procedures for site applications and wireless technology in early stages of organizational startup. Created strategies for technical implementation of cutting-edge telecommunications applications.

**Coordinated site acquisition project for contract completion in agreement with Teleport Communications Group that resulted in $2.5 million in revenues for ART.
Managed site equipment acquisition project for over 300 sites with a budget of $200,000. Led full life cycle from identification/acquisition to implementation and support. Supervised team of site acquisition specialists and directed the efforts of 3 field services teams.
Drafted comprehensive, yet simple lease agreement and supporting documentation to facilitate microwave radio site acquisitions and contract negotiations.**

EDUCATION AND TRAINING

Bachelor of Science (BS) – University of Washington
Scholarship Recipient

NCAA – All American Track and Field

101—WRITER

1769 Laurel Place Baltimore, MD 20945	**Dana Barnes** ~ Writer ~	410.555.0267 DBW@hotmail.com

~ Profile ~

Twelve years' experience as a professional technical and public relations writer.
Copy and content editor for four types of simultaneous publications.
Penned over 300 articles for magazines and periodicals.
Possesses a sharp eye for detail.

Marketing Microsoft / Windows / Internet	Web Content Graphic Programs	Technical Content Chicago Manual of Style

~ PROFESSIONAL EXPERIENCE ~

SENIOR COPY EDITOR
E-Finance, Inc., Elkridge, Maryland   **1997 to Present**
~ *E-Finance is a leader in developing Internet-based financial planning solutions, providing multiple service lines for professional advisors and consumers.*

- Edit Web site discussions on a range of financial planning topics: banking, investments, and trading. Meticulously edit for style, spelling, punctuation, and clarity. Input corrections. Proofread all written materials at various stages of production, e.g., annual and quarterly reports, official correspondence, Web marketing content, and discussions.

- Collaborated with the Editorial Director and drafted, implemented, and constantly monitored the corporate style guide—and staff members' conformance to guidelines.

- Interface with staff to apply guidelines ensuring consistency and grammatical integrity without altering a writer's meaning. Savvy knowledge of financial terminology.

PUBLIC RELATIONS SPECIALIST, Corporate Communications Department
Glendale Federal Savings and Loan Association, Washington DC (HQ)   **1990 to 1997**
* *A diversified financial services corporation and the nation's fifth largest S&L association with over $11B in assets and over 500 offices nationwide.*

- Generated leads, interviewed sources, researched, wrote and edited articles for four types of publications circulated in-house and to the public (weekly newsletters, monthly glossy/color 12-16 page newspapers, spot memoranda, and a 4-6 page bi-weekly financial bulletin). Prepared layouts and coordinated with the printer. Set up photo shoots, prepared press kits, and arranged media relations.

- Selected to draft initial Web content copy for the emerging company Web site. Worked closely with the financial and marketing staffs throughout the development process to identify documentation requirements. Implemented in-house style guidelines and edited all copy before uploading for public viewing. Provided recommendations for navigation.

(continued)

~ Accurate, interesting, concise writing educates professionals and wins business ~

Dana Barnes, Page 2

FREELANCE WRITER
Accepted various contract writing assignments, Baltimore, MD   **1988 to Present**
* Drafted proposals, wrote columns and articles for periodicals and magazines.

- Drafted a top-notch proposal for a major corporate to corporate deal. Designed a winning PowerPoint presentation. The deal closed with the company landing a $22M contract.

- Wrote a weekly finance FAQ's column in a city newspaper for four years. Offered banking and investment advice to readers (over 200 columns).

- Authored over 100 finance, banking, and investment articles for periodicals (paper and electronic), professional journals, and magazines including *Money & Sense* and *Home Office*.

- Wrote and self-published *Your Family Budget*, a practical guide to home finances.

~ Education ~

University of Southern California (USC)
MBA/Economics, 1990

Editor, Finance Club Journal

Instrumental in organizing a Finance Club Web site.
Wrote content copy and reviewed layout and navigation. Experienced with HTML

University of Maryland
Bachelor of Science in Journalism, Dean's List, 1988

Copy Editor, University Newspaper
Received the Best Writer Award

Editor, University Publication
Wrote and edited articles, shot and developed film, typeset, determined layout. and distributed a 60-page magazine style yearbook at the request of the Computer Club

~ An excellent Web site is brought to life each day with fresh, intoxicating copy ~

General Index

About the Authors

Jay A. Block, CPRW (Certified Professional Resume Writer), internationally certified career coach and resume strategist, is the contributing cofounder of the Professional Association of Resume Writers and Career Coaches (PARW/CC). He helped develop the PARW/CC national certification process and is a widely respected national speaker, author, and career coach. Contact him at www.jayblock.com.

Michael Betrus, CPRW, has been a hiring manager in the telecommunications industry for several years, and frequently engages in academic seminars for students on campus. Michael is the author of *The Guide to Executive Recruiters* and co-author, with Jay Block, of *101 Best Resumes, 101 More Best Resumes, 101 Best Cover Letters,* and *101 Best Tech Resumes*. Contact him at betrus@earthlink.net.